Someone Else's Empire

Verso is pleased to be working with the *London Review of Books* on an occasional series of volumes that draw on writing that first appeared in the paper.

The *LRB* is Europe's leading journal of culture and ideas. Subscribers can read all of Tom Stevenson's pieces, and every article ever published by the magazine, at lrb.co.uk/archive.

Someone Else's Empire

British Illusions and American Hegemony

Tom Stevenson

VERSO
London • New York

It should be manifest to every person that such a program for the subjugation and ruthless exploitation by one country of nearly one-half of the population of the world is a matter of immense significance, importance and concern to every other nation wherever located.

Cordell Hull, 1941

The mask of patriotism is allowed to cover the most glaring inconsistencies.

Edward Gibbon

First published by Verso 2023

Author and publisher are grateful to the *London Review of Books*
for permission to republish the following articles.

1 3 5 7 9 10 8 6 4 2

Verso
UK: 6 Meard Street, London W1F 0EG
US: 388 Atlantic Avenue, Brooklyn, NY 11217
versobooks.com

Verso is the imprint of New Left Books

ISBN-13: 978-1-80429-148-1
ISBN-13: 978-1-80429-151-1 (US EBK)
ISBN-13: 978-1-80429-150-4 (UK EBK)

British Library Cataloguing in Publication Data
A catalogue record for this book is available from the British Library

Library of Congress Cataloging-in-Publication Data

Names: Stevenson, Tom (Tom Finton), 1990– author.
Title: Someone else's empire : British illusions and American hegemony / Tom Stevenson.
Description: First edition hardback. | Brooklyn, NY : Verso is the imprint of New Left Books, 2023. | Includes bibliographical references and index.
Identifiers: LCCN 2023023188 (print) | LCCN 2023023189 (ebook) | ISBN 9781804291481 (hardback) | ISBN 9781804291511 (US ebk) | ISBN 9781804291504 (UK ebk)
Subjects: LCSH: Hegemony – United States. | United States – Foreign relations – Great Britain. | United States – Politics and government – 21st century. | Great Britain – Foreign relations – United States. | Great Britain – Politics and government – 21st century. | International finance – 21st century. | World politics.
Classification: LCC JZ1312 .S7 2023 (print) | LCC JZ1312 (ebook) | DDC 327.73041 – dc23/eng/20230622
LC record available at https://lccn.loc.gov/2023023188
LC ebook record available at https://lccn.loc.gov/2023023189

Typeset in Fournier by MJ & N Gavan, Truro, Cornwall
Printed in the UK by CPI Mackays

Contents

III. A Prize from Fairyland

Introduction

Most international affairs analysis comes from the perspective, if not from the capital city, of one or another powerful state. The view from the imperial metropolis has its advantages, but it tends to obscure the ruinous effects of the policies of the great powers themselves. In the present era, the United States and its allies have too often been spared scrutiny of their actions in favour of seductive abstractions or euphemisms about a 'rules-based' international order.[1] The discursive dominance of the United States is part of the problem. Much weight is put on the cultural or moral element of American power.[2] But American culture is hegemonic, and provincial elites in other countries adhere to it, because of American empire, not vice versa. Until very recently there was less interest in the underlying constants of the world situation: patterns in the flow of fossil fuels, German-Russian economic codependence, the implications of industrialised subcontinental states in China and India. Most significant of all, American maritime dominance over the industrial centres in the far west and east of the old world.

The world economy, in terms of both productive capacity and trade, is tripolar (the US, EU, and China).[3] But world power remains nearly unipolar. This inherently unstable configuration is the central fact of world politics. Just to list the very large number of overseas US military bases is to paint a misleading picture. The points of concentration in the US global position are more important than its general dispersal. In 1992, the US Department of Defense noted that a 'less visible' victory at the end of the Cold War had been 'the integration of Germany and Japan into a US-led system of collective security'.[4] The objective was to use 'the mechanisms for deterring potential competitors from even aspiring to a larger regional or global role' in order to 'prevent the re-emergence of a new rival'. Today, US military dominance over the world's major hydrocarbon reserves in the Persian Gulf is assured by garrisons at Udeid, Arifjan, and Bahrain. The global reach of the US Navy is evident in Diego Garcia, Singapore, and Yokohama. The instruments at the disposal of the US – military dominance, maritime primacy, nuclear superiority over all potential challengers, and financial centrality – remain. There has even been time for contemplation of far-future states: the US 'spacepower' doctrine outlines how it would dominate 'orbital warfare' and 'space access'.

There is no question that the mechanisms of American power have been transformed. Enforcement in the periphery has increasingly fallen to local proxies. American air power, often in the form of drones backed by the global surveillance system, works alongside proxy ground forces supplemented, where more artful work is required, by teams of US special forces. American foreign policy was once routinely attacked on grounds of incoherence, but more relevant has been its stability, even through the reckless dysfunction of the Trump years. Great noise continues to be made by ferocious tinkerers who favour this or that tweak to the US approach, but in the use of the main instruments of power there has been consensus. Donald Trump's 2018 nuclear posture review was very similar to a

2010 predecessor conducted under Barack Obama. The two wielded the sanctions weaponry in exactly the same way. NATO's 2022 strategic concept, with its talk of 'mutually reinforcing attempts to undercut the rules-based international order', approached paraphrase of the Trump-era 2017 US National Security Strategy.[5]

For the leaders of states that consider themselves 'allies' of American power, the renewed relevance of proxy armies has deeper connotations. The US has always involved surrogate states in helping to keep the world in order. One state in particular stands out in its willingness. After the loss of its own empire, the United Kingdom briefly sought to play the role of what David McCourt called a 'residual great power'.[6] But the job of field commander to the US better suited the martial values of the polity. In deference to local sensibilities, Britain's equite role must be couched in the more comforting language of partnership. Some British contributions to American power do resemble a shared project. Outposts on remote islands retained after the demise of the British empire make for useful listening posts in the global surveillance system run by the NSA and GCHQ. As the former head of MI6 John Sawers observed, 'politicians come and go, but the intelligence relationship stays really solid'.[7] Yet for what must ultimately be psychological reasons, British leaders and national security clerks have tended to dislike seeing Britain framed by American power. Refusal to acknowledge even the outlines of Britain's actual foreign policy has combined with a more recent build-up of irrelevant, nostalgic detritus around 'Britain's role in the world'. A great effort would be required to clear it away, and there is little sign of a beginning.

This book began as a series of essays written for the *London Review of Books*. Many of the chapters were originally reportage from places where the tensions of the world situation cannot be hidden in euphemism. To write about, or even just from, Libya, Iraq or Egypt is to be confronted with all the contradictions of Anglo-American power. Two themes were inescapable: the abiding presence of American empire, despite talk of its demise, and the consistency of British servility to US designs whatever the consequences. The first part of the book addresses the peculiarity of British foreign policy, which even before Brexit had tied itself to American power in more ways than the 'instinctive conjunction of financial interests' that Susan Strange once argued were the guts of the 'special relationship'.[8]

Even within the British establishment there is now some recognition that British foreign policy has somehow become both aeriform and distended. Nostalgia for global influence has produced a compulsive Atlanticism and a reflexive resort to military actions that the UK is near incapable of actually performing. While Brexit has been a very effective distraction from the fragilities in Britain's position, which now threaten the cohesion of the state itself, it has not broken the pattern. Arms procurement from the US has increased as British leaders double down on lieutenant status in a 'global NATO'. New British aircraft carriers sail to the 'Indo-Pacific' in accordance with American goals. Newly opened Persian Gulf bases are put to work by British military institutions working side by side with Saudi and Emirati forces engaged in the catastrophic Anglo-Saudi war on Yemen.

The Russian invasion of Ukraine in 2022, despite being in most respects an operational failure, was a gift to the permanent bellicose constituency within the Anglosphere. The invasion precipitated successive British pledges to raise military spending as a per cent of GDP. A badly run Russian invasion of an immediate neighbour justified rearmament and reaffirmation of strategic alignment behind the US alliance. Britain more than any other comparable power has talked Washington's pitch about a battle between democracies and autocracies.[9] This vocabulary will be of little help in Northern Ireland, in the interminable negotiations required by an ill-planned exit from the European Union, in addressing the problem of the British international corruption archipelago, or in restraining the worst tendencies of British militarism.

The significance of British participation in American designs should not be overestimated. Even British participation in the Iraq war was often a liability. As part two of this book shows, the American empire could get along fine without British assistance. After the 2008 financial crisis American planners worried about the potential loss of US economic power, and the effect that might have on its global position.[10] But instead the US emerged as the sole growth economy in the G7 (China and South Korea being non-G7 examples, adversary and ally respectively). The US also remained central to the architecture of international finance. Global trade plateaued as a percentage of GDP, but international dollar funding has in fact grown markedly.[11] An Atlantean thesis of American hegemony has recently gained much popularity, but for the most part it has not bothered to offer any concrete analysis of the US power position. In the global food crisis of 2022, Brazil still had to seek Washington's approval to buy much-needed fertiliser from Iran.[12] We are living not in the mossy ruins of empire but in its still-smouldering battlefields.

It is in the Middle East that the effects of Anglo-American machinations have been felt most keenly. Part three of this book focuses on the Persian Gulf and North Africa, where the rhetoric of benign hegemony runs up against the parlous state in which much of humanity actually exists. Control of Persian Gulf hydrocarbons has been critical to US grand strategy for more than seventy years. But what the US and Britain are actually doing in the Middle East is still a subject of contention and affected ignorance. Even left-wing critics have tried to argue that the US spends hundreds of billions of dollars a year maintaining its largest overseas military bases and keeping one of its three external naval fleets in the Middle East, not to mention conducting constant military interventions, for no real reason at all.[13] This is not credible. Tens of thousands of American troops are permanently stationed around the Gulf (the numbers for particular countries fluctuate, and are then said to demonstrate faux withdrawals[14]) because oil and gas are critical to global industrial production and neither of the other two poles of the world economy – Europe and East Asia – have very much of them.

This is the reason successive Anglo-American pivots out of the Middle East have not materialised. On the contrary, US Central Command has grown considerably since its inception in 1983. In local capitals, CENTCOM commanders are still looked on as viceroys. The Gulf monarchies have been flooded with American, British, and French weapons that require maintenance and munitions, and so strategic partnerships with their manufacturers. In Yemen those arms are put to use in an ongoing conflict that has left hundreds of thousands dead, and which continues solely because of the participation of the US and Britain.[15] The presence of British and American officials in the war's command rooms, and of their intelligence in the hands of the targeters, should be enough to call the war a joint Anglo-American, Saudi, and Emirati assault. This is only the latest in a series of atrocities committed by the US and its allies in the region that make backing for brutal autocratic regimes in Egypt and elsewhere appear mundane by comparison. More generally, the political and military influence of the US and its allies over the Middle East region has remained important through the Arab Spring years.

Whatever is said in Washington or London, American empire was never an ideological construct, or a commitment to rules, or to liberalism, let alone to democratic government. The general argument of this book is that American power and its British appendage is founded on brute military facts and centrality in the international energy and financial systems. These foundations are now strained by confrontations with Russia and China, nascent and incipient. In October 2022, the Biden administration's National Security Strategy described the US as being 'in the midst of a strategic competition to shape the future of the international order'. China is charged with harbouring intentions to remake the international order to its liking, and of 'working to undermine democracy'. The stakes are said to be winning 'the competition for the twenty-first century' and with it 'the contest for the future of our world'. At the same time, the US is carrying out a very high-risk strategy in Ukraine. Unlike China, Russia possesses a nuclear arsenal equivalent to that of the US. Ukraine has already suffered terrible damage. An attritional war implies long-term damage to European energy supplies and sustained damage to European industry. And the most hawkish analysis has to concede that it increases the likelihood of thermonuclear war.

The logic of the US order, supported to the greatest extent possible by Britain, has led us to this point. At greater risk than the world empire is the world itself. The accumulated experience of climatic breakdown has brought with it a resurgence of the original insight of geopolitics – not as a degraded synonym for international affairs but as the assertion that interactions between states are conditioned by physical geography. Still, comforting stories of coalitions of democracies uniting against autocratic menaces remain with us. So do transcendental ambitions to global power by individual states. The confrontations with both China and with Russia, however they develop, were elected by the US and its allies. It is clear in the black and white of strategic documents written prior to any subsequent ruptures. For some constituencies within the US and British security establishments, these confrontations are stimulatory. For everyone else, the risks are far from trivial. They will define the first quarter of the twenty-first century, should we get out of it.

I. Equerry Dreams

1
Eternal Allies

Grand strategy is for great powers. That is not a set to which Britain has belonged for decades, despite the occasional protests of local dignitaries.[1] All states have their self-delusions; the problem for British foreign policy is that elite descriptions of Britain's position in the world are incongruent with reality. In 1907, Eyre Crowe wrote that 'the general character of England's foreign policy is determined by the immutable conditions of her geographical situation on the ocean flank of Europe as an island State with vast oversea colonies and dependencies, whose existence and survival as an independent community are inseparably bound up with the possession of preponderant sea power'.[2] The vast overseas colonies didn't prove quite so immutable. Neither did the preponderant sea power. Within a generation, primacy at sea had been ceded to the United States. Britain fought repressive campaigns in colonial possessions in Palestine, Malaya, Kenya, Cyprus, and Aden into the second half of the twentieth century. But the ultimate effect was the same. The UK became what Crowe had called 'a small island kingdom . . . dependent for its food supply on overseas commerce'.

A new settlement had to be sought with the successor at sea, but of what kind? Far from Churchill's airy 'fraternal association of the English-speaking peoples', the relationship was in fact secured with formal military cooperation and intelligence agreements with the United States.[3] (The UKUSA agreement founding Five Eyes was signed the same day the Fulton speech). Just ten years after affirming the 'abiding power of the British empire', Churchill himself was admonishing the British government to 'never be separated from the Americans'.[4] Britain retained a prominent position in the institutions of the postwar order, from where it helped insert the cursed permanent member veto into the UN Security Council. But the disastrous and bathetic British machination at Suez soon dispelled rump illusions about Atlantic relations. In March 1957 President Eisenhower convened a conference in Bermuda 'to restore confidence in the Anglo-American relationship', that is to lay down the law for the future.[5]

In December 1962 two simultaneous events helped define the Anglo-American alliance. The first was the unilateral cancellation by the US of the air-launched ballistic missile programme Skybolt, which temporarily brought British nuclear status into doubt. The crisis lasted less than a month and was resolved with the American offer of Polaris as a replacement, but its significance lay in the feeling that a loss of face had been revealed in an area where revelations were not welcome. The second, and of greater import, was an outbreak of honesty from the US foreign policy planner Dean Acheson about the British position in world affairs. The anodyne statement that Britain had 'lost an empire and not yet found a role' caused a general furore.[6] That Britain's days as a world power were over and it would have to find a role in Europe should have been an uncontroversial statement, and that Acheson was regarded as an Anglophile is too often forgotten. But the outrage was real: so much so that it sometimes looked as though the entire Whitehall establishment organised itself around the rejection of a single comment. If what Tony Blair would later call 'Acheson's barb' stung, it was because it was well placed.[7] At issue was a rejection of the diplomatic fictions of the 'special relationship' around which Britain would build itself as subsidiary to American power.

Acheson was responsible for another statement far more consequential for Britain's future. Writing to US ambassador J. Robert Schaetzel, he described the value of 'getting Britain to act as our lieutenant'.[8] But what did that entail? Of considerable importance to the US was the transition from British to American hegemony in the Persian Gulf. Washington proposed joint British-American naval policing of the Gulf of Aqaba. Throughout the 1960s, the US urged the British government to keep military forces in the Far East, but British leaders were reluctant to bear the cost when the empire itself was dissolving.[9] Against this contention was the fear of a loss of status – of becoming what the diplomat Con O'Neill referred to as a 'greater Sweden'.[10] Harold Wilson's refusal to send British forces to Vietnam has received much focus, but provides a distorted view of British policy. At the outset, Britain had been keen to help the American effort in Vietnam and offered British military advisers and training to proxy forces.[11] The foreign secretary, Alec Douglas-Home, expressed British support for the war.[12] Britain agreed to redeploy military assets, including Royal Navy submarines, so as to free up US forces to be sent to Vietnam. In the early sixties British planes helped supply the proxy war in Laos.[13] Britain also provided direct assistance in Vietnam in the form of battlefield intelligence. That Wilson felt he could not commit troops for fear of appearing to be America's 'British stooges' was evidence of some element in national culture that resisted the role of lieutenant.[14] But whatever it was, it was systematically routed in the next three decades.

In 1979, the British diplomat Nicholas Henderson's influential final despatch noted Britain's decline relative to France and Germany, in part because of a foreign policy that gave preference to relations with the US and the former Anglo-settler societies over other interests.[15] But strategic concerns were not the only factor. Throughout the seventies Britain had been blithely supplying arms to Argentina on the basis of shaky commercialism.[16] The military historian John Keegan would argue that the Falklands War marked the beginning of Britain's 'late twentieth-century renaissance as an international power'.[17] The war was certainly not driven by American interests, but Britain struggled militarily against badly prepared Argentinian forces in a small war in the South Atlantic until Caspar Weinberger provided Sidewinder missiles, US electronic intelligence and refuelling, which were acknowledged as necessary by Margaret Thatcher.[18] British foreign policy could be said to have evolved, but it had not transformed. Over the 1950s Britain had given up the extremities of empire. In the 1960s it was forced to release the core possessions. The steady increase in provision of services to American empire coincided with these developments. In the 1990s and 2000s the strongest phase of the trend emerged as the architecture of American power built ostensibly to contain the Soviet Union was revealed to be just as useful in its absence.

In light of the extent of American power one of the central tasks would be finding ways for Britain to contribute without superfluity. In 1994 an internal intelligence guidance document argued that 'this may entail on occasion the applying of UK resources to the meeting of US requirements'.[19] Douglas Hurd's famous phrase about Britain punching above its weight belonged to this period – a quintessential nineties illusion. The two international conflicts that provided confirmation for the renaissance of British power – Kosovo and Sierra Leone – are looked on in quite a different light today. At the time both interventions were treated as virtuous humanitarian missions motivated by the highest principles. NATO intervention in Kosovo is still sometimes described as humanitarian cluster bombing, despite its blatant illegality, its contribution to deteriorating relations with both China and Russia, and the direct increase in the brutality of the conflict.[20] The 2000 intervention in Sierra Leone was also evidence of enlightened use of British military force and a justification for later expeditions to Afghanistan and Iraq.[21] It has since slipped back into a more modest position in the historiography befitting its minor significance. Looked back on today, the debates over humanitarian intervention have a surreal quality. It seems absurd, even maniacal, to rest any argument on the scope of British foreign policy on such flimsy stories.

The dominant trend of late twentieth-century Britain was not resurgence as an independent power but a new surrogacy. Britain responded to the magnitude of twentieth-century American power by seeking, contrary to Lord Palmerston's famous assertion, to make of the United States an eternal ally. In 1997, former US National Security Council official Charles Maechling described how Britain 'reduces its foreign policy to that of a satellite'. The question was whether 'British parroting of US foreign policy has so diminished Britain's standing as an independent force in world affairs as to make it more of a diplomatic encumbrance than an asset'.[22] The consequences were felt not in Britain but in Helmand and Basra. And reassessment of reflexive British contribution to the designs of American empire has been forestalled. At a talk at Cambridge in 2022, John Mearsheimer noted that 'if there's any country that does what the US asks, almost axiomatically, it is Britain.'[23]

In the British security establishment the commitment to inclusion in the execution of US strategy is given highest priority. For Emeritus

Professor of War Studies at King's College London, Lawrence Freedman, a guiding principle of British strategy has been to 'nurture a special relationship with the United States in the hope of shaping the exercise of US power'.[24] The image of the special relationship as a reciprocal cultural affinity, rather than a mercenary contribution to global order, has survived despite being a subject of ill-concealed humour to successive US presidents.[25] In effect, Britain did find a role: the equite role of attendant and occasional field commander to American global power. Britain is not exceptional, but it does occupy an unusual position in the international system in being one of few states organised primarily around the interest of another.

What does Britain offer the United States, given the capabilities already available to it? Diplomatic support, when the appearance of multilateralism is needed, is useful but can come from many directions. UK special operations forces work with a greater degree of secrecy than those of the US. The relative lack of parliamentary oversight of British special forces, combined with a culture of reverence for them, can be handy for rough and disreputable jobs.[26] Britain does not have global military infrastructure in the way the US does, but residual imperial possessions offer some military conveniences. The major Cyprus bases, Akrotiri and Dhekelia, are important beyond the Mediterranean as both staging and listening posts. In the South Atlantic, Britain has the Mount Pleasant military base on the Falklands and an airstrip on Ascension Island. In the Indian Ocean there is the small British presence at Diego Garcia, the Chagos Archipelago base leased to the US. The British army keeps a training facility in central Kenya, a fuelling station in Singapore on the site of the old Sembawang Naval Base, and a single infantry battalion at Brunei garrison in Belait. In Germany, the once major British army deployment has been withdrawn, leaving behind only a tiny base in North Rhine-Westphalia. The two naval bases in the

Persian Gulf, HMS *Jufair* in Bahrain, and Al Duqm in Oman, both of which are former imperial positions resurrected in the late 2010s, are a different matter. The significance of British overseas military bases should not be overstated, but they do sometimes offer logistical advantages. The US military also permanently deploys more than 12,000 military personnel to Britain itself (the majority airmen based in Lakenheath and Mildenhall).[27]

Peter Ricketts, a former permanent undersecretary in the Foreign Office, national security adviser, chairman of the Joint Intelligence Committee, permanent representative to NATO, and ambassador to France, represents the core of established British foreign policy. In *Hard Choices: What Britain Does Next*, Ricketts attempted an account of the present British strategy in world affairs.[28] Ricketts is clear that the special relationship is an 'incantation', which happens to be 'essential for British self-confidence'. In his view, the Obama administration's decision to lead from behind during the NATO military intervention in Libya was an inflection point, so much so that 'the global geometry of power had shifted decisively'.[29] Ricketts provided a cursory history of the Iraq war, and British involvement in war on terror operations. He then bemoaned how the Iraq war destroyed public confidence in military adventures 'either for Western security or for the countries Washington and London were trying to help'. He was particularly concerned by parliamentary refusal to bomb Syria in 2013, which he described as though it were a dangerous precedent. The net result of the 'Iraq effect' was Anglo-American 'reluctance to use military force' and a reduction in credibility.

Despite Iraq, and the imminent end of US global leadership, Ricketts still argued that 'on national security, Britain's unequivocal choice has to be to stand with the US'. In 2010, Ricketts was instrumental in the creation of a British National Security Council modelled on its American equivalent. At the time, this was seen as an attempt to curtail the influence of the Foreign Office in favour of prime ministerial discretion. The council was attended by senior cabinet ministers and had its own staff, the national security secretariat. The national security adviser was to be the prime minister's Kongming on international affairs. The mirroring of American institutions was more than metaphorical. David Cameron said he thought there were moments when President Obama seemed to think of Ricketts and his US equivalent Tom Donilon as though they were one person. It would be difficult to find a better encapsulation of the equerry dreams of contemporary British prime ministers.

For Ricketts, British strategy had become a lost art. Looking back, he contrasted embattled civil servants and politicians of the present with the Second World War Field Marshal Lord Alanbrooke, whom Ricketts saw as the last great British strategist (despite one of his achievements being the delay of an attempted cross-channel invasion of occupied Europe by the allies). Ricketts also contrasted Norman Brook's 1960 *Future Policy Study* with more recent declarative strategy documents produced by the British state.[30] Brook's study had argued that Britain should maintain its alliances with both the US and Europe. It also argued that Britain should be prepared to subordinate its own interests to those of the US, as the American ally most committed to remaining an 'opponent of Russian and Chinese expansionism'.

The idea that Britain has lost the art of grand strategy is worth consideration. For a figure as senior as Ricketts to conclude that 'the country's image of itself is significantly out of kilter with reality' marked a significant moment. The highest level of the establishment had identified how nostalgia for great power status had manifested in attempts to influence global affairs through partnership with the US. But it was far from clear that Ricketts's contribution improved matters. For one thing, he had devoted considerable space to the supposed existence of a 'triangle of tension' between Britain, the US, and China, reflexively falling back into the habit he purported to be criticising. And the implied comparisons between his writing and that of his predecessors was not flattering. Despite mentioning the idea that British military forces be confined to 'defending the UK and its Overseas Territories and fulfilling NATO obligations', Ricketts maintains that Britain's search for 'global influence' meant 'finding new ways to use its military power as an instrument of foreign policy'. This was principally to be through more investment in NATO, which Ricketts was unable to see as another instrument of American power.

The accordance of British foreign policy with American goals has if anything increased. New British aircraft carriers sail to the Indo-Pacific. Britain contributes to the American advantage over China in nuclear submarines through the AUKUS deal. British diplomats have sought to increase military ties with Japan.[31] In 2016, a marked turn in China policy saw a switch from offering Xi Jinping carriage rides on the Mall to full alignment with American policy. During Liz Truss's time as foreign secretary and then prime minister, British officials began to talk of the defence of Taiwan and officially designated China a threat to national security. In the Middle East, the newly opened Persian Gulf bases were complemented by a general shift towards American interests. The British 'Gulf Strategy Fund' was doubled in size, so that millions of pounds are spent cultivating relations with Saudi Arabia and Bahrain.[32] The Ministry of Defence worked with the Saudi Armed Forces engaged in the Anglo-Saudi war on Yemen. The UK operated joint squadrons with Qatar, near the major US air base at Al Obeid.[33] The British government also considered following the US in moving its embassy from Tel Aviv to Jerusalem.

In Eastern Europe, Britain followed the US lead in taking a military over a diplomatic approach towards relations with Russia. The 2015 creation of the Joint Expeditionary Force, led by the UK and participated in mostly by the Nordic and Baltic states, was a minor development in its own terms but significant as a signal of intention. In 2016 Britain decided to permanently deploy ground forces in Poland and the Baltics. In response to the Russian invasion of Ukraine in 2022, Britain adhered to American policy from the outset. American B-52 strategic bombers took off from British airfields to fly over Polish airspace. In June 2022, Britain added to the thousands of NLAW anti-tank weapons much appreciated by the Ukrainian resistance by pledging to commit another 1,000 troops to Estonia and a carrier group to the Eastern European theatre. Proponents of simultaneous negotiations with Russia were maligned until the US itself entertained them in October 2022. And even as Russia's poor performance in the Ukraine war was ridiculed, the threat of Russia served as a justification for long term increases in military spending by Britain. In November 2020, the British government had increased military budgets considerably. As a result, Britain already stood out amid a wave of increased military spending across Europe. Its military budget was significantly greater than that of either India or Russia. The Royal Navy planned to increase the overall tonnage of the British fleet by 50 per cent, while international aid to Lebanon, Syria, the Palestinian territories, and even Yemen were gutted.[34] The *Economist* noted that the outline of Britain's post-Brexit foreign policy appeared to be 'defence spending up, aid outlays down'.[35] The war in Ukraine only added impetus.

The main countervailing force to British militarism has been British economic malaise. In 1950, the UK still represented about 6 per cent of the global economy. By 1970 that figure had declined to 3.5 per cent, and the trend continues if at a slower pace. All the

North Atlantic economies have been afflicted by economic stagnation since 2008 except for the US itself. But the British case is particularly acute. The UK now compares poorly with Scandinavia, Finland, Switzerland, Austria, Germany, the Netherlands, and Belgium in life expectancy, infant mortality, doctors per capita, and other development indicators. It also compares unfavourably on most of these metrics with Australia and New Zealand. The British state's addiction to false economies and self-inflicted wounds is primarily responsible. The constraints of British decline are likely to take their toll on military spending. British military spending has been in long term decline as a percentage of GDP since the Second World War. The pledges of the early 2020s to return to military spending equivalent to 3 per cent of GDP would be a major reversal if it were possible.[36] But this obscures how much of a focus has remained on expeditionary military capacity. Defence spending may have reduced but the reduction pales when compared with other parts of the state. Successive cuts to the Foreign Office have seen the number of British diplomats halved in just thirty years. The most recent trend has been the prioritisation of the RAF and the Royal Navy over the army for the purposes of 'power projection'. Fortunately for the rest of the world, Britain isn't projecting power so much as decadence.

Frustration with relative decline was one of the factors that contributed to British entry into the European Communities in the early seventies. The same frustration played a minor role in the retreat. In September 2017, Michael Fallon promised that free of formal entanglement with the European Union Britain would 'spread its wings across the world'.[37] It is hardly surprising that ordinary politicians offered unserious assessments. Chaotic withdrawal has produced no global fanning out. That is to be expected given Britain's strategic posture. Even the very limited moves by European states to seek a course independent of the US have not been attempted by Britain. In Europe, the American approach after the collapse of the Soviet Union had been based on efforts to 'prevent the emergence of European-only security arrangements which would undermine NATO'.[38] British diplomats of the previous generation had a hand in the failure of the Treaty of Paris in 1952.[39] Except for a brief period around the Saint-Malo declaration in 1998, they played their part in hindering subsequent efforts to revive the principle. This effectively gave American security organisation free reign in Europe. After it left the European Union, Britain remained an organic constituent of the wider European economy, and other enmeshments persisted. The UK is still part of the Valduc initiative, under which it shares access to a French nuclear testing facility in Burgundy. Cooperation with France and Germany through E3 continues much as before. So far, Britain has not further diverged with the overall direction of European foreign policy because, despite the shaky arguments of the declinists, the latter too has tacked towards the US.

There is no denying that the net effect of Brexit has been an increase in vassaldom. The procurement of American arms by the UK has increased. During Liz Truss's time at the Foreign Office, and during her brief tenure as prime minister, there were calls for a 'global NATO' and for the G7 to become an 'economic NATO' under the US as 'leading light' of the free world.[40] This direction was not a necessary result of leaving the EU but it is obtaining. The British and French economies are of comparable size, but Britain's is much more reliant on international trade, resulting in a scramble for new trade agreements and ineffective yearning for CANZUK style resurrections of older formations based on former dominions. Such distractions have inhibited British planners from recognition of other fragilities. And as Scotland and Wales accuse Westminster of failing to match EU development financing (in the Welsh case perhaps half of EU levels) British foreign policy has become a clear threat to the cohesion of the state.

The appearance of choice between Britain as a 'global power' and as an insular European country is illusory. The impetus for so many disastrous decisions in British foreign policy has come out of a desire to maintain lieutenant rank with the United States. Questions that ought to be asked of British foreign policy – Why the Indo-Pacific tilt? Why did the UK become so heavily involved in the atrocities in Yemen? – have gone unarticulated. The reflexive expeditionary bellicosity so evident in Afghanistan, Libya, and Iraq is self-damaging. The Royal Navy's planned 'littoral response groups' and the army's proxy-war fighting ranger units are all evidence of the survival of this tendency.[41] That Britain has not faced a major threat since the 1940s has resulted in a frivolousness about war. The main military projects at present are nuclear modernisation and the acquisition of F-35 fighter jets for aircraft carriers – both in the interest of power projection. The UK has made a concerted, multi-generational effort to deal arms for autocratic US protectorates. The minor profits that result are concentrated in a few firms and contribute nothing to Britain's international position. The provision of international corruption and tax evasion services, conducted in the City and the rump colonies, represents the simple theft of wealth from less economically developed countries. Successive UK governments have been uninterested in relations with Ireland and have been willing to put the Northern Ireland agreement up for debate on a whim. The inability of the Northern Ireland executive to form for a full year was barely noticed in London.[42]

The tensions in the UK's position are clear: an economic role as Europe's Hong Kong, drawing in excess savings from the continent, sitting uncomfortably beside a strategic position as lieutenant to

American power. The relationship with continental Europe has now been badly destabilised. But what other problems of British foreign policy has the present environment made difficult to formulate? Avoiding expeditionary war must become a strategic priority. More thought should be given to managing dependence on EU markets, given the high British trade to GDP ratio. Territorial disputes arising from remnant imperial possessions, from Gibraltar to Belize to Montserrat, must also be avoided. There is a long term risk that the tax-avoidance archipelago becomes a strategic vulnerability, even though elites in other states tend to take advantage of it. The judgement of the International Court of Justice and challenges at the United Nations to the status of the Chagos Islands foreshadow this. In November 2022, the UK agreed to talks with Mauritius on the status of the islands but asserted that the military base on Diego Garcia would remain whatever the results of the talks.[43] It is obvious that the level of public investment, particularly in research and development, must be greatly increased as a percentage of GDP to cauterise wounds in the national economy. But long term relative decline must also be seen in a new light. That the UK will soon become a third tier economy, alongside the likes of Brazil, Mexico, and Indonesia, will mean proximity to countries with traditions of non-alignment. In no case are these traditions uncomplicated, or at all similar to that of the UK, but they show that other values exist and could come to the fore.

The question of military force is of primary concern. The British military could be reoriented towards island defence and away from the problem of maintaining expeditionary functions with declining economic power. The British armed forces have been a consistent source of evil in the world; any diminishment in expeditionary capacity would be a good in itself. An anti-expeditionary turn would have the advantage that the defence of the British Isles is a trivial problem, as evident in its complete absence in current planning and commentary. Talk of projecting British influence to the rest of the world should be dispensed with along with the retirement of expeditionary foreign policy. The Foreign Office and intelligence services could be directed to analysis and diplomacy, and away from the defence attaché model of ambassadorial arms dealing.

British foreign policy may have an inertial quality, but are other worlds possible? Britain has never experienced an Icelandic rebellion against NATO, and any move in that direction now seems remote. No element in the establishment favours any such break with the US project. Even at the height of Jeremy Corbyn's influence he could not include a more radical critique of British security policy.[44] On the other hand, the strategic community in the UK is nominally technocratic. Its preference for a strategy tethered to American power does not come from a class coalition, or any more general political tendency except in a very superficial way. Its effects are not of obvious economic benefit. And while most of the world has no decision to make about American hegemony, Britain is in the fortunate position that it could opt for much less cooperation, should it wish.

It is hard to argue that the British electorate has any interest in a new confrontation with China; it is not even an elite preoccupation.[45] The resurgence of enthusiastic Cold War–style rhetoric strongly favours technocratic Atlanticism. But the possibility remains that it could be challenged. Stripped of false grandeur, Britain could play a different role in the international system. That role would inevitably be based on what was immutable in Crowe's summation: the geographical condition of an island on the 'ocean flank of Europe'. This might entail a quieter pursuit of moderate prosperity. In the world as it stands it would also mean principled non-cooperation with American designs.

2

Someone Else's Empire

The invasion of Iraq was a generational disaster, but its effects will endure far longer. American and British armies descended in 2003, initiating the kind of cataclysm that registers in the fossil record. The war left hundreds of thousands of Iraqis dead, most of them civilians. There is still no authoritative count of the dead, only estimates with confidence intervals equivalent to tens of thousands of lives. The war's survivors were forced into violence or flight. A polity that had already endured a decade of genocidal sanctions suffered total collapse. The subsequent occupation was upheld through the use of torture and justified by the evidence of depleted uranium ammunition, a poor cousin of the weapons of mass destruction falsely held up as the reason for the invasion. Most former champions of the war now accept that it led to an increase in global jihadist activity, culminating in the rise of Islamic State. All these consequences were predicted by the anti-war movement. To speak of individual war crimes is to ignore the fact that the war itself was a terrible crime, a reckless assault of the sort that nations were once disarmed for committing.

During the first act of the 'global war on terror', which began late in 2001, British elites – along with their European, Russian,

Chinese and Japanese counterparts – could pretend that the US was engaged in an orderly action, even if it was motivated by retribution. The bombing and invasion of Afghanistan risked humanitarian catastrophe, but US 'allies' weren't inclined to oppose its exercise of authority. Terrorism was in any case a useful pretext for introducing domestic security measures of the sort to which all states are drawn. But Iraq was different. The arguments marshalled in favour of war in 2003 were dishonest. That its purpose was to reinforce US domination of the Middle East after the challenge mounted by al-Qaida was clear. The intelligence services knew, as the senior MI6 officer for the Middle East later admitted, that WMDs were a 'vehicle' for going to war.[1] The British government didn't hold its nose and accept that it had to join the invasion in order to retain its position in the US global order. In certain circles, enthusiasm for the war was high.

After seeing its terrible consequences, one might have expected the countries responsible to reflect on what had happened. But the UK has continued to evade scrutiny. Every prime minister since Blair has supported Britain's involvement; none has paid for it politically. Nor have pro-war intellectuals suffered. Much of the lingering criticism of the war falls back on legalistic critiques of process – the lack of UN Security Council resolutions, the misleading PR leading up to the invasion – where there ought to be condemnation. No convincing account of the British role in the war has yet been written. The Chilcot Report was delayed until it was so overshadowed by Brexit that the parliamentary debate on its findings was attended by only a handful of MPs. Patrick Porter's *Blunder: Britain's War in Iraq* showed that responsibility lay with the British elite as a whole and couldn't be limited to Blair.[2] But Porter's account also perpetuated the official story that the war 'exposed the deadliness of good intentions' and that it was prosecuted by principled idealists misled by a commitment to liberal democracy. Never mind that the honest idealists in the Bush camarilla were also Saddam Hussein's major sponsors in the 1980s, or that Blair's ideals stretched a few years later to selling his services as an adviser to other Middle Eastern and Central Asian dictatorships. The war's erstwhile supporters remain for the most part in a state of wishful forgetfulness, its uncounted victims not spoken of.

There have been more and better accounts of the military failures in Iraq than of the decision to invade in the first place. Ben Barry's *Blood, Metal and Dust: How Victory Turned into Defeat in Afghanistan and Iraq*, published in 2020, describes British military conduct in Iraq as a 'strategic folly on a level equal to that of Napoleon's 1812 attack on Russia and Hitler's 1941 attack on the Soviet Union'.[3] In 2009 the Ministry of Defence commissioned Lieutenant General Chris Brown to carry out a review of British strategy, later released under the Freedom of Information Act as the 'Operation Telic Lessons Compendium'.[4] Brown concluded that the army had not been prepared for the occupation, and that wars as unpopular as Iraq risked undermining 'the UK military's wider reputation'. This assessment stood in stark contrast to the confident war planning for Iraq that Donald Rumsfeld ordered in November 2001. Fresh from the swift removal of the Taliban with special forces and airstrikes, American military planners felt that its imperial tasks could now be managed by means of an air war and a modest number of specialist shock troops. Throughout 2002, plans for the invasion of Iraq were reformulated to put a greater emphasis on special forces operations. Iraq would require a larger ground force than Afghanistan but would be approached using the same tactics. In both cases, a fascination with the speed of the initial victory led to an underestimation of the problems of occupation.

Simon Akam's account of British military involvement in the

war for the greater Middle East, *The Changing of the Guard: The British Army since 9/11*, begins with a portrait of the British army at the start of the millennium.[5] The UK's contribution to the Iraq invasion force involved the 7th Armoured Brigade, 16 Air Assault Brigade, 3 Commando Brigade and 102 Logistics Brigade. Akam reconstructs the path to war of one of the armoured regiments, the Royal Scots Dragoon Guards. Before Iraq, the regiment was part of the British force based in North Rhine-Westphalia. Its main function was 'sitting in Germany boozily waiting for the Russians' (Akam seems to have a puritanical interest in the drinking habits of soldiers). It's a cliché that generals are always fighting the previous war, but the Royal Scots Dragoons seem to have been preparing for World War Two. The tank exercises they conducted on the Alberta plains would prove unsuited to engagements in the Middle East. They wasted time on intra-regimental squabbles. Officers were more concerned with ritual and class nonsense than professional soldiering. Infantry training was already less interesting to the army than special forces operations. As Akam puts it, exaggerated stories of recent special forces feats, particularly in Sierra Leone, had reinforced the idea that 'going far away and trying to do good with a rifle actually works'. And whatever state it was in, the British army was sure of its own superiority.

The UK spends more on its armed forces than the vast majority of countries, but since the 1980s the army has steadily reduced in size.[6] In recent years the army has struggled to fill its recruitment quotas. The median recruit is likely to be from a rural background, disadvantaged, and probably from the north-east of England. It was not always so. In the 1830s, more than 40 per cent of the army was drawn from Ireland and a disproportionate number of soldiers came from Scotland. In England, the standing army was originally a product of the Restoration. The country entered the final years of the seventeenth century with an oversized royal army accustomed to fighting continental wars. After the Peace of Rijswijk, parliament cut down the armed forces by more than 90 per cent. The army inflated again during the War of the Spanish succession but was still outnumbered by mercenary auxiliaries. At Waterloo, only about a third of Wellington's army comprised British soldiers.

Akam provides a picture of the contemporary British army as a decaying institution, but there is a sense that the decay doesn't matter much. His book is largely based on interviews with the officers who conducted the wars in Iraq and Afghanistan: a history through the eyes of the invaders. It was no surprise that the formal defences of the Iraqi state disintegrated when faced with the might of US forces. But even with a clear technological advantage over a poor and half-starved enemy, the war exposed British incompetence. The army was tasked with capturing and securing Basra, a city of about a million people, because anything else was beyond it. The British supply chain could only reach 95 kilometres from staging grounds in Kuwait. Their tanks required constant maintenance and couldn't be relied on to go further than that. Some of them crashed, or were delivered into ditches, and the operators lacked the plastic explosives necessary to drive them out. In April 2003, a Special Boat Service unit had to be rescued by coalition helicopters near Mosul.[7] Before the invasion the talk had been of demonstrating British prowess to the Americans. But claims of expertise and finesse soon ran up against reality, even when faced with a military as badly equipped as Iraq's: the Iraqi army could only field T-55s, designed in 1946, and many of the tanks destroyed by the British on the approach to Basra had already been abandoned. Unlike the defenders, the invasion force had air support. Akam neglects to say that British forces fired more than 2,000 cluster bombs at Basra, and never properly investigated the civilian casualties.

Having overcome Basra's flimsy defences, the army had to administer an occupied city. The British and American forces seemed to see the resistance they faced as inexplicable, nihilistic violence. The looting and burning of Basra Central Library in the first days of the occupation came to stand as a symbol of the disorder the invaders had unleashed. British officers told the Americans that they knew what they were doing thanks to their exploits in Northern Ireland. Yet they failed either to pre-empt or recognise the emerging Shia resistance. The British army proved incapable of securing the city, and not for lack of trying. In September 2003 British forces arrested a group of men, including the hotel receptionist Baha Mousa, and took them to battalion headquarters. There, Akam writes, 'Mousa died of his injuries' – one way to describe torturing a prisoner to death. Mousa was hooded and suffered ninety-three distinct injuries. Here were the skills acquired in Northern Ireland. The army was warned by its lawyers to prevent the abuse of prisoners, but Akam reports that the divisional commander, General Peter Wall, refused to give this order to the forces under his command. He was later promoted to chief of the general staff.

British behaviour in Basra inspired widespread hatred. Officers deceived themselves by talking of their good works, such as repainting schools (which their own forces had damaged). But the occupation forces never achieved the minimum objective of rebuilding Iraq's domestic security services. The number of British soldiers killed began to rise. Local militias soon had a freer hand than the occupiers. By 2005, IED attacks were common. In 2006 the British made a push to re-establish their authority, but their own soldiers couldn't move around safely. Akam describes an institution in a state of constant insecurity about its reputation with the Americans, but the US military had long since become disillusioned with British claims to expertise. American generals produced their own counterinsurgency manuals, with the aim of building up Sunni tribes against the Shia militias in classic colonial mode – the ramifications are evident today. They ramped up troop levels with the so-called surge, an option that wasn't available to the British. By early 2007, the forces in Basra were holed up in a garrison under constant shelling. When Blair left office in June that year, the British army was releasing prisoners to the city militias in exchange for temporary cessations of attacks on its positions. Akam describes all this well, but gives little sense of what any of it was like for Iraqis.

It took about eight weeks to remove British military equipment from central Basra, but the soldiers withdrew from the city in a single night like criminals leaving a burgled house. Their departure had been negotiated in advance with the Shia militias. British forces exercised so little control over the city by September 2007 that to leave without such an arrangement would have been very difficult. The midnight convoy was subjected to just one IED attack, which given the circumstances was counted a success. Basra was left to the militias. Having invaded Iraq's second city and occupied it for four years, British soldiers ended up sitting in an out-of-town airport while militiamen took pot shots at them with rockets. In the spring of 2008, American forces had to move south to support reconstituted Iraqi army divisions in retaking Basra. The British force was gone from Iraq within a year. In military circles this episode is seen as a total humiliation. Akam calls the Basra debacle 'the nadir of the post 9/11 wars', but there is also a sense in which it was a fitting end.

The war in Afghanistan began in October 2001 with seventy-six consecutive days of bombing in which the US Air Force and Navy dropped 17,500 bombs. One of the USAF's B-2s conducted a forty-four-hour sortie, the longest air mission in history. Warnings from aid agencies and the UN that the bombing and invasion risked worsening 'impending mass starvation' were brushed aside. After the first eleven days of air strikes, US special forces teams were brought in to begin their work with the Northern Alliance, the proxy force employed by the US and the UK to overthrow the Taliban. Kabul had fallen by 13 November and Kandahar by early December. The speed of this apparent victory encouraged the use of similar tactics in Iraq, Libya and Syria. The Afghan warzone was also a test case for armed drones and for the mass use of battlefield assassination. The combination of special forces, local proxies and air power is now the standard American model of war. But as in Iraq, success was an illusion. Twenty years later the war continues, with an estimated death toll of 241,000 and counting, according to Brown University's Costs of War project.[8]

British involvement in Afghanistan began with special forces raids in support of the bombing and as part of the hunt for senior members of al-Qaida. There were also missions of less obvious value: basic reconnaissance work and a raid on an opium factory in Kandahar. Akam focuses on the later deployment to Helmand province. From 2006 the British, Canadian and Australian armies controlled the province as part of the International Security Assistance Force. If the two main forms of colonial war are urban occupation and rural fort-soldiering, Basra exemplified the first and Helmand the second. British officers knew that they had too few troops in Helmand. The armed forces often claim that the civilian state asks them to do too much with too little, but in this case the military leadership had insisted on the deployment. In 2007 the chief of the general staff, General Richard Dannatt, told the British ambassador to Afghanistan that this decision was a result of the army's fear of further troop cuts. They believed soldiers who had finished their tours in Iraq would be dismissed if the generals didn't put them to use elsewhere.

Neither the British nor the Americans had much understanding of the civil war into which they had waded. Mike Martin, a former officer commissioned to research British military operations in Helmand (he published his findings in *An Intimate War*, despite the MoD's attempts to suppress it), described the British approach to the conflict as 'so far removed from the Helmandi understanding that Helmandis considered them to be trying to destroy the province through an alliance with the Taliban, rather than their purported aim of reconstruction'.[9] Had there been any realistic strategic aim in Helmand – a doubtful proposition – it would have required considerable diplomacy to pull it off. But the British sent in the third battalion of the parachute regiment: the regiment responsible for Bloody Sunday (and known for employing a soldier who collected human ears during the Falklands War). Akam describes 3 PARA as 'the most bellicose section of the British army'. In the first few months of 2006, the regiment fired half a million rounds, setting the general tone for subsequent deployments. Officers would refer to colonial-era campaigns in Malaya and Kenya. Medals and citations were handed out to officers who got into needless entanglements and then fought their way out of them. Helmand came to be seen as a place where violence was licensed.

After the US troop surge in 2009, the war in Afghanistan was overseen by American generals who had directed major operations in Iraq. Both Stanley McChrystal and David Petraeus considered themselves experts in counterinsurgency – the respectable term for trying to suppress domestic resistance to a military occupation. British soldiers were supposed to fall in line with American thinking and avoid making too many enemies, but they often failed. In September 2011, a patrol from the Royal Marines Corps came across an Afghan man who had been wounded in a helicopter strike. The patrol leader, Alexander Blackman, executed him, admitting unabashedly that he was violating the Geneva Conventions. He didn't realise that one of his men was wearing a helmet camera. The execution was treated as an outrage even within the army: Blackman was arrested and sentenced to ten years in prison. Some tried to treat the case as an aberration – the deputy commandant of the marines called it an isolated incident. But Blackman's immediate commanding officer believed the culture within 42 Commando, the unit to which Blackman belonged, was likely to produce war crimes. He resigned; the company and brigade commanders were promoted. Conservative MPs and the *Daily Mail* launched a campaign defending Blackman. As a result, his sentence was cut to eight years and then reduced to a conviction for manslaughter. He was released in 2017 and soon appearing as a guest on morning TV.

Akam contends that there was as little accountability within the military hierarchy as there was outside it. Individual soldiers were sometimes disciplined. But generals who oversaw strings of failures were rewarded. None was ever fired. The commander of joint operations during the Basra debacle, Nick Houghton, became chief of the defence staff in 2013 and now sits in the House of Lords. His deputy went on to become head of the army.

The Ministry of Defence tried to prevent the publication of Akam's book: the original publisher, Penguin Random House, pulled out before Scribe agreed to publish it. The military would obviously like to avoid a close examination of this unbroken string of catastrophes, but Akam's book is a gentle account – critical but not unsympathetic. The establishment reaction to it was unsurprising: Akam is too harsh on brave fighting men, the failures were the fault of politicians, or of too little money or insufficient militarism among the general population. But a pro-military position could be formulated another way: the army was asked to engage in criminal recklessness, and we must ensure that doesn't happen again. The generals don't say this and nor does Akam. Such criticisms can't be expressed even in a history that the MoD tried to pulp.

In March 2021, the British government published the results of its Integrated Review of Security, Defence, Development and Foreign Policy. This major national strategy document contains the usual overtones of imperial nostalgia and platitudes about 'British leadership in the world', but, even at this distance from the Iraq and Afghanistan wars, it is striking how much of the review is taken up with US priorities. An 'Indo-Pacific tilt' is mentioned. South Korea is described as 'a highly significant area of focus'. And the government pledges to 'work with our international partners to maintain secure global oil supplies, particularly in the Middle East'. Since the mid-2010s, the UK has sought to facilitate US requests by 'returning' military forces to bases in places of American interest: in particular the Persian Gulf and Far East. In 2018 a permanent British naval base was opened in Bahrain, with the intention, so it appears, of serving the needs of the American empire more efficiently. There's also a commitment to increase the UK's stockpile of nuclear weapons – a decision not discussed in public, and one which has received too little attention.

After the publication of the Integrated Review the MoD released a 'command paper' with further details on plans for the armed forces.[10] The paper included an illustration entitled 'The Threat' that listed 'electro-magnetic railguns' and 'over exposure through globalisation' in infantile bubbles. The MoD outlined some reductions in the numbers of soldiers, tanks and helicopters (the air force is to receive more overpriced, subsonic F-35s), as well as plans for a new special forces Ranger Regiment responsible for 'training, advising, assisting and accompanying local forces': an indication that it intends to fight more proxy wars. The defence secretary, Ben

Wallace, announced that UK armed forces would 'no longer be held as a force of last resort, but become a more present and active force around the world'.

Perhaps the most significant commitment was the deployment of a new aircraft carrier group in 'the Indo-Pacific', which would be 'permanently available to NATO'. One of the carriers set out for the South China Sea at the end of May 2021. British politicians were persuaded to spend £7.6 billion on the new vessels, HMS *Queen Elizabeth* and HMS *Prince of Wales*, despite having too few planes with which to equip them and only one ageing store ship to supply them. The military leadership also pushed for the Royal Navy to form 'Littoral Strike Groups' for international interventions. Baroness Goldie clarified in a written answer to Parliament later that year British patrol vessels would be stationed in the Indian and Pacific Oceans, and there would be a frigate in the area by the end of the decade. The reason given for these deployments was 'projection of power' – but whose power? In the 1960s, the US secretary of defense Robert McNamara and the secretary of state Dean Rusk urged their British counterparts to retain British military forces in the Far East.[11] The British ministers were reluctant, given that 'the empire was no longer there to justify it'.[12] The current government has no such reluctance.

It is one thing to station military forces around the world to maintain your empire, but quite another to do so for someone else's. It's not a new observation that those in power in Britain have become more culturally militarist as the UK has been shorn of actual global military influence. It's harder to explain the persistence of imperial lackeydom after Iraq. Part of the reason is a refusal, in most parts of society, to confront the reality of the post-9/11 wars. An aphakic view of the British military's role in the world persists. The UK remains a country in which the phrase 'east of Suez' is used without irony. A country that claims having soldiers in forty-six countries is necessary to keep its citizens safe. A country where professing a willingness to use nuclear weapons is considered a precondition for political office. A country that passes legislation to protect itself from prosecution for torture and war crimes (the Overseas Operations Act was criticised by the UN special rapporteur on torture as 'one of the most corrupt ideas the UK has come up with in modern times'). A country that has an undercover domestic police force to spy on and interfere with anti-war activists. It's not enough to say that British society has learned nothing from the way its distorted view of itself and of its relationship with the US contributed to the horrors of Iraq. After that debacle the UK was a leading advocate for destroying a state and half-heartedly instituting a new regime in Libya. There is no reason to think it won't happen again.

3
The British Defence Intellectual

Many countries find a special place for civilians who share the interests of the state's military, intelligence and diplomatic bureaucracy but operate outside its hierarchy. In Britain they are spread among a network of security think tanks and academic departments that include the Royal United Services Institute (RUSI), the International Institute for Strategic Studies (IISS), the Royal Institute for International Affairs (Chatham House) and the Department of War Studies at King's College London. From fine old buildings in Whitehall, Temple, St James's Square and the Strand, they shape much of the foreign and defence policy analysis produced in Britain. Each institution has its own flavour (the Chatham House sensibility is more mandarin than military), but they have a great deal in common. All have close connections with the intelligence services – after John Sawers retired as head of MI6 in 2014, he took up posts at King's and RUSI – and an equally close relationship with the national security establishment of the United States.

Among the British defence intelligentsia, Atlanticism is a foundational assumption. A former director of policy planning at the US State Department and a former director at the US National Security

Council are on the staff of the IISS. Until he stepped down in July 2022, Chatham House was led by Robin Niblett, who spent time at the Centre for Strategic and International Studies in Washington. RUSI's director-general, Karin von Hippel, was once chief of staff to the four-star American general John Allen. In 2021, RUSI's second largest donor was the US State Department. (The largest was the EU Commission; BAE Systems, the British army, the Foreign Office and some other friendly governments account for most of the remaining funding.) IISS's main funders – aside from the EU Commission, the State Department and, notably, Bahrain – are mostly arms companies. Chatham House gets more money from the British government and oil companies than from arms sellers, but its list of backers is similar. Despite these US links, however, and despite the fervency of their commitment to American national security priorities, British security think tanks have next to no influence across the Atlantic. Staff from UK think tanks sometimes take temporary jobs in more prestigious offices in Washington, but they very rarely become insiders.

During the invasion of Iraq, the most significant Anglo-American project of the past fifty years, the security think tanks didn't counsel prudence. In the run-up to the war, RUSI's director of military science, Michael Codner (King's via the US Naval War College in Rhode Island), described it as 'an intervention of choice designed to make the world on balance a safer and better place'. Britain was involved, Codner wrote, because 'one of successive British governments' highest-level grand strategic objectives is to enhance the security of the UK by influencing the execution of US security strategy'. (He also noted that 'this objective is not formally stated in public documents'.) In May 2003, Jonathan Eyal, now associate director at RUSI, complained that 'persuading international public opinion that a military action against Iraq was necessary should have been easy'. But for some reason, even within the Anglosphere, large numbers of people were opposed to it. Eyal ascribed this to 'atavistic anti-Americanism'. In a retrospective analysis, the then director of RUSI, Michael Clarke (King's, plus a brief period at the Brookings Institution in Washington), claimed that Blair had been 'guilty of confused optimism'.[1]

After Iraq, a number of senior figures in the British military had misgivings about intervening in Libya in 2011, but the defence intelligentsia didn't share their concerns. RUSI's major report on Libya, which dealt with the details of the military campaign not its possible consequences, was published under the title 'Accidental Heroes: Britain, France and the Libya Operation'.[2] Military performance aside, NATO could claim 'justifiable credit': 'whatever happens next in Libya, there can be no doubting that the allied air operation was critical to saving many innocent lives and removing a dictatorial regime'. The enthusiasm for intervention remains. In January 2022, as a Russian invasion of Ukraine seemed increasingly likely, RUSI's research fellow for European security, Ed Arnold, argued that the crisis in Ukraine would provide an opportunity 'to demonstrate exactly what Global Britain means'. At RUSI's annual land warfare conference in June, the chief of the general staff, Patrick Sanders, praised the British army's response to the crisis and said he would now have an answer for his grandchildren if they asked what he did in 2022.

These institutions do make some less boosterish contributions. Chatham House publishes *International Affairs*, a journal once indispensable and still very well regarded. The IISS publications *Survival* and *Strategic Comments* are usually of a good standard. The King's Department of War Studies has produced some novel scholarship.[3] But, with the British defence intellectual in greater demand than ever from newspapers and broadcasters, book-length projects have become rarer and some areas of research are neglected in favour of those that will play well with the media. Here's a sample of the headlines from recent think tank comment pieces: 'Terrorism Is Less of an Existential Threat than Russia and China' (RUSI), 'The Middle East: Exploring the Limits of Pragmatism' (IISS), 'Geopolitical Corporate Responsibility Can Drive Change' (Chatham House).

The most influential recent piece of work connected to the think tank nexus was *Global Britain in a Competitive Age*, the government's 'Integrated Review of Security, Defence, Development and Foreign Policy', published in March 2021.[4] Its principal author was John Bew, a fixture at the King's war studies department, where he is professor of history and foreign policy (he used to hold the Henry A. Kissinger Chair in Foreign Policy and International Relations at the Library of Congress), and foreign policy adviser to both Boris Johnson and Liz Truss; in September 2022 he was commissioned to lead yet another defence policy review. In 2016, Bew published a biography of Clement Attlee, whom he described as looking to the US on foreign affairs and as being a gatekeeper against elements in the British labour movement who were too soft on the Soviet Union.[5] The Attlee government spanned the period when NATO was founded, Britain worked to acquire nuclear weapons, and the general transfer of British imperial positions to the US occurred. Bew praised Attlee's 'unobtrusive progressive patriotism'. He described Jeremy Corbyn's leadership as 'a distinct break from the political tradition in which Attlee stood' and the movement around him as 'faddish radicalism'. Attlee, by contrast, was to be admired as a British socialist who was proud to have a signed photograph of Harry Truman in his study.

The 'Global Britain' slogan, the Indo-Pacific tilt, and the commitment to increase the UK's nuclear weapons stockpile (the ambition to become 'the European partner with the broadest and most integrated presence in the Indo-Pacific') were all included in the Integrated Review. 'Global Britain' is advertising speak, of course, not strategy: states with international influence don't need to boast about having it. Despite its commitments to 'British leadership in the world', the review seemed to follow American priorities. Britain would deploy an aircraft carrier to 'the Indo-Pacific' to be at NATO's service, and would pay special attention to America's East Asian allies. This led to the UK sending a warship into the Black Sea in June 2021, and through the Taiwan Strait in September 2021 in 'freedom of navigation' operations intended to rile Russia and China. The British government also continued to sponsor the catastrophic Saudi-led attack on Yemen with billions of pounds in arms transfers, technical support, training and operational direction, all while cutting humanitarian aid to the victims.

The Johnson government's decision to raise the defence budget by £16 billion over four years was celebrated by the Department of War Studies and at the chief think tanks. One of the central tasks of the British defence intellectual is to challenge signs of declinism and suggestions that the UK might be demoted from the 'top table'. The Integrated Review argued for reductions in the number of soldiers, tanks and helicopters, but at the same time promised that British armed forces would be a 'more present and active force around the world'. Although Britain claims to be committed to countering nuclear proliferation, the review announced a unilateral increase of 40 per cent in its nuclear weapons stockpile. There was no reassessment of relations with the US and the disastrous wars Britain was involved in by blindly adhering to US priorities.

Lawrence Freedman is the most distinguished figure in the British defence intelligentsia. He has written authoritatively on the history of nuclear strategy and was the official historian of the Falklands campaign. As a contributor to various magazines and

TV programmes he succeeds in treating vulgar matters without vulgarity. Before moving to King's, he worked at IISS and Chatham House. The major influence on his work was Michael Howard, who held the Regius Chair of Modern History at Oxford, translated Clausewitz, and founded both the Department of War Studies and the IISS. Howard supervised Freedman's PhD thesis and remained his mentor until his death in 2019. Howard was an elegant example of the conservatism of military historians: he didn't accept that the malfeasance of elites played much of a role in starting wars. For him, they were an inescapable product of the division of the world into states.

Freedman's most recent book, *Command: The Politics of Military Operations from Korea to Ukraine*, looks at the problem of leadership in wartime, and in particular the line between political and military authority.[6] He insists that there is a permeable barrier between the two because 'soldiers unavoidably influence the politics and civilians influence the operations'. Charismatic generals can erode the distinction between military and political leaders. In some states, this can take the form of a coup, and generals will sometimes start anti-systemic parties. As Gibbon said, men habituated to organised violence are generally unfit guardians of a civil constitution. What about the strategic decisions made by generals? Freedman discusses General MacArthur's disastrous decision during the Korean War to push to the Yalu river after capturing Pyongyang. He covers French campaigns in Indochina and the Algerian war of independence – at one point described as France's 'counterterrorism campaign in Algeria'. His chapter on the Cuban Missile Crisis provides good detail on the naval blockade, and on the American soldiers tasked with searching out Soviet submarines in the Sargasso Sea. One of those was the submarine B-59, about which there are conflicting accounts, some of which claim that the captain was preparing to fire a nuclear-armed torpedo before being talked down at the last minute. What is clear is that B-59 was detected by a US aircraft carrier group and that the US used depth charges and hand grenades against it. It's also clear that the sub had lost contact with Moscow and didn't know whether war had begun. As Freedman says, it wasn't a unique incident: 'numerous field commanders, on both sides of the US-Soviet confrontation, had the capacity to fire nuclear weapons'.

Freedman's work is most interesting where it touches on British history, especially its military calamities. He argues that the Falklands War was a close-run thing but gives a more or less positive assessment of Margaret Thatcher and Admiral Terence Lewin, as well as the British commanders in the field. (He doesn't mention the fact that the Royal Navy deployed ships with nuclear weapons to the theatre against Foreign Office advice.) He praises the productive relationship between the British government and the army, while also treating the Argentinian side as a study in the effectiveness of military dictatorships in wartime. One of the paradoxes of military dictators, he points out, is that they can end up making their national armies less efficient in an attempt to protect themselves from coups. But he doesn't offer a more general critique of the way the war was prosecuted.

The analysis provided by intelligence services will only be fully reliable if it's detached from the exigencies of government. But it never quite can be. The temptation is for judgements to become responsive to policy rather than to inform it. A similar problem afflicts the defence intellectual. Freedman paraphrases Hedley Bull to the effect that 'good scholarship is likely to be subversive of all causes, good or bad'.[7] But the institutions Freedman and his colleagues represent are not neutral: they have a structural role within the British establishment. As a public commentator Freedman often supports the consensus policy. He backed the First Gulf War on the basis that it was useful for the US to manage the balance of power in the Middle East. His chapter on Kosovo begins with the standard analysis of the NATO bombing of Yugoslavia, that it was conducted to stop the persecution of Kosovar Albanians. He doesn't mention the fact that the intervention only increased the level of persecution, or that American and European leaders repeatedly stressed that part of their motivation was to enhance 'NATO's credibility'.

At the height of the Kosovo war, Freedman made some edits to Tony Blair's Chicago speech on the 'Doctrine of the International Community'. His memo, which was disclosed by the Chilcot Inquiry, shows the difference between Freedman's published work and his private counsel.[8] The rhetoric – 'our fighting men and women', 'the Western alliance' – comes easily to him. Blair incorporated some of his suggestions in the speech. 'Many of our problems', Freedman wrote, 'have been caused by two dangerous and ruthless men, Saddam Hussein and Slobodan Milošević', who underestimated 'the resolve of democracies'. British military operations were all about 'delivering humanitarian aid, deterring attacks on defenceless people, backing up UN resolutions and occasionally engaging in major wars'. This sentence defined the Western view of liberal interventionism. In *Command*, Freedman acknowledges that humanitarian interventions were not seen that way elsewhere in the world. He argues that the Kosovo conflict destroyed any delusions in Moscow that the US would be constrained by international law. The accidental bombing of the Chinese embassy in Belgrade, he admits, 'had a long-term effect on Chinese attitudes towards the West'. But NATO's part in the war is seen as a humanitarian effort blighted by political and inter-military friction. For Freedman, one of the main problems with the bombing was that there were too many decision-makers, including 'committees of lawyers at the NATO HQ in Belgium' checking for violations of international law.

Command also includes Freedman's analysis of the war in Ukraine, much of which has been very good. He acknowledges the much fretted-over fact that one factor in the invasion was Russia's fear of Ukraine drifting closer to the West, and potentially joining Western institutions such as the EU and NATO. He explains the importance the Russian leadership put on the Donbas republics, Donetsk and Luhansk, as a way of exerting influence on Ukraine. He is strong on the operational and strategic mistakes made by Russia and on the state of the Ukrainian defences. What he fails to discuss is the relevance to the conflict of US-Russia relations – all he says is that the Ukrainian defenders depended on NATO supply lines to stay in the fight. But any full assessment of the invasion has to include some account of the breakdown of those relations in 2021. Freedman argues that Russia has demonstrated the danger of 'leaders supremely confident in their wisdom and insight, egged on by sympathetic courtiers who share the same baleful worldview, while disregarding any naysayers who warn of the pitfalls'. That observation could apply to others.

His account of the war in Afghanistan opens with the tiffs between Donald Rumsfeld and the military hierarchy. Rumsfeld was an unwavering advocate of the combination of air strikes, special forces teams and local proxies. His preferred approach prevailed. Freedman accepts that there were alternatives to war, such as persuading the Taliban to abandon Osama bin Laden, and that this 'might have prevented a lot of later grief'. But he's more interested in the operational failure of American and British special forces to find bin Laden at Tora Bora. At least the military leadership got it together well enough to pursue the global war on terror. Freedman argues that US leaders wanted to invade Iraq because they were 'reluctant at this time to tolerate any conceivable risk'. This despite the absurdity of the suggestion – and the lack of any evidence – that Iraq posed a risk to the US. He fails to give a general strategic picture of the US position in the greater Middle East region. And there is nothing about overconfident leaders with baleful worldviews incapable of heeding criticism.

His discussion of the Iraq conflict ends up focusing on the divergence between American and British approaches to the war in 2007, when the US opted for the surge and Britain for a humiliating exit from Basra. Here Freedman seems to suggest that one reason for the British decision to withdraw was that the UK realised the presence of its soldiers was the problem before the US did. But by 2007 the British army was incapable of doing anything much. The chapter on Iraq is headed with a wistful quote of Blair's, voicing regret that Britain did not 'play a far greater part'. But the anxiety of inferiority is only on the surface. Freedman's own language is calm: 'The United Kingdom took on a commitment to Iraq out of solidarity with its closest ally.' After the occupation, 'unfortunately, the violence only got worse'. He finds Britain at fault for failing to commit enough soldiers and equipment, but in general the UK is, as so often in the writings of British analysts, the restraining hand on American savagery.

Freedman's experience on the Chilcot Inquiry led him to think that the lesson for British policy was 'don't do it again', which is fair enough – though when have aggressive states learned that lesson? Joining the invasion of Iraq was, he says, 'the entrance fee into American decision-making', which Britain would use to 'moderate the tough line'. But Freedman never rejected the framework of US military operations against 'terror'. In the *Financial Times* in 2005, he argued strongly against changing foreign policy 'in response to terrorism'.[9] After all, 'if we wanted to be sure that the terrorists left us alone, then the necessary appeasement would go well beyond Iraq and require a series of immediate and probably catastrophic policy reversals, followed by a lifetime of grovelling'.

During the later stages of the occupations of Iraq and Afghanistan, American generals turned their attention to counterinsurgency operations. One of the military groups that thrived as a result was the Joint Special Operations Command, a collection of thugs, kidnappers, and battlefield assassins that continues to do a good deal of America's dirty work. Freedman describes its members as 'intensely patriotic'. Stanley McChrystal is a former JSOC commander who now runs 'an elite advisory team that improves the performance of organisations', drawing from 'experiences gained while transforming the US counter-terrorism effort from a . . . hierarchical apparatus into a high-performing team'. McChrystal, Freedman writes, 'understood the unique needs of this type of war'. But as head of US forces in Afghanistan in 2009, McChrystal pushed for the deployment of tens of thousands more troops to the country. He then publicly criticised those in the White House who had opposed that course, and had to resign as a result. There isn't much evidence that McChrystal or any of his successors understood what was happening in Afghanistan. In Iraq, Freedman writes, the American air campaign against Islamic State reduced much of Mosul to rubble. The drone operators had no idea who, or what, they were hitting. They still don't. This was also true in Afghanistan. Targeting decisions are made after looking at a few seconds of aerial video footage. Drone operators make mistakes, like misidentifying farm equipment as explosives factories, and have killed thousands of civilians. The air campaign against Islamic State continued long after it had lost the ability to hold territory. Freedman contrasts American bombing with Russia's air strikes in Syria, and says that Russia had 'fewer concerns over collateral damage'. But avoiding collateral damage was hardly the concern when the US continued to bomb a country it had already destroyed in the hope of winning over its population.

A book on command by a British military historian will inevitably be compared with John Keegan's 1987 classic *The Mask of Command: A Study of Generalship*.[10] Keegan taxonomised commanders as heroic, anti-heroic, false heroic or unheroic, all in the romantic sense of heroism. Freedman is more interested in human fallibility. In his best work, *Strategy: A History*, he challenged the notion of the master strategist: 'Operating solely in the military sphere, their view could only be partial. Operating in the political sphere they needed an impossible omniscience in grasping the totality of complex and dynamic situations as well as an ability to establish a credible and sustainable path towards distant goals that did not depend on good luck and a foolish enemy.'[11] But recognising human limitations can easily shade into sympathy, and for all Freedman's subtlety, his sympathy is often with British and American leaders. David Deptula, the architect of the American bombing campaign in Iraq in 1991, is thanked in his acknowledgments. Freedman claimed that one of the central themes of Michael Howard's work was 'urging Americans to keep a sense of proportion and use their power with care'. This, again, is the tired idea of Britain as wise adviser to American power. Freedman is sharper than most of his Atlanticist contemporaries, but he has much in common with them.

The British defence intelligentsia has an endorheic quality. As a whole it forms a permanent constituency in support of excessive military responses. This is inbuilt in the discipline: there isn't much point in a defence intellectual without an army. The think tanks welcomed Truss's policy of drastically raising military spending, with the aim of reaching 3 per cent of GDP by 2030. In the US there is detailed public debate about foreign policy, admittedly within a limited ideological range. In the British media there usually isn't. The influence of RUSI and other similar institutions in the media and on the professional class as a whole is partly responsible: supposed technocratic expertise is too often accepted on its own terms. The British security establishment experienced the Brexit vote as a mild shock but soon fell back into its old patterns. Freedman imagined that leaving the EU might lead to an introspective retirement from international posturing, but there has been no move in that direction. Instead, the reaction of the defence intelligentsia was to double down on Atlanticism regardless of the character of the US government or the ensnarements into which it leads the UK.

The British defence intelligentsia is a monolith. There is no prospect of significant disagreement between, say, IISS and RUSI on any significant question of foreign policy. Dissident work on military history and contemporary security is rare. The policy of the day always happens to coincide with the personal opinions of the *grand choeur*. Passionate Atlanticism proceeds on the assumption that the interests of American power are necessarily coterminous with those of Britain. The effect has been to preclude any re-examination of the special relationship, even during foreign policy overhauls of the kind required by Iraq and Brexit. The illusion of British 'leadership in the world' as counsel to American violence is stubborn as well as vain.

4
The Anglo-Settler Societies and World History

The existence of Five Eyes was not officially acknowledged until 2010, but accounts of its activities have been circulating for years. The sheer extent of the global surveillance system overseen by the US and its allies made it difficult to hide. The physical infrastructure alone operates at a Promethean scale: a network of satellite monitoring facilities shielded by radomes stretching from Point Barrow on the Arctic coast of Alaska to the Rideau River in eastern Ontario to the Hartland Peninsula on the north coast of Devon to Kojarena in Western Australia to the Waihopai Valley on New Zealand's South Island. An NSA analyst sitting in an office in Fort Meade, Maryland, receives signals from radio interception antennae in Tangimoana and taps on subsea internet cables on the bed of the Sea of Okhotsk. The system collects a massive volume of information: phone calls, satellite communications, emails, internet traffic, webcam images, billions of mobile phone location records, and tens of billions of text messages every day. This global data collection wouldn't be possible without the collaboration of the state intelligence agencies of Britain, Canada, Australia and New Zealand. The Five Eyes members share listening posts and much of the signals intelligence they collect. A reader of a Five Eyes brief may not know which state has collected the information they're looking at without consulting the technical data. The NSA is by far the most powerful signals intelligence agency in the world, but global surveillance is a shared effort of the Anglosphere.

The birth of the Five Eyes is usually dated to 1941, when US military intelligence officers visited Bletchley Park, bringing with them a 'Purple Machine' used to break encrypted Japanese communications. British cryptanalysts had already broken Enigma (though not yet the more sophisticated naval version). The Bletchley meeting became the basis for a wartime agreement between the US and UK to share codebreaking methods. In his history of the Five Eyes system, Richard Kerbaj goes back to 1938, when an MI5 officer decided to tip off the US embassy in London about a minor German plot to steal secrets from an American colonel in New York.[1] After the culprit was arrested, another MI5 officer, Guy Liddell, travelled to the US to discuss the case with American officials and to push for more co-operation between British security services and the FBI. But as Kerbaj's account shows, he didn't get very far. It was the Bletchley meeting that led to the BRUSA agreement, which codified the 'exchange and dissemination of all special intelligence derived by cryptanalysis of the communications of the military and air forces of the Axis powers'.

Many of the early efforts at transatlantic co-operation were less about intelligence-sharing than about drawing the US into the war. MI6 tried to improve links with American security officials with the help of the Canadian-born pilot turned industrialist William Samuel Stephenson. The plan was for American and British intelligence agencies to share the burden of monitoring the world by drawing up zones of influence – a version of the principle still applies today.

In 1940, William 'Wild Bill' Donovan, the head of the OSS, the wartime intelligence agency that preceded the CIA, visited Britain. The British wanted American money, radios, and boats. Donovan's visit led to the 'destroyers for bases' deal, under which Britain received American ships in return for the leases to some imperial outposts. The deal was celebrated in the UK because American support was critical to the war effort, but the US didn't do badly out of the arrangement. Given the speed at which American naval yards were churning out ships, fifty old destroyers was a price the US could easily pay. And the land it received in return came with benefits. The bases in various outposts were later used for tracking Soviet submarines, as stations for Strategic Air Command's nuclear weapons, and for launching reconnaissance flights during the Cuban Missile Crisis.

Neither Washington nor London saw any reason to end intelligence co-operation at the end of the war. Besides, the US had bigger plans. The UKUSA Agreement – the official name of the Five Eyes founding document – was drafted as a permanent replacement for BRUSA in November 1945. It became an important part of the postwar security architecture established by the US at the height of its power. What the US needed was territorial reach. Canada, Australia, and New Zealand, the three colonial territories granted dominion status by Britain in 1907, were to play a significant role. In the nineteenth century the British Empire had compensated for the loss of most of its American colonies by expanding eastwards. Capital from London had been poured into the Anglo-settler projects in the Antipodes (and what remained of its North American possessions: in the 1840s Toronto tripled in size). As James Belich showed in *Replenishing the Earth: The Settler Revolution and the Rise of the Anglo-World*, more British investment went to the Australian colonies in the 1870s and 1880s than anywhere else in the world.[2]

In 1835, Melbourne had no permanent residents; fifty years later its population was almost half a million. Within two generations, Sydney grew from a village to a city of 400,000. In the 1880s, Victoria was richer and more populous than California. The settlers were building Gladstone's 'many happy Englands' at a furious pace. The Anglo colonies were imagined as a transcontinental cultural system, much like the one the Mongols had built on the steppe, with the connections supplied by steamship instead of by horse. As British primacy faded, the US put these connections to use in the postwar architecture of surveillance.

Signals intelligence is supposed to be shared seamlessly among the Five Eyes members, but that's not the way it always works in practice. The NSA automatically receives the feed from other stations, but sometimes withholds what it knows. On occasion it takes in intelligence from another Five Eyes country and then reclassifies it as NOFORN, revoking the access of the ally that originally collected it. The greatest hits of Anglo-American intelligence work are well known: the NSA's monitoring of Egypt and Syria, the 1953 coup in Iran, a failed attempt at a redux in Syria in 1957, the Anglo-American operation to tunnel under East Berlin and tap its telephone lines, covert support for the mujahedin in Afghanistan, the false claim about the existence of Iraqi WMD. Kerbaj adds little to the histories of these cases. But his account contains useful information on some of the ruptures in the alliance.

In 1973, Henry Kissinger was infuriated by the Heath government's public stance against US actions in the Arab–Israeli war. He responded by temporarily cutting off British access to the Five Eyes feed. But US leaders rarely found it hard to keep the British in line. The more difficult question was whether the bogans in the dominions were really to be trusted. In 1942, the US had helped establish Australia's signals intelligence agency, the Central Bureau, in order to decrypt Japanese communications. But after Soviet spies were discovered in Canberra in 1948, the US downgraded Australia's access to intelligence as a disciplinary measure. In order to keep its place in the club, the Australian government was effectively forced to set up a professional intelligence apparatus – the agencies that would become the Australian Security Intelligence Organisation (ASIO) and the Australian Secret Information Service (ASIS). These institutions nurtured a generation of Australian Cold Warriors.

The general direction of US policy in Oceania was set with the signing of the ANZUS agreement, a deal between the US, Australia, and New Zealand in which the junior signatories received no security guarantees. In 1956, Australia and New Zealand were made full parties to UKUSA, completing the Five Eyes set. Australia was tasked with monitoring East Asian communications; New Zealand's agencies were trained on South Asia and the south-west Pacific. Seven years later, the US opened a jointly operated naval communications base on the North West Cape peninsula in Western Australia for messaging its ballistic nuclear submarines in the Indian Ocean. In 1966, the most important satellite facility in the region was established at Pine Gap, just south of Alice Springs. In 1969, Australia assisted with the construction of the Nurrungar listening station north of Adelaide, intended to help the US detect missile launches. At first Australian intelligence agencies were enthusiastic assistants, even supporting the CIA by running agents in Chile. But in 1972 the matter was again put in doubt when Gough Whitlam, a principled opponent of the Vietnam War, became prime minister. Nixon despised him, and there were serious concerns in Maryland and Virginia that Whitlam might try to close Pine Gap. Fortunately for the Americans, in 1975 Whitlam was removed from office on flimsy grounds by the governor-general, John Kerr, and intelligence co-operation resumed. Kerbaj refrains from judgement on whether the CIA had a hand in the matter.

In New Zealand, there was a more sustained challenge to the country's position as a far-flung auxiliary in the US-led military and intelligence system. The detonation of British and French nuclear weapons on Pacific atolls had contributed to a widespread scepticism about the bomb. In 1984, the new prime minister, David Lange, announced that he would make the country a nuclear-free zone – a policy hated by the US but popular, then as now, in New Zealand. When New Zealand began to refuse permission for nuclear-powered ships to enter its ports, the US suspended New Zealand from ANZUS and downgraded its access to Five Eyes intelligence. In theory, all intelligence flows to the New Zealand agencies were stopped. The official story was that intelligence-sharing was only reinstated after New Zealand agreed to participate in military operations in Somalia in the early 1990s. But in fact the NSA quietly continued to exchange intelligence because it wanted to maintain intercept facilities in New Zealand. The main Five Eyes facility at Waihopai opened in 1989. The balance of power among the Five Eyes countries was always clear, but on both sides the exigencies of global surveillance proved more significant than principles. New Zealand got to keep its nuclear-free policy and the listening stations remained.

On 12 September 2001, the heads of MI6, MI5, and GCHQ were flown to Langley to discuss how they could contribute to the war against al-Qaida. Kerbaj says that British intelligence agencies had expertise to offer from their work in Northern Ireland that was thought valuable to American efforts. That was certainly the belief in the UK, though questionable in reality. What was more important to Washington was that the already substantial resources the US devoted to its own intelligence agencies should be increased. By 2013, the NSA's budget had doubled and thousands of new staff had been hired. Many of the revelations in the papers leaked by Edward Snowden (which Kerbaj refers to as 'stolen documents') had to do with systems brought in for the new era of mass surveillance. The general scope of the established programmes had already been revealed by the brilliant work of the investigative journalist Nicky Hager in the late 1990s. But the Snowden leaks exposed the workings of the system – PRISM, XKEYSCORE, ECHELON, Stellar Wind, DISHFIRE, Tempora, MYSTIC and others – in remarkable detail. Kerbaj seems uninterested in the physical and computational architecture of global surveillance. He describes the NSA-funded satellite interception base at Morwenstow in Cornwall, which is jointly operated by the NSA and GCHQ, but doesn't really dwell on its function. He seems to prefer the thrills of stolen papers and vignettes about defectors and hairdressers turned spies. This leads to some unintentional comedy. 'As the world was preoccupied with the US nuclear attacks on the Japanese cities of Hiroshima and Nagasaki, which had killed more than 200,000 people,' Kerbaj writes, 'a young cipher clerk at the Soviet embassy in Ottawa was fighting for his own survival.'

Secrets tucked into trench coats miss the point of the Five Eyes and obscure its political implications. The history of Anglo-American surveillance matters, from its late imperial beginnings to the contemporary needs of American power. The idea that the existence of a vast system of global surveillance might be problematic doesn't have much purchase in any of the Five Eyes countries. Kerbaj includes a brief discussion of British and Canadian involvement in the CIA's post-9/11 rendition programme, which involved fifty countries and torture sites from Poland to Tashkent. In the British case the collusion went as far as tracking people who were to be rendered by the CIA. But the advantages of Five Eyes membership are supposed to outweigh other considerations. What are they? According to Kerbaj, the achievements of American-led signals intelligence include 'the defeat of the Soviet Union, combating Islamist terrorism and exposing Russian interference in Donald Trump's presidential campaign'. It is bad enough to equate a world historical event such as the fall of the Soviet Union with the non-achievement of 'combating' terrorism. But it's ludicrous to suggest that Russian interference is of any significance in the history of mass surveillance. It's revealing of Kerbaj's political allegiances that he makes no mention of the US's continuing global assassination programme, which makes use of drone and missile strikes, and is fully dependent on the Five Eyes system. After all, 'the Five Eyes is equivalent to a band of brothers and sisters drawn together by common values, language and cause'.

Clinton Fernandes's approach in his book *Sub-Imperial Power: Australia in the International Arena* is different.[3] He points out that the foreign policy of states – his focus is Australia – is often bound up in liberal technocratic euphemisms about the 'rules-based international order'. But such rules, he suggests, are also 'instruments of control and exclusion'. His argument is that Australia has taken on the role of a 'sub-imperial' power within the US-dominated system. As a former Australian military intelligence officer, he knows that US congressmen have easier access to information about Australian intelligence facilities such as Pine Gap than members of the Australian Parliament do, thanks to some autocratic laws about secret operations. As in Britain, to which Fernandes ascribes the more senior rank of 'lieutenant with nuclear weapons', military operations in Australia can be approved by the executive without parliamentary approval. Unlike New Zealand and Canada, Australia was an enthusiastic participant in the invasion of Iraq. It also signed up for duty in Afghanistan, with Pine Gap providing tactical intelligence. When Australian forces withdrew from the country in the summer of 2021, the head of the army, General Angus Campbell, said they had helped to improve security for millions of Afghans. Fernandes argues that their mission was really the 'pursuit of relevance to the United States'. A generation earlier, Australia sent sixty thousand troops to Vietnam. Australian strategic documents include some awareness of the more cynical side of American power, but there has been little attempt to change the trajectory.

Unusually for a developed country, the Australian economy is powered to a significant extent by the export of basic commodities – in particular, iron, coal, gold, and wheat. Most of these raw materials are sold to China, Japan and South Korea. This might seem to offer the opportunity to establish a foreign policy that isn't US-facing. But Australia's corporate economy is firmly integrated into American financial institutions. The major mining companies are for the most part US-owned. This led, for example, to Australia denying India access to its uranium until the US changed its policy on the Indian nuclear programme and then began building nuclear reactors in India in 2016. Fernandes argues that instead of developing Australian mineral deposits with a broader national development goal in mind, the state has preferred openness to private investment, 'to make Australia a better quarry'.

When it comes to their country's involvement in international affairs, Australian politicians have tended to stress lofty principles and the protection of human rights. But in the region where Australia has most influence, East Timor and the south-west Pacific, there has been little evidence of either. Fernandes writes about Australia's support for the Suharto dictatorship in Indonesia, its collusion in the invasion and destruction of East Timor and its opposition to West Papuan demands for self-determination. The Australian contingent in the Five Eyes put considerable resources into intelligence operations in East Timor in the early 2000s, and successive governments have refused to negotiate a maritime boundary there, wanting to continue to reap the benefits of oil and gas in the Timor Sea. According to the terms of a treaty signed in 2018, Australia is not required to pay compensation for its past exploitation of hydrocarbons. And despite Australia's economic interest in pursuing links with China, the signs are that here, too, the state will continue to follow the US's lead. Fernandes quotes a former Australian minister of defence, Peter Dutton, to the effect that Australian participation in any potential conflict between the US and China is seen as preordained.

Australia's future military plans put considerable emphasis on submarine warfare. The AUKUS deal, signed between Australia, the UK, and the US in September 2021, includes an arrangement to provide Australia with the technology for nuclear submarines. An existing submarine deal with France, signed in an outbreak of simple-minded commercial logic, was unceremoniously jettisoned – the US is more interested in having nuclear-powered boats armed with Tomahawk missiles patrolling the South and East China Seas. This is the first time the US has agreed to share nuclear technology with a non-nuclear state. As the US Centre for Strategic and Budgetary Assessments noted, 'US defense strategy depends in large part on America's advantage in undersea warfare. Quiet submarines are one of the US military's most viable means of gathering intelligence and projecting power.'[4] The AUKUS deal enables Australia to host US submarines in Western Australia until its own submarines arrive sometime before 2040. In its 2022 National Security Strategy, the US said the deal would contribute to 'iron-clad commitments' in the Indo-Pacific. China perceived the deal as just another example of America marshalling its forces around their territory. In Australia, it has been justified on the basis that an island nation has to protect its seaborne trade. But, as Fernandes notes, there is an irony here. Since China is Australia's major trading partner, Australia is in effect claiming to be 'protecting trade with China from China'.

But there is also a more general project: making Australia as useful as possible to American power. The head of the US army in the Pacific, General Charles Flynn, has declared his aim to make Australian armed forces interoperable or even interchangeable with those of their allies. Like its British counterpart, the Australian army is part of Project Convergence, which aims to 'merge joint capabilities' with US forces. In April 2021, Australia expanded four of its military bases to enable military exercises with the US, and that same year hosted Exercise Pitch Black, a joint drill in the Northern Territory. It has signed arms deals for billions of dollars' worth of US helicopters and HIMARS rocket launchers. The Australian government has also spoken of a desire to acquire hypersonic missiles, and for guided missiles to be constructed in Australia in partnership with Lockheed and Raytheon. As the defence minister, Pat Conroy, put it, 'Quite frankly, we need more missiles in Australia.'[5]

For the US, there has been political value in co-opting the former Anglo-settler societies. When the Biden administration stepped up sanctions on Nicaragua it helped that the UK and Canada followed suit. When the US pressed its allies to ban Huawei from involvement in their communications infrastructure, Australia, New Zealand and Canada readily agreed, and the UK capitulated after some rough diplomacy. Obedience is usually guaranteed in the end. In 2005, Canada opted out of the US homeland missile defence programme, but the Trudeau government is now revisiting that decision. In November, the US threatened that if Australia were to join the Treaty on the Prohibition of Nuclear Weapons its security arrangements would be at risk. Only Jacinda Ardern's government in New Zealand showed any resistance to lining up behind America's increasingly aggressive policy on China.[6]

Talk of historical ties and fraternal co-operation is the standard vocabulary of diplomacy. But how much of it is sincere and how much merely jockeying for position among subordinate nations in the Anglosphere? In Britain's case, keeping up appearances has come to seem essential now that the former Anglo-settler societies are in most respects wealthier than the UK – all have higher GDP per capita, in Australia's case considerably higher. It's a competition, dressed up in the language of intimacy. The former Australian prime minister John Howard spoke of the 'cultural affinity' between the Five Eyes countries based on 'the commonality of values among Anglosphere countries'.[7] But what are these values? For those in favour of constant global surveillance, the answer is often a willingness to allow the erosion of democratic principles.

5
Green Bamboo, Red Snow

In the spring of 2021, the UK government decided to greatly increase the size of its nuclear weapons stockpile. In keeping with local custom, this important strategic decision was slipped into page 76 of the government's Integrated Review of Security, Defence, Development and Foreign Policy. As we have seen the Integrated Review was long awaited, but few expected a major revision to Britain's perspective on nuclear weapons. The only reason to smuggle a major strategic decision into national policy in this way is to avoid scrutiny and attention, which is exactly what happened. The UK was committing itself to maintaining a larger stock of nuclear warheads than China (according to estimates by the US Department of Defense at the time) and the policy passed with very little examination.[1]

Until recently, Britain's record on nuclear weapons had some points in its favour. The UK was the only nuclear state that had limited itself to a single deterrence system (submarine-launched ballistic missiles). Between 2010 and 2019 successive governments held up Britain as a principled supporter of disarmament, pointing to 'step by step' reductions in the UK nuclear stockpile since 1980.[2] In 1998, the nuclear stockpile had been nominally capped at 200 warheads (though in fact 225 remained). In the 2010 and 2015, Conservative governments committed to reducing the stockpile to 180 bombs, even though upgraded warheads were being added. In the words of the director of the Nuclear Information Project at the Federation of American Scientists, Hans Kristensen, the UK had 'suddenly reversed decades of gradual disarmament policies'.[3] In fact the decision to increase the cap to 260 nuclear weapons represented a volte-face into open illegality because of Britain's commitments under the Non-Proliferation Treaty, not to speak of international efforts against nuclear weapons under the new Treaty on the Prohibition of Nuclear Weapons, adopted by the UN general assembly in 2017.

Britain's new nuclear turn was justified only by unspecified 'technological and doctrinal threats'. Later, the secretary of state for defence, Ben Wallace, claimed that one of the reasons was Russia's improved defences against ballistic missiles, which remain untested. The defence intelligentsia presented some arguments in favour of a high number of nuclear weapons. One argument is that more warheads would allow for the deployment of low-yield 'tactical' nuclear weapons, which the UK has not had since the 1990s. But no plans for the procurement of tactical nuclear weapons have emerged. Another argument was that increasing the stockpile to 260 would allow for two fully armed nuclear submarines to be on patrol at the same time (each submarine can load sixteen missiles, each of which carries eight warheads, for a total of 256 on two submarines). But the strategic need for this is unclear. As are some of the practicalities. It is not yet known what will become of the warheads awaiting decommissioning at the Royal Naval Armaments Depot in Coulport, nor whether the work of nuclear decommissioners in Burghfield is to stop. Will the stockpile be filled over time with new bombs? It is likely that at least some previously disassembled warheads will have to be reconstituted. Answering these questions is made harder by an associated decision, following the lead of the United States, to keep the exact number of warheads in the stockpile a secret.

Associated with a larger nuclear stockpile was a general project to modernise the British nuclear arsenal. This was a government programme to devote at least £31 billion to nuclear renewal and a major commitment. Over the next ten years, the programme is to cost considerably more than 25 per cent of the government's Defence Equipment Plan.[4] In May 2022, BAE and Rolls Royce got the contract for four new submarines, the first of which was to be named HMS *Dreadnought*, which are to replace the current Vanguard boats in the 2030s. The Dreadnought-class submarines are to be equipped with 'Quad Pack' missile compartments designed in council with the US Navy, which is keeping the same specifications for its own Columbia-class boats. The theme of similarity with American military equipment is ever present in discussion of British nuclear weapons. In addition there is greater co-operation with the American global deployment of its incomparably larger nuclear weapons capabilities. Most consequential of all, and also most quiet, was the decision to return US nuclear-armed bombers (stored in the UK until 2006) to the Suffolk Fenlands at RAF Lakenheath.[5]

A rare note of dissent was struck by the two LSE academics, Christine Chinkin and Louise Arimatsu, who had been commissioned by the Campaign for Nuclear Disarmament to provide a legal opinion on whether UK policy is in breach of article VI of the Non-Proliferation Treaty, which requires that signatories take effective measures 'in good faith' towards nuclear disarmament. Chinkin and Arimatsu found that the UK is in breach of the NPT under both treaty law and the law of state responsibility.[6] The office of the UN secretary-general came to a similar conclusion. Chinkin and Arimatsu's argument that the UK is breaking international law was a necessary challenge to the government, but it was not sufficient.

There is no reason to confine a critique of UK nuclear policy to the limited strictures of international law, which are themselves usually a weapon of the strong. Political critiques from pragmatism, from hypocrisy, from strategy, and from principle are needed. The UK has unilaterally moved to increase its nuclear weapons stockpile and changed its nuclear weapons doctrine, and no such critique has been made. Vague references to 'the prevailing security environment' were all the cover the government needed.

The history of British nuclear weapons is at every point fraught with auxiliary meaning – what Peter Hennessey once called 'one of the great running psychodramas of the United Kingdom'.[7] At its heart is the central question of what point there is in a non-superpower possessing nuclear weapons, a question that cannot be dismissed only because Robert Mcnamara once posed it.[8] In the earliest days of the British nuclear programme, this was complicated by the idea that Britain might still be a world power (a thought that animated both Clement Attlee and Ernest Bevin). But in the years after the Second World War it became unavoidable. The US had abruptly terminated nuclear co-operation with Britain in 1946, and it was not reinstated until after the Sputnik launch. The first nuclear weapons deployed by the UK had been smaller yield atomic bombs designed to be delivered from the air. The bombs and their delivery systems had colour names: Blue Danube, Red Snow, Yellow Sun, Violet Club, Green Bamboo. The development of thermonuclear weapons by first the US and then the Soviet Union changed the calculus. Harold Macmillan wanted the 'great prize' of a British thermonuclear weapon, which was achieved at considerable cost in November 1957.[9] But the delivery systems would prove more difficult: for those Britain would be dependent on the US.

The reliance of Britain's nuclear weapons programme on American industrial support immediately raised questions as to its nominal independence. The former Liberal Leader Jo Grimond asked, 'In what sense it is an independent deterrent which depends entirely upon whether the Americans make it?'[10] And what purpose did the prize serve? On this point there was disagreement with the US, which has tended to view British nuclear weapons as, at best, addenda to its own nuclear forces. British leaders have wanted to assert an 'independent nuclear deterrent'. But the question of independence is inextricable from that of utility. In a memorandum written in 1962, Under-Secretary of State George Ball suggested that the UK state clearly that it would only be able to use nuclear weapons 'in the event of a dire national emergency – an emergency which we might have to face alone' but 'always, of course, after adequate notice to all their allies'.[11] Macmillan refused this language out of a desire not to appear a 'satellite' of the US, but he knew that the refusal itself was a form of face saving. Tony Blair would later give voice to a variety of the same idea when he said it was 'frankly inconceivable that we would use our nuclear deterrent alone without the US'. And in any case, British nuclear weapons were to be 'targeted in accordance with NATO plans'.[12]

The Integrated Review included the standard rationale for having a 'nuclear deterrent' (what the UK has is nuclear weapons, deterrence is a conceptual matter): the weapons are to be used in 'extreme circumstances of self-defence', and not for threatening non-nuclear states so long as they are not in breach of the NPT. But the Integrated Review also included another striking revision to British policy. Under the new policy the UK 'reserves the right to review' its assurances not to use nuclear weapons against non-nuclear states 'if the future threat of weapons of mass destruction, such as chemical and biological capabilities, or emerging technologies that could have a comparable impact, makes it necessary'. It is possible to read this as opening the door to the use of nuclear weapons in response to a non-nuclear attack. Nuclear policy is supposed to be based on the principle of deliberate ambiguity, but this line of reasoning crosses from ambiguity into recklessness.

The UK nuclear programme has been based on submarine-launched ballistic missiles since the 1960s. They are the centrepiece of Britain's 'minimum, credible, independent nuclear deterrent, based on a continuous at sea posture'. The question of the utility of nuclear weapons for a non-superpower seems to be answered in the second-strike capacity of British SLBMs against Moscow: the hypothetical ability to respond to a nuclear first strike with surviving nuclear missiles. As early as 1960, Thomas Schelling had observed that SLBMs might offer considerable benefits in this respect: if the submarine-launched nuclear missile 'should prove to be both undetectable and highly reliable, it would have the advantage of not needing to strike first to strike at all'.[13] This has proven to be so for both American and British nuclear armed submarines. Trident D-5 missiles are MIRVed, meaning they are well suited to second-strike counterforce against an attacker's remaining nuclear force. (The combined cancellation of the unproven air-launched ballistic missile Skybolt and the British IRBM Blue Streak were in this sense fortuitous.) But to apply this analysis to the British context is to assume that the UK is in a nuclear dyad with Russia. In fact it is the US and Russia, in possession of the two major nuclear arsenals, which form the true dyad of the global nuclear balance. Pre-delegation for the use of nuclear weapons is widely discussed in the technical literature, even if lied about in public. In the UK case, 'letters of last resort' are issued to submarine commanders on leaving port containing written advice such as 'put yourself under the command of the US, if it is still there'.[14] And Britain's SLBMs are strongly dependent, in material and programmatic terms, on America. The missiles are leased from the US and stored in a communal pool in a US naval base in coastal

Georgia. The warhead, known as Holbrook, is made in the UK, but built using rebranded American designs for the W-76. In the words of the former national security adviser Stephen Lovegrove, 'it's not exactly the same warhead but . . . there is a very close connection in design terms and production terms'.[15]

There was once a belief that the proliferation of nuclear weapons to most of the world's states was inevitable.[16] Instead very little nuclear proliferation has occurred, with the majority of developed economies choosing to seek nuclear breakout capacity (the ability to produce a nuclear weapon in short order) rather than weapons themselves. As former imperial powers, Britain and France opted for the opposing route of maintaining their own weapons. France can plausibly claim that its nuclear weapons are not just modest numerical additions to the US arsenal. In the current strategic balance, the UK represents a tool of US power in a way that France does not. But France too is constrained by the reality of American power. In some great rupture to the international system, it is possible that the strategic position of the UK might change, but no one advocates for nuclear weapons on that basis, for obvious reasons. Instead nuclear weapons are more often a matter of current international status.

When it comes to national security, prestige is not a good in itself, but the argument has the merit of superficial coherence. Prestige was certainly present at the beginning of the British nuclear weapons programme, not least in Bevin's need for a union jack flying over a British bomb. Macmillan too openly admitted that there had been an element of 'keeping up with the Joneses' in Britain's decision to acquire and maintain thermonuclear weapons in July 1954, a project led by William Penney under Operation Grapple, which saw the detonation of nuclear bombs of various designs – Green Granite, Orange Herald, and Green Bamboo, among others – over the coconut palms of Pacific atolls.[17] Acquisition of thermonuclear weapons was framed as critical to British relations with the US. A British thermonuclear bomb was supposed to make US planners factor Britain into their strategic calculations. Similar arguments remain, with the direct tying of Britain's status as nuclear power to its permanent membership of the UN Security Council.

Concomitant with the reversal of Britain's pretensions to nuclear disarmament in favour of a larger stock of nuclear weapons has been a general degradation of state capacity. The MENSA warhead assembly and disassembly plant in Aldermaston has been delayed by six years. The Pegasus and Hydrus facilities, suspended and scuppered respectively, have likewise seen British hydrodynamics capability set back considerably. Another facility for handling enriched uranium components still hasn't been completed. The withering of British state capacity is not particular to the nuclear domain: despite talk of overdeveloped states, what is evident in contemporary Britain is signs of undevelopment (privatised water systems, the hosting of intelligence sites by Amazon, the relative decline of the Royal College of Defence Studies, once very well respected, now a shell as a result of funding cuts).[18] But nuclear support facilities are not an area in which imprecision is encouraging, or acceptable. The renationalisation of the Atomic Weapons Establishment in July 2021 was a necessary step, and no less concerning for its necessity. The prospect of Britain as an irresponsible nuclear power even in the narrow sense of safety and competence opens a new avenue of critique against the pro-nuclear weapons consensus.

The prevailing view on Britain's nuclear weapons remains that they are what Admiral Ben Key recently called 'the ultimate guarantee of security'.[19] But this view has been sustained as much by pride as by practical consideration. Recognition of the strategic role of British nuclear forces as supplementary to US forces is lacking. And talk of national interest and prestige obscures the vulnerability implied by a minor power possessing nuclear weapons. Due to the threat of species extirpation, the prevention of a NATO–Russia nuclear escalation should be one of the central tasks of contemporary international affairs. A confrontation between NATO and Russia that is in some respect limited to Europe represents a crisis just one rung lower on the escalation ladder than one of all-out war between Russia and the US itself. This has the concerning effect that the odds of nuclear weapons being used between the UK and Russia, while still low, are probably slightly higher than those of a full exchange between the two main nuclear powers. The possibility that the attack dog takes the first slashes is a significant risk to the general population of the UK, but scarcely acknowledged.

Concrete analysis of the effects of nuclear possession on Britain as a minor nuclear power within a global strategic picture in which there are only two significant thermonuclear powers, in fact shows not a guarantee of security, but vulnerability. Put simply, the world is subject to a global nuclear dyad in which minor nuclear weapons states are mostly subordinate to one of the major powers, both of which are capable of total destruction of all others. The destructive power of nuclear weapons means the missiles of other states are either directly or implicitly targeted at other nuclear forces. In the case of the breakout of nuclear conflict, possession of nuclear weapons thus makes a state a target in a way its non-nuclear neighbours are not. For a non-superpower, strategic analysis should show considerable strategic gains in the retirement of nuclear weapons. Opponents of disarmament have tended to be disinclined to note that in the worst-case scenarios having nuclear weapons is simply disadvantageous to the population of a smaller nuclear state, even in the sterile terms of national security.

II. Instruments of Order

6
The Economic Weapon

The global economy contains a striking asymmetry. We have noted that in terms of trade and GDP, the world has three poles: the United States, the EU, and China. But the international financial system is decidedly unipolar. The vast majority of transnational payments are routed through US banks. US Treasury bonds are the de facto reserve asset around the world. The Fed is the global supplier of liquidity in times of crisis. National economies respond on a hair trigger to US monetary policy. Giant American and European financial institutions, based for the most part in the US, control a large share of international corporate activity. New York is in effect the organisational headquarters of global capitalism, a permanent Bisenzone fair. Almost all transactions between nations are priced and settled in just a handful of currencies, of which the dollar makes up by far the biggest share. Colombian pesos are as much use in Karachi as Pakistani rupees are in Bogotá, but dollars count in both. Even large economies such as those of India, Brazil and South Korea conduct about 85 per cent of their trade in dollars.

In *Trade Wars Are Class Wars*, Matthew Klein and Michael Pettis showed that the US functions as the world's importer of last resort – absorbing the trade surpluses of Europe and China – and that the American working class pays the price.[1] But they didn't discuss the power that accrues to the US through its financial dominance. Economic sanctions were treated in a single line: 'The dollar's role in the global payments system has given the Treasury immense power to impose financial sanctions on targets anywhere in the world.' The fact is that Washington controls access to the international financial system. Much as a naval blockade denies access to the seas, US sanctions are based on monopoly power over a global commons: the world's reserve currency and medium of exchange. Sanctions are also a weapon. As a component of US strategy they are often seen as an alternative to military violence, promising, in the words of a recent *Washington Post* editorial, 'the achievement of foreign policy goals without the use of armed force'.[2] In reality, sanctions usually accompany military action (Libya in 2011, Syria from 2012) or are a prelude to it (Haiti in 1994, Bosnia in 1993, Kosovo in 1999, Afghanistan in 2001, Iraq in 2003).

Sanctions have long been the 'instrument of first resort' of US foreign policy. During Obama's second presidential term 2,350 new sanctions were declared. Over Trump's term there were 3,800. The current system of American financial weaponry developed alongside the rapidly growing security state during the war on terror. The Treasury, eager to keep rank with the national security apparatus, looked for ways to contribute. Ideologically, sanctions complemented the 'rogue state' discourse of the 1990s. Under cover of UN consensus, they were applied to devastating effect in Iraq, where pretensions of peaceful coercion resulted in hundreds of thousands of civilian deaths. When Iraq invaded Kuwait, sanctions were built around an embargo on Iraqi oil, but after 9/11 new methods were deployed. A combination of presidential decrees and provisions under the Patriot Act compelled banks to provide financial intelligence to the US Treasury. Swift, the main global network for inter-bank payments, agreed in secret to hand over transaction data to the government. Section 311 of the Patriot Act gave the Treasury the power to sever the link between the US financial system and entire national jurisdictions. Since international banks are almost all reliant on America's financial infrastructure, this was a significant innovation. Ostracising countries from the banking system became the capital punishment of the financial world.

What did this look like in practice? Iran had been subjected to an asset freeze after the revolution in 1979. The US imposed traditional trade sanctions during the Iran–Iraq war, and blocked all trade with Iran in 1995. The following year, an embargo effectively killed the country's liquid natural gas industry. But it wasn't until the Treasury's new weapons were turned on Tehran that it became clear how potent they could be. In 2006, the US began isolating Iranian banks from the international monetary system. In 2011, the Obama administration launched a 'sanctions onslaught'. Iran's oil exports, ports, petrochemicals industry and central bank were all targeted; Iranian banks were cut off from Swift. It was a complete financial stranglehold. US allies – the UK, France, Germany, Japan, South Korea, Australia and Canada, together with the Gulf monarchies – were enlisted to lend a veneer of multilateralism. Only some of these sanctions were lifted after the Iran nuclear deal came into effect in 2015, and these were reimposed when the Trump administration withdrew from the deal in 2018. This time, America's allies objected strongly: Europeans briefly tried to institute an alternative payments system, INSTEX, to get round the sanctions, and an effort was made to block them through the UN. But dissent in the Security Council was quashed with breezy truculence by the then secretary of state, Mike Pompeo: opposing the US position, he said, was 'just nuts'.[3]

In 1979, Iran's GDP per capita was slightly higher than Turkey's. It now stands at less than 25 per cent, despite a succession of government breakdowns and economic crises in Ankara. The trajectory of the Iranian economy has more closely resembled that of Iraq, which suffered from a decade of brutal traditional sanctions followed by outright conquest and civil war. In Iran's case it's difficult to disentangle the causes, since revolutionary politics had their own effects. But the Obama-era financial punishment of 2011–12 was responsible for an immediate drop in Iranian GDP, wiping out a third of economic activity. In *The Art of Sanctions: A View from the Field*, the former director of Iranian affairs at the National Security Council, Richard Nephew, described the sanctions as based on 'objectives for the imposition of pain', accompanied by instructions for 'the conditions necessary for the removal of pain'.[4] It's the torturer's schema, taken straight from the war on terror handbook. (Until December 2021, Nephew was Biden's deputy special envoy to Iran.)

The term 'economic sanctions' fails to capture the nature of these measures: they are a full financial blockade, stopping the flows that allow an economy to function. When the EU imposes 'sanctions' on employees of the Russian military contractor Wagner Group, or considers imposing them on the Bosnian Serb leader Milorad Dodik, these are forms of diplomatic pressure. The UK's restrictions on Belarusian state companies are economic sanctions, but they are effectively an industrial penalty – quite unlike the financial weaponry wielded by the US. (The UK was unlikely to do a lot of business with the Minsk wheeled Tractor Plant in any case.) Blocking access to London's financial networks is a major inconvenience but is hardly comparable to severing access to the international financial system itself. The EU claims it runs a 'fully autonomous sanctions regime' in the service of 'safeguarding EU values'.[5] But for the most part its sanctions, and those of the UK, are applied in conjunction with US power. The structure of international finance means that even the largest banks can't afford to provoke American ire.

Iran is far from the only case. One of the first subjects for Section 311 was Myanmar.[6] In November 2003, two Burmese banks, described as 'financial institutions of primary money laundering concern', were targeted for isolation. Within weeks, the Burmese government had shut down the banks and introduced regulations that conformed to American desires. But as Nicholas Mulder shows in *The Economic Weapon*, a much longer history lies behind the invention of modern sanctions.[7] When war broke out in 1914, the British Empire had been the dominant naval power for almost a century. London's capital markets financed 60 per cent of global trade: like New York today, it was at the centre of the infrastructure of industrial capitalism. France joined Britain in imposing blockades against German heavy industry, which relied on imports from as far away as the Malabar Coast. Thanks to Dutch and Swiss neutrality, a full maritime blockade of European ports was impractical. Instead, Britain imposed a system of naval stop and search in the North Sea. Beginning in 1916, all ships refuelling at British coaling stations were subject to cargo inspections to check for contraband destined for central Europe.

This was a material blockade, but it soon became a monetary one too. The British government confiscated financial assets held in London and forced banks to sign guarantees to prevent them dealing with the Central Powers. Until 1916, financial flows were routed to Germany and Austro-Hungary through Dutch, Swiss, and Scandinavian banks. Now the British exercised its power over neutral countries by threatening to exclude their banks from the London-Paris financial system. At first the effect was limited, but the threats became more potent after the US joined the effort in 1917. A Dutch bank was blacklisted for working with German clients. Crédit Lyonnaise had its transactions interdicted.

Estimates of the deaths caused as a result of the blockade of central Europe range between 300,000 and 400,000. (Ludendorff said that without food supplies from Romania the situation would have been much worse.) Of course the balance of forces meant that the war was a losing proposition for the Central Powers in any case: the outcome can't be attributed to either the trade embargo or the financial blockade. But as Mulder shows, such measures were decisive in the eastern Mediterranean, where large parts of the Ottoman Empire were dependent on imported grain. Unlike in northern Europe, Britain and France were able to impose a total naval blockade. The Levant experienced a brutal famine during which up to 500,000 people died. In Mount Lebanon, only one in two survived. Here was the economic weapon in full force.

The leaders of the major powers were impressed and sought to build sanctions into the design of the League of Nations. Before the war, 'arbitrationists' – mostly jurists in France – had searched for ways to enforce international law without committing to military action. In the starvation methods of the Anglo-French blockade they believed they had found one. The US president, Woodrow Wilson, thought economic 'suffocation' would be impossible to resist. The French minister of commerce, Étienne Clémentel, commended the notion of subduing 'unruly' peoples by manipulating the supply of raw materials. The Versailles powers spoke about law and order, but were eager to make the wartime blockade a permanent form of imperial discipline. League of Nations officials had no illusions about the effect on civilians. As the head of the economics section put it, recalcitrant nations could reliably be brought into line through 'the starvation of the general population'.

The US decision not to join the League of Nations impeded the full realisation of this dream. Even so, Britain and France had a few successful moments in their attempt at rule by sanctions. In 1921, the threat of a League-endorsed British naval blockade prevented a war between Yugoslavia and Albania. In 1925, Greek border incursions into Bulgaria were seen off by a combination of the threat of League sanctions and the prospect of Royal Navy manoeuvres off Piraeus. But these were minor episodes, and Mulder perhaps exaggerates the extent to which they represented a change in the way the great powers exercised control. In Ireland and Afghanistan, Britain was still suppressing independence movements with military force. France and Italy both occupied neighbouring territory in Europe. Anglo-American ships bombarded Nanjing. Mulder wants to argue that the autarkic turn taken by Japan, Italy and Germany in the 1930s was partly a reaction to the threat of material blockades. But if he is right then it was an overreaction, since the threat was largely empty. The only time League sanctions were actually applied was following the Italian invasion of Ethiopia – and they were largely ineffective because the US refused to enforce an oil embargo. No serious effort was made to use economic weapons against Germany in 1936, Japan in 1937, or Germany in 1938.

In the absence of US support, the failure of rule by sanctions as attempted by the British and French empires was hardly surprising. Industrialisation had altered the composition of the global economy and with it the balance of power. Only America had the financial might to constrain other nations by economic means. This was first demonstrated in 1941. Before joining the war, the US froze assets belonging to countries under German control and imposed an oil embargo on Spain to manoeuvre it away from the Axis. In July 1941 the US and Britain cut off Japan's oil supply, leading to the suicidal attack on Pearl Harbor. The postwar settlement was enforced by US air power rather than by economic coercion, but sanctions had proved their usefulness. When the UN Security Council was set up, sanctions were incorporated into its design as the penalty of first recourse for rebellious nations.

The UN gave sanctions the appearance of multilateral legitimacy. But in practice the economic weapon was a dollar weapon. During the Cold War, the presence of the Soviet Union and China on the Security Council inhibited the US from deploying its weapon under UN auspices – that didn't come until the 1990s. But the US could impose its own trade embargoes, with the Soviet Union and China each targeted at one point or another. The biggest American sanctions programme, however, was reserved for Cuba – a target that receives curiously little attention in the historiography of sanctions, as if the American embargo were a natural feature requiring no explanation. Cuba necessarily plays no part in Mulder's account, which ends with 1945. But *el bloqueo* – starting with the arms embargo of the 1950s, becoming near total in 1962 and maintained ever since – is the oldest and harshest sanctions programme in the world. It is embedded in US law, making it 'unique among country-based sanctions', as the Treasury proudly puts it. Its costs to Cuba over time are difficult to tally but they certainly run into hundreds of billions of dollars in today's money.

Judged as an attempt to bring down the political structures of the Cuban revolution, economic sanctions obviously failed. Much the same could be said about Iran. And the efficacy of sanctions as a tool of coercion has often been criticised within the US establishment. In 1997, Robert Pape, a political scientist much admired by policy-makers, published the influential paper 'Why Economic Sanctions Do Not Work'.[8] Pape argued that even the most severe economic measures would inevitably run up against nationalist resolve, and that no matter how strict the blockade, a country's well-connected elite would still be able to procure the luxuries to which they were accustomed. The people most affected would be the poor – and alleviating the suffering of poor people is rarely a government's highest priority.

Even countries subjected to the harshest US sanctions have found ways of adapting. Despite decades of economic assault, Iran has managed to raise life expectancy to the level of a standard industrialised economy through a commitment to public health that is exceptional by regional standards. Life expectancy in Cuba, thanks to its famed health service, is the same or higher than in the US. But to criticise sanctions on the basis of what they achieve is to ignore the logic behind the infliction of pain, as former US officials describe it. Torture is more often about punishment than coercion. Pape maintained that sanctions could have a further use, to 'disarm criticism of the use of force later'. In other words, American military action would be more palatable if it were presented as a last resort after sanctions 'failed'. Principled criticism based not on the usefulness of sanctions but on the suffering inflicted on civilians has been quite rare. In 2017, the Trump administration passed the Countering America's Adversaries Through Sanctions Act with just five dissenting votes in the House and the Senate.

National trade restrictions may be unwise, even cruel, but a government's ban on its own trade with another country is a legitimate part of statecraft. American embargoes are of a different order, since the US is in effect asserting that it is illegal for anyone, anywhere, to deal with countries or entities it has placed under sanctions. Large international banks including Lloyds TSB, Credit Suisse, Standard Chartered, HSBC, RBS, BNP Paribas, Commerzbank and ING have all paid fines for violating American sanctions, as have Bank of Brazil, Bank of Tokyo Mitsubishi and Bank of China. The fines sometimes run into the hundreds of millions of dollars. Outside the

US, these 'secondary sanctions' are quite reasonably interpreted as extraterritorial expansion, with no justification beyond America's brute power. Secondary sanctions are a 'weapon out of control', as Tom Ruys and Cedric Ryngaert have argued in the *British Yearbook of International Law*.[9] But although European leaders often express their outrage at being subjected to US whims, they never show signs of actual resistance. It is taken as a given that the US will infringe the rights of all other states.

China and Russia are not so inhibited: both vehemently condemn the 'long-arm jurisdiction' of the American legal system. As critics in China put it, US financial sanctions are the equivalent of papal excommunication.[10] Such thinking is surprisingly novel: Russia once went along with the strangulation of Iran and in 2006 Chinese banks complied with the US attempt to finish off North Korea's economy. The turning point came in 2014, when the Obama administration imposed sanctions on Russia after the annexation of Crimea. While not full isolation on the Iran model, in combination with low oil prices these measures contributed to a Russian recession. China saw the situation as Russia did: a line had been crossed. The US might punish peripheral states such as Iran or Cuba for their disobedience, but attempting to treat a major nuclear power the same way was another matter.

Late in 2022, as Russian military forces began to mass from Rostov to Pinsk, the US threatened to extend its sanctions to a full blockade of the Russian economy. When Putin recognised the independence of the Donbas separatist regions on 21 February, Biden responded by sanctioning the Russian state investment company VEB and the state-backed Promsvyazbank. The following day, he announced that the US had 'worked with' Germany to cancel the Nord Stream 2 pipeline, which had been due to deliver enough Russian natural gas to supply 26 million European homes. The moment Russian troops crossed the border into Ukraine, the US brought out the heavy financial weaponry. On 24 February, the major Russian banks – Sberbank, VTB and Gazprombank – had their access to the international financial infrastructure revoked. This was an attack on Russia's whole financial system, not to mention the majority of its citizens. Sberbank's European subsidiaries collapsed overnight. The US followed up by banning all transactions with the Russian Central Bank and freezing its assets. By 27 February, Russian banks were being cut off from Swift.

Since 2014 Russia has taken steps to make its economy relatively sanctions-resistant. Spending on imported goods and services was deliberately suppressed and Russia's foreign currency reserves were nearly doubled to $640 billion. It's hard to know exactly where these assets are held, but as much as 65 per cent are thought to be with financial institutions based in the US, UK, EU, Japan and Switzerland. The remaining 35 per cent are held in gold or on Chinese territory. These reserves may be vulnerable to the edicts of the US Office of Foreign Assets Control, and some pressure has been brought to bear by Chinese state banks, which have refused to finance purchases of Russian oil for fear of US secondary sanctions.

Yet despite these harsh measures, Russian energy exports were initially exempted from US sanctions. Biden declared that the programme had been 'specifically designed' to allow Europe to keep paying for the Russian oil and gas on which it depends: American officials told international banks that they wouldn't be penalised for processing energy transactions.[11] The energy ties between Russia and Europe are such a central feature of world politics that it seemed unlikely that even a war could interrupt them. European imports of Russian hydrocarbons have barely shifted since 2014. On 8 March, Biden went further, issuing an executive order prohibiting the purchase of Russian oil, coal and gas. This move is unlikely to hurt the

American economy. Europe, deeply divided and still considering its options, is in a far more difficult position.

The Kremlin has acknowledged that these are 'heavy sanctions'. On 28 February, the rouble lost nearly a third of its value and the central bank was forced to double interest rates. US officials began to worry not that the sanctions weren't working but that they were working too well: could putting Russia under this much pressure provoke further military escalation? No one knows how damaging sanctions might be to a state of Russia's size and importance. The Russian government has taken action to shore up the currency by forcing exporters to buy roubles with the proceeds of foreign sales. Some of the defensive measures put in place over the past eight years are as yet untested. Russia's own alternative payments system, Mir, has allowed domestic transactions to continue unimpeded even though Mastercard and Visa have suspended Russian operations. But despite the name – it means 'world' – Mir is of little use outside Russia and Armenia. The Russian transfer network SPFS is unlikely to be an adequate replacement for Swift. It's clear that US sanctions against China wouldn't cause the degree of economic damage seen in a smaller country, such as Iran. But what of Russia?

The biggest victims of financial blockades will always be the ordinary citizens of the sanctioned state. Whether or not America's financial weaponry is capable of inflicting mass suffering on Russia, it continues to do so in smaller countries. In 2017, as part of an attempt to force Nicolás Maduro from office, the US imposed a financial blockade on Venezuela, with sanctions that were referred to as 'smart' and 'targeted'. The Washington-based Centre for Economic Policy Research has since reported that they were in fact responsible for more than 40,000 deaths: they 'reduced the public's caloric intake, increased disease and mortality (for both adults and infants) and displaced millions'.[12] The echoes of wartime starvation were unmistakable – but the EU and the UK supported the policy anyway. The Caesar Syria Civilian Protection Act sanctions, which came into effect in 2020, were just as indiscriminate. The World Food Programme found that the number of Syrians without enough to eat doubled.[13] Aid groups reported that the sanctions were restricting the supply of humanitarian aid. None of this has altered the policies of the Syrian regime.

This kind of power remains an American prerogative. US analysts have begun to speak of China's increasing use of sanctions – which have involved trade restrictions and tit-for-tat travel bans on American and European officials – as though they were comparable with those imposed by the US. But the renminbi accounts for only 2 per cent of international transactions. Bans on wine or basketball coverage are not an economic threat. This hasn't stopped some American courtiers claiming that China and even Russia are the real masters of the discipline, just as they do with space militarisation and proxy warfare.

Last year the Biden administration conducted a review of US sanctions programmes. Janet Yellen, the secretary to the Treasury, suggested only one improvement: that exceptions should be made for humanitarian assistance – 'where possible and appropriate'.[14] Biden has persisted with Trump's sanctions on Syria and Venezuela. Saudi Arabia's blockade of Yemen in 2017, in concert with a proxy war backed by the US and UK, contributed to miserable conditions for the majority of the Yemeni population. The Biden administration is now considering reimposing sanctions on the Houthis. After its withdrawal from Afghanistan last year, the US froze $9.5 billion in Afghan state assets under old anti-Taliban sanctions. Afghanistan's financial institutions can now barely function and the country is facing a general famine. The US has ignored appeals from the UN and the World Food Programme to unfreeze assets. And yet despite

Biden's faithful adherence to Trump-era policy, he has been criticised by the American right for doing nothing to prevent the 'brazen defiance' of Chinese firms purchasing Iranian oil.

The financial blockade originated as a tool of imperial control, and this is what it remains, even when used in response to a clear act of aggression. Russia's invasion of Ukraine has shown that sanctions not only have widespread support, but are now considered an inevitable, even natural, force in world politics. The current arrangement of the global economy is not inevitable, however. At some point the US may no longer be in a position to exploit its financial centrality as it does now. For large parts of the world that moment will be cause for celebration.

7
Keys to the World

The oceangoing ship has been one of the principal engines of history. Breakthroughs in hull, mast and rudder design, not to mention navigation techniques, led to the galleon and so to the early European maritime empires. Since at least the fifteenth-century naval strength has been a central component of national power. Sea power isn't just a matter of building a bigger navy. Nor is it reducible to the skill of admirals. Even the best ships with the ablest captains will struggle without conveniently located ports and the infrastructure they provide. Without secure access to the relevant seas a large navy is just a lot of metal to clean. The best summation of the importance of naval position was given in 1904 by the British admiral John Fisher: 'Five keys lock up the world! Singapore, the Cape, Alexandria, Gibraltar, Dover. These five keys belong to England.'[1] But if you leave strategic bases aside, it is often the show of naval force, rather than its application, that has proved most potent.

The modern tool of naval power projection is the aircraft carrier. The biggest of them, which belong to the US Navy, are 333 metres end to end (longer than the Shard would be if it were laid horizontally) and displace 100,000 tonnes of water with their bulk. They rarely travel alone. An aircraft carrier is usually escorted by cruisers, destroyers and submarines, as well as fighter jets, attack aircraft and helicopters. US carriers are nuclear-powered so don't need regular deliveries of fuel. Naval enthusiasts tend to take emphatic pride in their nation's carriers: the Royal Navy refers to HMS *Queen Elizabeth*, launched in 2014, as '4.5 acres of floating sovereign power'. The US has eleven full-size fleet carriers, more than the rest of the world combined. It wasn't always so. Japan had ten carriers by 1940 and Japanese admirals pioneered the carrier group, before the US sank almost all of them in the Pacific. In a sense American aircraft carriers are throwbacks: relics of the military-industrial production of the Second World War, when US shipyards built thousands of warships. The point of them today is to transfer the advantages of military power far out of sight of land, beyond the range of strategic ports, bestowing on their masters the power to set the rules at sea.

Because most countries have coasts and about 80 per cent of physical trade depends on the seas, the question of who governs them is critical to international relations in general. The balance of sea power matters to everyone, most of all to large island countries (New Zealand, the United Kingdom, Madagascar) and archipelagic states (Indonesia, Japan, Malaysia, the Philippines). David Bosco opens *The Poseidon Project: The Struggle to Govern the World's Oceans* with the question of the Senkaku Islands, eight uninhabited rocks between Taiwan and Okinawa which are in themselves no good to anyone but are nonetheless bitterly contested.[2] Under US occupation from 1945, when the islands were sometimes used as a bombing range, the Senkakus were given over to Japan in 1972. They are still subject to territorial claims by China and Taiwan. Islands that lie between major powers have always been a good pretext for national disputes, but there are also practical reasons for wanting them. Most states struggle to assert claims to the seas far beyond their own shorelines, and the possession of islands, even islets like the Senkakus, may allow for a better claim to what would otherwise be treated as open ocean.

The seas have often been thought of as 'lawless'. But Bosco, who has an American law school background, contends that an international legal regime for the oceans has been in place for at least two centuries. Iberian, Dutch, French, and then Anglo-American maritime empires usually favoured a Grotian 'freedom of the seas', which in practice often meant their freedom to conquer by sail. European powers adopted a lofty language of the global commons while insisting on retaining advantages for themselves. Britain perfected the practice after the Napoleonic Wars, and the US continued where Royal Navy admirals left off. Franklin Roosevelt said it best: 'All freedom – meaning freedom to live, and not freedom to conquer and subjugate other peoples – depends on freedom of the seas. All of American history – North, Central and South American history – has been inevitably tied up with those words, "freedom of the seas".'[3] Bosco is concerned that the idea of that freedom is vanishing. Russia is planting flags on the bottom of the Atlantic, China is harassing fishermen in the South China Sea, and Turkey and India are making maritime territorial claims based on arguments about continental shelves. It isn't a coincidence that the upstarts all sit outside areas of US hegemony and the traditions from which it drew. 'If open conflict does break out in Asia,' Bosco says, 'it is likely that "freedom of the seas" will be a battle cry.'

The doctrine of free seas has some predecessors in the ancient world. The extent of Roman influence around the Mediterranean necessitated freedom of access – for Romans. One forerunner of modern maritime codes was seventh-century Byzantium's Rhodian Sea Law, which dealt with liability for lost or damaged cargo. The twelfth-century Rolls of Oléron provided indemnity for captains whose sailors got drunk in port and injured people in fights. But it was difficult for navies to lay down the law in the ocean expanse until the development of better naval weaponry. Bosco implies that ships had a limited ability to engage one another at sea until the end of the Age of Sail. This underestimates the trireme ram, Korea's armoured *geobukseon* and the innovations of the Portuguese Navy. It also misplaces the introduction of naval artillery by almost 300 years, making nonsense of the 1588 Battle of Gravelines, the defeat inflicted by England on the Spanish Armada, achieved with the use of naval cannon.

As soon as there were global maritime empires there were attempts to claim ocean territory, or at least the land found while exploring it. The Treaty of Tordesillas (1494) and the Treaty of Zaragoza (1529) divided the Atlantic and then the Pacific into Portuguese and Spanish domains. Anglo-Dutch competition led to the seventeenth-century argument between Hugo Grotius, the Dutch jurist who saw the seas as global commons, and the English lawyer John Selden, who argued for a right to claim territory close to the mainland. *Mare liberum* or *Mare clausum*? Writing in the early eighteenth century the Dutch legal theorist Cornelius van Bynkershoek provided a synthesis of sorts in the cannon shot rule, which declared that states could claim the seas 'as far as cannon will carry' from the shoreline. At the time that meant about three miles, which happens to be approximately the distance of the horizon as seen at sea level. The three-mile rule, with freedom of the seas beyond, suited Britain when it became the principal naval power from the mid-eighteenth century onwards, and Admiralty charts were closely guarded assets until the British felt comfortable enough in their navigational advantage to start selling their maps for good fees in the 1820s. In 1841 Britain asserted dominion over Hong Kong and twelve years later Matthew Perry steamed into Edo. This is what was meant by freedom.

Bosco's book, with its legal slant, doesn't really explain how Anglo-American maritime dominance came about. In the late sixteenth century, John Hawkins, a privateer who became treasurer of the British Navy, transformed what was primarily a coastal defence force into an ocean-going fleet capable of plundering Iberian colonial trade. But it was the English Civil War that provided impetus for the creation of a large professional navy at the service of the state. As the result of a remarkable shipbuilding effort the navy doubled in size between 1649 and 1651.[4] It was immediately put to work against the Dutch and in a bout of colonial expansion in the Caribbean. At the turn of the eighteenth century the British and French navies were roughly equivalent in size. By its end, Britain had 500 ships to France's 200.[5] In 1759, at the Battle of Quiberon Bay, Britain inflicted a major defeat on the French Navy that set up its victory in the Seven Years' War. By the time the two powers relitigated the matter during the Napoleonic Wars Britain's advantage was too great. Trafalgar made the decision final.

British naval dominance was always accompanied by rhetorical flourishes about freedom of the seas. Yet it was Britain's control of the Atlantic that made it possible for its merchant ships to transport more than three million slaves to the Americas. Under the Slave Trade Act of 1807, abolition became a pretext for boarding foreign ships anywhere at sea. After US independence the British Navy intercepted supply ships in the Atlantic, which in 1780 provoked the anti-British League of Armed Neutrality between the northern European naval powers and then the war of 1812. The interceptions represented no more than a shift from the traditional British practice of authorised privateering, as effected since the days of Francis Drake, to the state carrying out piracy on its own account. While Britain was bombarding North African towns in response to the wrong kind of (Barbary) piracy in the eighteenth and nineteenth centuries, its leaders adopted ever more vaulted commitments to free seas. And British sea power had never been greater. The requirement that foreign ships salute when passing through the Channel had been magnanimously dropped after the Battle of Trafalgar: why limit symbolic deference to the Channel? Britain was to be what the diplomat Eyre Crowe later, ominously, called 'the neighbour of every country accessible by sea'.

Britain remained unchallenged as the pre-eminent naval power until the onset of the First World War. When towards the end of the nineteenth century the German Empire mounted a challenge by building a navy, acquiring overseas colonies, and establishing a coaling station in the Zhoushan Islands at the mouth of the Yangtse, it proved to be a grave strategic mistake. Bosco has very little to say about the effects of the war. Referring to the British naval blockade of Europe he asks why it was that 'the edifice of norms protecting freedom of navigation' was allowed to crumble. The answer couldn't be simpler: the world was at war. But Bosco reduces it to 'British and German restrictions on free navigation'. His treatment of the interwar period, and the arms race that dominated it, is also lacking. The 1922 Washington naval conference and its successor in London in 1930 gave Britain and the US 30 per cent of global naval tonnage, and a far greater advantage in destroyers and other smaller ships. Britain and the US dictated the sizes of ship that other states were allowed to build. There were limits on the size of submarines and the kinds of weapon they were allowed to carry. At the Washington and London conferences, the US and UK froze the global balance of naval power in their favour. The major powers effectively stopped building battleships until 1936. Because warships take a long time to build, the balance set in 1922 was still in effect in 1939: a remarkable feat for Anglo-America.

Bosco mostly leaves out the Second World War, skipping straight from 1939 to the Truman proclamations of 1945. The US emerged with total dominance on the seas and in the air. The Soviet Union didn't really become a naval power until the 1960s and never rivalled the US on water. Truman asserted exclusive rights to continental shelf waters, while still claiming to uphold freedom of the seas. Other states in the western hemisphere, from Mexico to Chile, made similar claims to continental shelf waters. The USSR followed suit, extending its territorial waters to twelve miles from the coast. In 1970 Brazil declared a 200-mile territorial sea. States were playing by the new rules the US had ushered in. But the idea of freedom of the seas was too useful to be jettisoned. Whenever it was convenient, the US opposed the territorial claims of other countries on the basis of commitment to free commons. When in the early 1970s Canada tried to impose environmental controls on shipping in the North-West Passage, the US State Department's executive secretary, Ted Eliot, said it was unacceptable that a neighbour 'feels it can undertake such action in the face of United States opposition'.[6] The US Navy blockaded Guatemala and intercepted ships in the Taiwan Strait. But maritime freedoms were regarded rather differently by small states that had experienced the dangers the seas could bring to their shores. Freedom of the seas, Peruvian officials argued, meant 'colonial subjugation'.

In 1948 the UN established the International Maritime Organisation to deal with the great expansion in merchandise trade, which became more urgent with the rise of containerisation in the late 1950s. The logistics and regulation of global shipping became a central fact of industrial capitalism. But deciding who was responsible for enforcing laws at sea was made more complex by the use of flags of convenience. Since 1927, thanks to a ruling by the Permanent Court of International Justice, ships have been subject to the laws of the state of whichever flag they fly. As a result companies found it useful to register their ships in Liberia, Panama or the Marshall Islands: anywhere with open registries. Panama was attractive to US shipowners because of the convenience of the canal and because its currency was pegged to the dollar, but especially because its safety regulations were lax. By 1970 flags of convenience were flown on a quarter of merchant ships by total tonnage. Sometimes they had immediate practical value: during the Iran-Iraq war, the US allowed Kuwaiti oil tankers to fly American flags for their protection. But for the most part they were an instrument of labour subjugation: foreign laws made it easier to screw over sailors. France and the Soviet Union mounted campaigns against the practice but the US overruled them.

In the 1970s momentum began to build at the UN for a multilateral treaty on the laws of the sea. Bosco provides an entertaining account of the Maltese diplomat Arvid Pardo's efforts in that direction, inspired by hallucinogenic visions for undersea development including fish farms staffed by dolphins. Pardo was instrumental in beginning the nine-year drafting process that produced the 1982 UN Convention on the Law of the Sea. Unlike early efforts at a maritime convention, this was a full treaty. Flags of convenience would continue to be permitted. States would have the right to claim up to twelve miles of sea as sovereign territory, overthrowing the three-mile cannon shot rule favoured by Britain.

The convention also introduced Exclusive Economic Zones as a way of mediating the areas between national waters and the high seas. An EEZ could stretch as far as 200 miles from the coast, allowing even small islands to make great claims. Coastal states could assert rights to the hydrocarbons and fish in their zones. But in practice the EEZ was a troublesome concept: states tend to interpret their zones as their own territorial possessions but object when their adversaries do the same. Another principle the convention codified was the right of 'innocent passage' in the territorial waters of other states. The arrangement was to the US's advantage, but American nationalists were opposed in principle to the idea that the US should be subject to international rules. So the US ended up voting against the convention while also declaring its own EEZ covering seven million square miles. The convention didn't come into effect until 1994 and the US still hasn't ratified it, though it recognises its provisions when they accord with its interests. Hundreds of EEZs have since blossomed. Ultimately the convention allowed commercialised enclosure by all without infringing on the control of the commons exercised by the US.

The conventions and legal disputation Bosco is interested in are only so much marginalia when set beside the brute fact of US naval hegemony. Paul Kennedy's account of the naval history of the Second World War, *Victory at Sea: Naval Power and the Transformation of the Global Order in World War II*, makes this clear.[7] For Kennedy the main story of the war at sea is the ascent of the US, having started out as one naval power among many, to 'naval mastery at the close of the war years'. In 1939 there were six major powers at sea: the Royal Navy, the US Navy, the Imperial Japanese Navy, France's La Royale, Italy's Regia Marina and Germany's Kriegsmarine. The British fleet was the only truly global navy, ranging from Jamaica to Sydney. Having many colonies to police, Britain naturally favoured light cruisers for the work of maritime empire. German and Italian admirals favoured heavier ships for battles closer to home. Early in the war the Royal Navy struggled to compete with its Italian and German equivalents, but the Italian part of the alliance eventually collapsed thanks to its inferior ships and submarines. Germany's submarines were more advanced but it had too few of them, no more than fifty in the first year of the war. (Contrary to the usual narrative, Italy ended up sinking more British submarines than Germany did.) Following a strategy put forward by Wolfgang Wegener in his book *Die Seestrategie des Weltkrieges* (1929), which argued that Germany could not break a Royal Navy blockade in the North Sea directly, the Kriegsmarine focused on a campaign to seize Norway and break out of the North Sea through Norwegian harbours.

Germany took Norway in 1940, but at the cost of much of its navy. Wegener hadn't foreseen how vulnerable ships would become. Air attacks and torpedoes neutered the German surface fleet within the first two years of the war, and German submarines were able to sink British battleships. Without air cover large surface ships were sitting ducks that could be sunk with a single torpedo. Between November and December 1941, the Royal Navy lost six capital ships, four of them to submarines. The war demonstrated the redundancy of the battleship and the value of destroyers and escorts. Allied supply transports continued to be under serious threat from the Kriegsmarine until the adoption of small centimetric radar and air escorts. But the central contest of the war, between the Soviet Union and Germany, put limits on German submarine production. Despite the pleas of Admiral Karl Dönitz, Germany wasn't able to build large numbers of submarines until well into 1942. By then, technical innovations in anti-submarine warfare were turning against them, definitively so after the deployment of the acoustic torpedo in March 1943.

In keeping with the traditions of Anglosphere scholarship, Kennedy makes too much of the contribution of British and American actions in the Atlantic to the Soviet victory over Germany. Raw materials and equipment (especially Western trucks) supplied by sea were helpful to the war effort, but much of the Lend-Lease aid arrived after the great battles of 1941 and 1942. The importance of efficient, domestic Soviet arms production cannot be overstated. The Soviet Union would have won regardless of the sideshow in the Atlantic. But the Pacific War was a different matter. The British assault on the Italian fleet in Taranto had demonstrated what aircraft carriers could do. More dramatic was Japan's aerial attack on HMS *Prince of Wales* and HMS *Repulse*, which showed that surface battleships were useless against modern aircraft and good torpedoes. Britain realised it couldn't hold the empire's eastern possessions against sustained pressure. The Imperial Japanese Navy was professional and well equipped. Japan had a fine war record up until 1942; it had conquered a great deal of territory. It had the best fighter aircraft and the best torpedoes. In the Kidō Butai it had a carrier fleet. But it was completely overwhelmed by the US Navy.

Just as the USSR overwhelmed Germany on land by producing more munitions and tanks, the US would overwhelm all other states in shipbuilding and aircraft production. The American shipbuilding programme begun in 1940 was unprecedented in scale. The naval yards in New York and Philadelphia could turn out ships at a speed no other power could approach. Some naval yards had a dozen destroyers on the docks at any one time. A single production yard in New Orleans built nearly 9,000 landing craft of the kind used in Normandy. In 1941 the Japanese, British and American navies had been similar in size – about two million tonnes of warships for Japan and 2.5 million each for the US and UK. By 1944 the US had ten million tonnes of warships. Britain's navy had barely grown and Japan's had been depleted. In 1944 alone the US launched nine aircraft carriers while producing more aircraft per year than Germany, Japan and Britain combined.[8]

Kennedy doesn't believe that American war production was in itself decisive, but the effect was clear enough. The major carrier battles in the Pacific, Coral Sea and Midway were the proof. US aircraft launched from fleet carriers in the Philippine Sea eliminated the prospect of Japan as a world power. The US approached

Okinawa with 200 destroyers, eighteen battleships, and more than forty carriers to face down no surface opposition. By 1945 only the US and British navies were major forces, and the US dwarfed all other states in terms of naval and air power. It soon acquired nuclear-powered aircraft carriers and submarines. As Kennedy says, 'shifts in the productive balances' didn't just change the face of the war, 'but were going to be large enough to alter the strategic landscape of the twentieth century itself'.

Until the 2010s, there was little talk of challengers to American sea power. It is only recently that China has credibly been described as an aspirant rival at sea. During its continued period of dominance, the US has advanced an image of itself as the protector of freedom at sea, just as Britain once did. Under the Proliferation Security Initiative launched by George W. Bush in 2003, the US Navy has interdicted, boarded and searched ships as a matter of course. In December 2020, the US military published an official strategy document titled 'Advantage at Sea' which claimed that American sea power had assured 'free and open access to the world's oceans', bringing about 'an extraordinary era of wealth and peace for many nations'. But, it went on, 'that system is now at risk'. As a result, the US must 'maintain and exploit sea control in contested environments from the littorals to open ocean, including critical chokepoints'.[9] The contemporary equivalents of Fisher's five keys – Malacca, Yokosuka, Hormuz, Suez and Panama – are all either in American hands or as good as. In East and South-East Asia the US has major military facilities on Guam, naval bases in Japan at Yokosuka, Sasebo, Okinawa, Misawa and Atsugi, bases in Thailand and Sembawang, and access to military support facilities in South Korea and the Philippines. To these can be added the US position in the Indian Ocean, based on Diego Garcia, and the Fifth Fleet's permanent presence in the Persian Gulf.

But in a report to Congress in November 2021 the US Department of Defense declared that China now had 'numerically the largest navy in the world'.[10] That line, widely reported in international media, is misleading, since much of China's fleet comprises patrol and logistics vessels. It's difficult to make a direct comparison between the US and Chinese navies because their ships play different roles. The US has many more destroyers, amphibious assault ships and guided-missile cruisers, as well as by far the best submarine force in the world, with eight times as many nuclear attack submarines than any other state. The majority of China's submarine force runs on diesel. China didn't have a domestically built aircraft carrier in service until 2019 and both its carriers (one of them a refitted Soviet ship built in 1985) are half the size of any one of the eleven US vessels. A third Chinese carrier is now being built, but again without nuclear propulsion. China has developed anti-ship ballistic missiles to counter the US carrier fleet, but it's too soon to know whether they will be decisive. If they are, China will have spent a lot of time and money in foolish emulation of US carriers. In any case the Chinese Navy has conducted no military operations of any scale and almost nothing outside its immediate sea perimeter. The US Department of Defense assessment was that the Chinese Navy's 'ability to perform missions beyond the First Island Chain is modest but growing'. In other words it remains a regional navy.

What is now at stake between the US and China is not global pre-eminence but the shackles the US has constructed around China: the 'defense perimeter' around the East and South China Seas, at some points just a few kilometres from the Chinese coast. That explains the focus on Taiwan, to which America sends more than just octogenarian politicians. In February 2021 the US conducted naval exercises in the South China Sea with two aircraft carrier groups. In early August, the US Navy assembled thirty-eight ships and 170 aircraft from allied countries for naval exercises in the Pacific. It's probably a sign of confidence that American planners have been happy to supply Taiwan with F-16 fighters but haven't paid much attention to its shore defences. That may now be changing. In August last year, the US signed a deal to supply Taiwan with American howitzers. It has also considered placing large numbers of missiles on the territory of its East Asian allies, and permanently deploying attack helicopter squadrons and artillery in South Korea.

Since 2015 the US has regularly conducted 'freedom of navigation operations' in the seas surrounding China. And China has continued to face legal battles over its territorial claims to islands in the South China Sea. When brought to international tribunal by the Philippines, China rejected the tribunal's jurisdiction, as large powers tend to do. In July 2020, Mike Pompeo accused China of attempting to build a 'maritime empire', a statement which ought to have elicited general laughter.[11] As I write, a US carrier group is passing through the South China Sea. The US claims it is conducting a principled defence of free seas; China says that such moves are merely provocations. On 13 July 2022, China claimed that a US destroyer, the USS *Benfold*, had entered waters off the Paracel Islands, which China claims. The US insisted that the *Benfold* was in international waters. China sent a frigate to follow it all the way across the Taiwan Strait. These incidents happen so often that they now rarely qualify as news. At its core the dispute is an iteration of an old argument as to whether the claims of maritime empires to freedom of the high seas are anything more than a predatory pretext.

8
The Proxy Doctrine

To fight a war this century you need proxies on the ground. From South America to Central Africa, the Middle East and Eastern Europe, nations have chosen to pursue their objectives through local confederates. The catastrophic Anglo-American invasions of Afghanistan and Iraq are remembered as conventional wars. But the war in Afghanistan began with the raising of a proxy army. Although the invasion of Iraq was conducted by traditional armed divisions on a grand scale – nearly 180,000 troops from the US, UK, Australia, and others – the occupation that followed devolved into an exercise in proxy management. The temptation to use direct military force to contend with the provocations of another state is ever present; injunctions to 'arm the rebels' – from proponents of interventions in civil wars around the world – are now almost as common.

Powerful states have used local auxiliaries to pursue their foreign policy aims since ancient times. The Athenians engaged Cretan archers – they had better bows. The Roman Empire used Ghassanid tribesmen to combat the Lakhmids, themselves proxies of the Persians. Almost every kingdom in Renaissance Europe enlisted halberd-waving Swiss Reisläufer. Turning regional political factions into proxy armies was a standard tactic of European empires. But war by proxy is a strategy depended on now as never before.

Until his assassination by US drone strike on 3 January 2020, it was generally agreed that the modern master of proxy warfare was Qasem Soleimani of the Islamic Revolutionary Guard Corps, the general in charge of Iran's extraterritorial and clandestine military activities. President Donald Trump justified turning the US global assassination machine against Soleimani on the grounds that he had been 'saying bad things about our country', but his reputation as mastermind wasn't without basis.[1] Unlike his equivalents in the CIA and MI6, Soleimani liked to dodge mortar fire near the front lines. He spoke reasonable Arabic and was able to inspire loyalty in ragtag bands of foreign fighters. His activities led to the belief that where Americans and Brits were amateur proxy warriors, Iranians were professionals. Sepah-e Quds, the directorate of the IRGC responsible for running forces abroad, was founded during the Iran-Iraq War; Soleimani took command in 1997 and built on a tradition that had been developing in Iran since the revolution. In Iraq, the Quds Force has influence over the Hashd ash-Sha'bi, a group of forty or so militias also known as the Popular Mobilisation Committee. In Syria, it works through Afghan and Syrian Shia irregulars. The Zaidi Shia of the Houthi movement in Yemen and Taliban factions in Afghanistan both work with the Quds Force, though – like Hizbullah in Lebanon, which has grown to be more of an ally than a proxy – they are better described as supported by Iran than as its puppets. Most of the fighters for these groups are drawn from local Shia communities, but the Quds Force doesn't insist on doctrinal purity.

The logic of the strategy is faultless. For four decades Iran has been the declared nemesis of the global superpower. It is encircled by US military bases and hostile Sunni Arab states. Its economy has been strangled by US sanctions. By keeping the Americans occupied with its proxies across the Levant, Iran has protected itself from US interference within its own borders. Acting through proxies has another benefit: by stopping short of direct confrontation, the Iranian government has been able to make periodic overtures to the US, recognising that a degree of accommodation with American power is necessary for long-term survival. Iran's proxy strategy is primarily defensive, but it has also allowed the country to have greater influence over its neighbours than it would otherwise have had, reinforcing Bashar al-Assad in Syria and boosting Shia political forces in Iraq.

The IRGC has a term for its approach: 'effects-based operations', a term it has used in public. What's interesting is that the concept is derived from American military literature: 'effects-based operations' were defined by the former US Air Force general David Deptula during the First Gulf War as a means of applying the minimum conventional force to achieve the greatest strategic effect.[2] In US government planning, 'proxy warfare' is the preserve of wily enemies, Iran and Russia in particular. The US National Defense Strategy 2018 notes the threat that competitors may use tactics short of open war to achieve their ends, including 'information warfare, ambiguous or denied proxy operations and subversion'. The most recent report of the US National Defense Strategy Commission describes 'the growing prevalence of aggression and conflict in the grey zone – the space between war and peace'. In Western national security circles this is sometimes referred to as the 'Gerasimov doctrine', a term invented in jest, and later regretted, by the Russia analyst Mark Galeotti after a speech by the Russian general Valery Gerasimov. National security officials in Washington and London – including the former UK national security adviser Mark Sedwill – have used the term to describe what they see as Russian plans to destabilise Europe and America. The irony is that

Gerasimov wasn't talking about Russian strategy at all: he was, quite reasonably, accusing the West of 'blurring the lines between the states of war and peace'. Whenever America's enemies are said to be using 'asymmetric' or unconventional tactics and proxy warfare, it's easy to forget not only that America is the world's most prolific sponsor of armed proxies but that it is the US – not Russia or Iran – that has done most to develop the proxy war doctrine.

In January 2018 the US military introduced the 'by-with-through' approach.[3] It was the work of J-2, the intelligence directorate of the Joint Chiefs of Staff: 'the US military must organise, resource and train' local forces and 'operate by, with and through' its 'partners' and 'nations that share our interests' (note that the word 'proxy' is avoided in favour of more anodyne terms). Using proxies has been common practice for the CIA for decades, but the J-2 doctrine describes an increasingly common style of war. The model depends on American air power, often in the form of drones backed by satellite surveillance, deployed to support proxy ground forces of local grunts, supplemented by teams of American or American-allied special forces where more artful work is required. The US used this approach in its interventions on the rebel side in the Libyan and Syrian civil wars, and in support of Kurdish and Iraqi militias to defeat Islamic State. In Yemen, the air war itself was farmed out to vassal states – Saudi Arabia and the UAE – with US and British advisers providing direction, training, tactical advice, munitions, and the services of their engineers. Saudi military personnel are trained by the RAF in Shropshire and flown back to fight in Yemen.

The UK military has adopted similarly euphemistic terminology to describe the approach it has agreed with its more powerful ally. In a speech for the think tank Policy Exchange, the head of the British armed forces, General Nick Carter, said that Britain faces 'authoritarian rivals' that employ attacks below the threshold which would prompt a war-fighting response in 'a continuous struggle in which non-military and military instruments are used unconstrained by any distinction between peace and war'.[4] In Carter's telling, 'our natural aversion to putting people in harm's way' is a weakness that is exploited by enemies – an amorphous Russo-China that doesn't exist outside Anglophone propaganda. The British solution is an Integrated Operating Concept that envisions the armed forces working permanently in 'partnered operations against common threats'. If official adversaries were doing all this it would be called proxy warfare. But in the parlance of the armed forces the British approach involves 'a campaign posture that involves continuous operating on our terms and in places of our choosing'.

There is every sign that the US plans to prosecute future conflicts along these lines, and other powers have sought to emulate American practices as far as they can. The Arab monarchies of the Gulf enlisted their own proxies in Syria, and Russia used proxy militias in eastern Ukraine. More recently, Turkey has repurposed its failed Syrian proxy army and put it to work in Libya. Military analysts are forever declaring the onset of new ages in warfare. Perhaps this really is one.

The United States emerged from the Second World War in possession of by far the most powerful conventional military forces ever assembled. It controlled the world's oceans and had an air force that would soon become so far superior to the air forces of other states that it could have come from the distant future. The USAF's early large-scale deployments were dedicated to the burning of East Asian cities. It wasn't just the apocalyptic demonstrations at Hiroshima and Nagasaki that announced America as the pre-eminent superpower, but the even more destructive aerial firebombings of Tokyo, Nagoya, Yokohama, Osaka, Hamamatsu, and Kobe – each a Dresden in its own right. In Korea, General George E. Stratemeyer commanded the air force to destroy 'all buildings capable of affording shelter', with the expressed intention of turning the entire peninsula into a desert.[5] Kanggye, Pyongyang, Sakju, Huichon, Chosan, Hoeryong, and even Seoul were almost completely destroyed between 1950 and 1953. The head of Strategic Air Command, Curtis LeMay, said the US had 'burned down just about every city in North and South Korea', and in the process killed one million civilians.[6] There were generals, LeMay among them, who favoured doing the same to the Soviet Union.

The Cold War that followed the age of firebombing is the source of common conceptions of proxy war, limited engagement and clandestine operations. The US military, possessed of more garrisons around the world than any state before it, turned to covert action and war by surrogate. The two superpowers – really one superpower and one recalcitrant – launched outright attacks on small states in the global periphery. The US attacked Cuba, the Dominican Republic and Grenada, and waged a war of total destruction on Indochina. The Soviet Union invaded Hungary, Czechoslovakia and Afghanistan. But there were relatively few interstate conflicts between peers. Those that did occur either had little to do with US-Soviet competition (Iran-Iraq, the Arab–Israeli war, Israel's many invasions of Lebanon) or used it as cover for struggles over the rubble of the old empires or for the projection of national power. But there was a proliferation of civil wars, and in a world of pseudo-bipolarity they served as a battleground for global competition by proxy.

The study of proxy warfare is still the domain of military historians and tacticians. Most of the histories of it are shaped by the procession of Cold War interventions. They also tend to degenerate into studies of imperial administration. Eli Berman and David A. Lake's edited collection *Proxy Wars: Suppressing Violence through Local Agents* purports to take an academic approach (the title is a bad start, since in most cases a state involved in a proxy war has no interest in suppressing violence).[7] The editors make clear that the central question is how to counter threats – or 'disturbances' – to US interests around the world. They argue that the incentive to turn to proxy war is for the most part budgetary. For the US, naval and air superiority is a given, but a ground force large enough to intervene anywhere in the world is expensive to maintain. Proxy wars are cheap, but are they effective?

Good examples are hard to find. In a chapter on the war on drugs in Colombia that's been going on since the early 1990s, Abigail Vaughn praises the use of proxies for achieving the grand goal of a slight reduction in cocaine production at the cost of tens of billions of dollars. The inept vigilante criminals with whom the US worked aren't mentioned. Nor are the feral Colombian *paramilitares*, many of whom were themselves engaged in the drug trade. The war necessitated an extensive propaganda campaign inside the US to persuade Americans of its worth, and its main achievement was to drive production into neighbouring Peru. To the extent that overall cocaine production was reduced it shifted American consumption to other stimulants, methamphetamines chief among them.

The proxy war in El Salvador is presented by Ryan Baker as the archetypical 'small footprint' intervention. Beginning in 1979, the CIA provided enormous sums to increase the security services of the Salvadoran dictatorship to six times their original size. New paramilitary units were set up by US military advisers to serve as direct proxies of Washington. But even after a couple of years it was clear that the strategy wasn't working. Rather than pacifying the rural Salvadoran opposition the programme had created a more skilled guerrilla movement. The government paramilitaries came to be seen as death squads and the conflict grew into an all-out war on the peasantry, crowned by such atrocities as the assassination of

Archbishop Óscar Romero and the massacres on the Sumpul river. In 1981 a US proxy known as the Atlácatl Battalion executed the entire population of the village of El Mozote – just one episode in a conflict that caused perhaps 60,000 civilian deaths.

Searching the history of US intervention in Latin America for models of successful proxy wars means making some questionable decisions. The Nicaraguan Contras aren't mentioned at all in Berman and Lake's book, perhaps because the CIA provided them with torture manuals and instructions on 'the selective use of violence for propagandistic effects'. These manuals have since been discovered and can now be read in their entirety. The Contra affair is often remembered today for its farcical elements – arms sales to Iran – but by 1987 the 10,000 or so US-backed Contras had left at least 30,000 dead. And by any measure the war failed. The Sandinista government survived and instituted social reform programmes that still determine the politics of Nicaragua today. There are glimpses of insight in Berman and Lake's collection, but they are for the most part unintentional. In noting that the US relies on proxy ground forces in politically unstable places, one contributor remarks in passing that proxies are often chosen because they are unrepresentative. Savage reprisals are not a by-product but a feature.

If the Cold War were the ideal environment for proxy war stratagems, it would be reasonable to expect fewer of them after it ended. But recent Western-led wars in the Middle East have raged alongside civil wars of terrible brutality in Algeria, Somalia, Liberia, Yugoslavia, Sierra Leone, Congo, Libya, Syria, and Yemen. Many of these conflicts have been intensified by proxy interventions – either by local or great powers – to the point of becoming international conflicts. At the peripheries of the global economy the US has been able to intervene at will. More and more of these interventions are carried out using a sophisticated combination of proxies, drones and special forces. Though the J-2 doctrine is rarely mentioned, scholars and analysts have sought to frame the tactical question of how best to wage a modern proxy war.

Tyrone Groh's *Proxy War: The Least Bad Option* contains advice of this kind.[8] The first step is to establish intentions. The aim of a traditional invasion is victory, but that isn't the case with proxy wars. Groh defines four types of proxy war and argues that planners should know which kind they're getting into. The first, 'in it to win it', is self-explanatory: the proxy is used to defeat an enemy's forces. The second, 'holding action', involves the idea that the aim of an intervention by proxy may be to prolong a civil war in order to maintain the status quo. The third type, perhaps the most common, is 'meddling'. Here, the ideal outcome is for a proxy to change the course of a conflict, perhaps by overthrowing a government, although this is considered unlikely given the present balance of power. Even so, a proxy force can still be useful in interfering with the designs of others. The last type, 'feeding the chaos', is in most cases a matter for covert operations and occurs when a state has no achievable strategic aim but sees an advantage in prolonging the violence indefinitely.

Managing a proxy force is easier when a proxy and its backer have the same goals. But even then it's crucial to establish a system of punishment and reward. If the goal is to take control of a country's seat of power, and hold it, then the political legitimacy of the proxy force is relevant – but not if the aim is to create chaos. It's wise for those waging a proxy war to keep their vassals entirely dependent on them, so there must be appropriate incentives. But care must be taken not to overcommit to a proxy, at least in public, and in covert proxy wars lower-level intelligence officers must not be given the sort of autonomy that might lead to the collaboration being revealed.

Above all, the backer must retain the power to abandon the proxy when its usefulness has ended.

Groh presents the US proxy war in Laos as a successful example of proxy management. From 1959, Washington sought to prop up the right-wing government in Vientiane. Faced with 'a largely pacific, Buddhist population', the CIA exploited Laotian geography and trained mountain-dwelling Hmong soldiers in camps in Thailand to supplement intensive bombing by the USAF. Isolated and dependent, the Hmong remained firmly under US control. Although the strategy escalated the war, the operation remained an official secret for ten years. In Groh's judgement the CIA achieved 'significant benefits from the arrangement with comparatively small costs'. Thailand was insulated from the left-wing nationalist movements that troubled its eastern neighbours. The damage done to Laos is well known. The Hmong themselves saw no benefit and paid a great cost in lives.

From the perspective of a proxy, the risks of accepting patronage are clear. Proxy warfare involves exploitation. A local militia, almost always comprised of willing volunteers, is motivated by grievances that it might not otherwise have the opportunity to act on. The training, weapons and other enticements offered will serve to recruit more volunteers. But outside interventions have a tendency to extend conflicts rather than resolve them. In the context of a civil war this can be disastrous for a group accused of being a puppet of a foreign power. If it fails to subdue its enemies, a proxy force is likely to suffer for its vassalage.

Battlefields are messy places even for regular armies. Proxy forces only increase the confusion. Undisciplined troops may not try as hard as one would want, or they may act to further their own interests. Flashy weapons have a way of going missing and turning up on black markets rather than being used for the purposes for which they were intended. 'Mercenaries and auxiliaries are at once useless and dangerous,' Machiavelli wrote, 'disunited, ambitious, insubordinate, treacherous, insolent among friends, cowardly before foes.'[9] There is a common tendency to conflate proxies with mercenaries since you have to pay both. The difference is that mercenaries have no programme of their own and so are easier to control. About half the US troops in Afghanistan are technically mercenaries: they are deployed for private profit, but they are still American soldiers. The use of contractors derives from the ideology of privatisation, not proxy war.

America's recent use of proxies in the Middle East is part of a history that began with its sponsorship of paramilitary groups in Afghanistan. To impede the 1979 Soviet invasion the CIA provided finance – often rucksacks filled with cash – and more than 2,000 Stinger missiles to Afghan and Arab mujahidin. For the most part the job of controlling them was left to Pakistan's intelligence services. In 2001 the militias of the Northern Alliance acted as direct US proxies to overthrow the Taliban. They were well suited to the work of insurgency but proved a hindrance when it came to forming a new governing authority. The US was forced to commit large numbers of its own troops, with consequences that still resonate two decades later.

In post-invasion Iraq, the collapse of the state compelled the occupation forces to arm and train the reformed Iraqi army, in the hope of turning it into an institutionalised proxy force. At the same time, the US army and intelligence services recruited local armed groups from outside the official military. In Anbar, they organised Sunni tribes to counter al-Qaida and enforce order. By the time of the siege of Mosul in 2016, the US was co-ordinating a multi-proxy assault involving Iraqi security forces, Kurdish Peshmerga and Iran's Shia paramilitaries, backed by US air strikes, to seize the city from Islamic State.

The Syrian civil war typifies the age of proxy war like no other conflict. At least nine countries raised proxy militias to attempt to influence the course of the war. On the loyalist side, Iran's Badr Organisation and Russia's V Corps sought to reinforce the Syrian government's forces with volunteer fighters attracted by monthly salaries of a couple of hundred dollars. The Gulf states and Turkey funded conservative religious militias. The US and UK funnelled support to rebel brigades through operations rooms in Amman and Gaziantep. The complexity of the conflict made control of the factions, and control of their media messaging, a constant problem: one CIA-supplied militia recorded a video of its fighters beheading a 12-year-old boy. In Afghanistan and Iraq local proxies had the overwhelming benefit of US air support. That wasn't usually the case in Syria – a difference that proved crucial when the Russian Air Force entered the war. Most Syrian proxies were expendable, in the sense that their cause had little strategic significance to their American backers. By contrast the Syrian Kurdish forces supported by the US in its campaign to relieve Islamic State of its caliphate weren't just pliant proxies but worked seamlessly with US intelligence to co-ordinate air strikes. The distinction between these two cases – the failure of the loose coalition known as the Free Syrian Army; the success of the Syrian Kurds – has probably contributed more to the current proxy doctrine than any other recent experience. The Syrian Kurds were nonetheless discarded once their usefulness was at its end, along with the promises the US had made to champion their interests.

The usual way of explaining the onset of a new age of proxy war is that the US-dominated international order has fractured. Startled by electorates raising brash showmen – Donald Trump, Boris Johnson – to the highest offices in Washington and London, patrician analysts of the status quo have been quick to declare the imminent end of the American epoch. Executive competence has never been a strength of Anglo-American societies, but present chaos combined with the growing power of Chinese trade is said to portend a new anarchy of international competition. There is general consensus that the world is descending from a state of unipolarity towards a more equitable balance of power: a Concert of Eurasia resembling the European order of the nineteenth century. In this order war by proxy occupies a different place.

But while there has been some erosion of American power, the US still has reason to see the world as being under its control. Trump was derided as an isolationist by Democrats who claimed a commitment to 'free trade', but US withdrawal from international organisations and agreements has looked more like an assertion of strength than a retreat. The US has not dismantled NATO or left the Middle East (despite fantasy talk in the American press). The global architecture of American power is still in place. At international level, the US operates a near feudal model of diplomacy (hence the existence of a Lake Trump in the Balkans). There are more than a dozen US naval facilities around East Asia alone. There is no Iranian, Russian or even Chinese sphere of influence that can stop America from exercising its will by force anywhere on earth. In the US and UK, the preference for proxy warfare has been driven by the experience of the disastrous domestic political consequences of full-scale military intervention – the invasion of Iraq, the war in Vietnam – rather than by any actual military rationale. Over the past decade or more, internal politics, rather than the increasing size of the Chinese economy, have deterred Western states from direct military intervention abroad. Minor powers have a different motive: proxy warfare offers an outlet for pursuing national interests while avoiding the wrath of the powerful. But that has always been the case. During the Cold War, apartheid

South Africa waged proxy wars in Angola and Mozambique. At the height of American unipolarity one of the bloodiest civil and proxy wars in history was waged over Congo. Laments for the 'rules-based international order' rest on pious myth-making. The Pax Americana was never peaceful.

In *Surrogate Warfare: The Transformation of War in the 21st Century*, Andreas Krieg and Jean-Marc Rickli subscribe to a version of the thesis of hegemonic decline, in which a West riven by identity crises has seen proxy warfare as a way to minimise the cost of war to its citizenry.[10] What they refer to as 'stand-off' postmodern warfare has served as a 'substitution of the burden of warfare' for governments which in public must now scrimp. To this they try to add an explanation for the evolution of proxy warfare based on technology. They argue for an expanded concept of surrogate war that includes forms of technological surrogacy such as cyberwarfare and autonomous weapons. War, they argue, has moved 'into the cyber and media domains'. The development of precision-guided munitions, unmanned vehicles and artificial intelligence, they say, is replacing armed divisions.

It should by now be a truism that wars begin with talk of high technology and end with the drudgery of infantry pushes. Advances in military technology are often exaggerated, in part to justify budgets. Wild claims for the accuracy of 'precision munitions' have been a standard feature of new adventures for half a century and more. Even so, the invention of armed drones was an important development. In conjunction with the greater innovation of mass electronic surveillance it has enabled the current capabilities of America's global assassination programme. But drones are still planes. (In Arabic they are known more prosaically as 'tayerat bidoun tayar', 'planes without pilots'.) A great deal of funding has gone towards the development of weapons systems that can operate with near autonomy, but only one working model has been deployed: the Harpy, designed by Israel Aerospace Industries, a 'loitering munition' that seeks out and attacks enemy radar systems without humans pointing them out. The American military didn't bother to buy it. It may one day be possible to field armies of killer robots – assuming a human points them in the right direction – but for now surrogates have to be of the human kind.

The notion of 'cyberwar' is a different problem. It has become common to refer to the work of hackers as a form of war. Even propaganda campaigns on social media are classed as warfare. What are called 'cyberweapons' involve attacks on electronic security systems linked to important infrastructure. Introducing a virus into the computers of a nuclear facility is a dramatic act of sabotage. But sabotage, while useful in war, is a tool of espionage rather than of warfare per se. The same goes for stealing the schematics for a fighter jet. All states conduct cyberespionage, just as they do traditional espionage, but as with proxy warfare it is often described as an activity unique to official adversaries. Since 2011, when the White House published its 'International Strategy for Cyberspace', the US has asserted the right to respond to hacking with military force.[11]

Krieg and Rickli are on firmer ground in describing the near constant state of conflict that has existed across large parts of the world since 2001. 'War, or more precisely the absence of peace, has become a permanent state of affairs that requires a simmering commitment by some states to maintain their strategic, sometimes peripheral interests.' Despite all the talk of the soldier disappearing from the battlefield, for decades American and British troops have been shepherded without respite from one conflict to another. It is only logical that these states would supplement their own forces by acting through proxies. Though Krieg and Rickli don't mention it, the older technology of nuclear weapons is more relevant to the current state of affairs than any recent advance. Nuclear weapons, more than anything else, removed the option of the US Air Force destroying Soviet cities by fire. Nuclear weapons – judged, for now at least, to be too powerful to be used – seem to preclude wars of destruction between major powers today. But the constraining effect of nuclear weapons on direct confrontation between great powers has only encouraged the spread of constant but limited violence. The soldiers of nuclear-armed India and China fight with sticks and clubs in the Himalayas. Proxy wars are conducted outside the territories of the nuclear states.

Mentioned only obliquely in the academic literature is the fact that proxy wars are attractive in part because they insulate military action from domestic scrutiny. National leaders are given to believe that strength lies in the ability to take decisions without the interference of the public, which too often fails to divine the wisdom of military expeditions. In societies where the higher echelons of the state are accountable to the opinions of the general citizenry, proxy warfare offers a form of violence less inhibited by pacific tendencies. A proxy war need not be clandestine to subvert public accountability. It's usually easy to find out who is backing whom, and even when support for a proxy force is an official secret the information is likely to be uncovered at some point. But a proxy force allows rulers to circumvent scrutiny of costs and casualties. Intervention within the borders of another state is usually illegal under international law, but the use of local auxiliary offers protection against legal challenges. Krieg and Rickli write that 'the need to remove military action from society's checks and balances is the single most important driver and aspect of postmodern surrogate warfare'.

That proxy wars are essentially anti-democratic goes some way to explaining the adoption of a proxy doctrine, traditionally the preserve of the intelligence services, by the conventional US military.

Proxy warfare is officially condemned in Washington and London as a device of undemocratic enemies, but it is precisely for its anti-democratic possibilities that the West embraces it. For US allies, rejection of proxy warfare would be a contradiction. At the strategic level, the British armed forces and the armed forces of Australia and Canada have no discernible vision beyond serving as adjuncts to US power. Which in a sense makes them proxy forces too. The armies of many small states are available to the US as proxies under the justification of fighting 'terrorism', controlling 'ungoverned spaces' and other phantoms. The new model of local proxy ground troops backed by air power, global surveillance and special operations forces has become a fixture of the times. For political leaders, it's tempting to see this type of military action as the Goldilocks option: neither the heat of full-scale war nor the cool of unmanly indifference. But all violence tends to escalate, and it's hard not to imagine that this developing doctrine will in future lead to more damaging – and more criminal – foreign interventions that avoid the limited checks of public scrutiny.

9
On Thermonuclear War

To build a nuclear bomb you need uranium. That's the easy part. Uranium ore is plentiful, but it isn't very useful in its naturally occurring state. For bomb-making it must be enriched to increase the concentration of the isotope uranium-235. Weapons-grade uranium is about 90 per cent enriched, but at a pinch you can make do with a lesser grade, enriched to 50 per cent or so. Uranium can also be run through a reactor and reprocessed to obtain plutonium-239, the other main candidate for a nuclear bomb. Enrichment is not straightforward. At one point the Manhattan Project's gaseous diffusion plants accounted for 5 to 10 per cent of all electricity use in the United States. But if you can acquire the fissile material, you can make a bomb. Most people probably know the outline: a nuclear reaction involves a split atom emitting a number of neutrons, which in turn split the nuclei of other nearby atoms, and so on. A nuclear bomb produces a fission reaction in a supercritical mass of nuclear material contained in a tamper to make the reaction more efficient. The initial explosion heats the fissile core to billions of degrees Celsius. The bomb expands to create either an enormous fireball or a tiny sun, depending on how you look at it. A shockwave radiates outwards. As the fireball rises, air and dust are sucked into a pillar below, forming a mushroom cloud. Witnesses to nuclear tests say it feels like the air is tearing.

The nuclear weapon used at Hiroshima was primitive: sixty kilograms of enriched uranium slammed against itself. The Nagasaki bomb was of the more advanced implosion type. It contained just six kilos of plutonium, about the size of a shot put. But all fission bombs are primitive when compared to a thermonuclear (or hydrogen) bomb with a yield measured in megatons rather than kilotons. It comprises a fission bomb separated with polystyrene from a secondary fusion device. The secondary is a core of fissile material surrounded, these days, by lithium deuteride. When the first stage is detonated, the radiation emitted by the fission explosion sets off a fusion reaction in the hydrogen isotopes of the secondary. The two stages of the bomb feed off each other, like a pair of autotrophic matryoshkas.

Large thermonuclear bombs are a thousand times more powerful than the first nuclear weapons. One will destroy a few square miles of city, the other hundreds. The first victims are killed by the sheer force and heat of the blast wave. Its diffraction causes the entire human body to be compressed, resulting in embolisms in the arteries and crushing the lungs and heart.[1] Then there is the thermal pulse, which causes flash burns on exposed skin. A large proportion of the victims in Hiroshima and Nagasaki were killed by the heat. A smaller number were trapped in rubble and burned to death. Along with the blast and heat there is ionising radiation, which creates defects in individual atoms, morphs the blood and bone marrow, breaks chromosomes and irreparably damages cells. Victims vomit and suffer ataxia and delirium. Less is known about longer-lasting nuclear fallout. Marshall Islanders subjected to fallout in 1954 suffered 'beta-burns' within twenty-four hours and nuclear testing rendered their atolls uninhabitable.

The usual fate of revolutionary weapons is for their startling effects to be quickly nullified, or at least blunted, either by the invention of countermeasures or by everyone acquiring them. But effective defences against thermonuclear weapons have been hard to come by. Instead, their very power has constrained their use. War has always been destructive for the losers. It's sometimes destructive for the victors too: the Soviet Union lost 13 per cent of its population in the Second World War. But until the invention of nuclear weapons, victory didn't also mean annihilation. There is an irony in the fact that city-killer weapons arrived at the precise moment that humanity became a predominantly urban species.

Nuclear weapons haven't been used in war since 1945, but there have been many close calls. In 1956, a B-47 bomber disappeared over the Mediterranean with two nuclear weapons on board. It was never found. In 1960, US nuclear early warning systems were accidentally triggered by the Moon. The same happened with flocks of migrating geese. In 1966, a B-52 crashed mid-air and dropped three thermonuclear bombs on a Spanish village (the cores didn't detonate). These are the accidents. The times when intentional nuclear war seemed imminent are better known. Countries with nuclear weapons often claim that only their head of state or government can order their use, but in practice states recognise that this would make them vulnerable: what if the national leader is dead? Most have allowed some delegation, so that *in extremis* subordinates or military commanders can order nuclear strikes.

Fred Kaplan's 1983 book *The Wizards of Armageddon* was an invaluable account of early American nuclear strategy.[2] In the immediate postwar period, US military theorists were impressed by the power of what Kaplan called the 'absolute weapon', but they saw it principally as an advance on the proven techniques of incendiary bombing. Bernard Brodie, an academic at Yale and then the RAND corporation, described the implications of nuclear weapons in 1946: there can be no winners in the conventional sense, and the advantage is in the threat rather than the execution.[3] In order to deter attack, all you have to do is show that if you're hit, you will hit back. When a state lets it be known that it has the capacity to carry out a second-strike retaliation it's almost unthinkable that it would be subjected to nuclear attack in the first place.

The US lost its nuclear monopoly in 1949 but remained by far the most powerful state in the world. The American homeland was by any measure very secure. But development of nuclear technology, and of ICBMs, was a potential challenge to its position. If security of the population, or even the state, was the main concern, it would have been rational for the US to push for arms controls on nuclear weapons technology. This was never seriously considered. The first thermonuclear device was detonated by the US on the former island of Elugelab in 1952. The Soviet Union built its first thermonuclear weapon three years later.[4] By the 1960s the superpowers could launch them using missiles travelling at 16,000 mph.

The question for the US was this. In a world with nuclear weapons, how should it continue to exercise its global power, from Guam to Congo? It was essential to retain the imperial protectorates, which included Western Europe. During the Eisenhower administration, US policy was to threaten the Soviet Union with 'massive retaliation' over disagreements at the periphery of the Soviet bloc. The political leadership expressed what was already military policy. Admiral Arthur Radford summed up the thinking in American military circles when he described nuclear weapons as 'the primary munition of war'.[5] The Joint Chiefs of Staff had already started on target lists of Soviet cities, power plants and oil installations.

Kaplan was responsible for raising the reputation of William Kaufmann, a civilian nuclear strategist and critic of massive retaliation. Another RAND corporation man and an influential adviser to the Department of Defense on nuclear matters, Kaufmann argued that threatening to respond to minor aggression with total nuclear war was an ineffective bluff. The US was saddling itself with a choice between 'the immeasurable horrors of atomic war' and loss of prestige if its bluff were called.[6] A nuclear response to non-nuclear aggression far from the homeland was like 'a sparrow hunt with a cannon'. Practical maintenance of America's imperial and quasi-imperial positions required conventional military forces and alliances in Germany, Taiwan, and South Korea.

There were other ways of waging 'limited war'.[7] In 1957, Henry Kissinger argued for smaller, tactical nuclear weapons. Kaufmann and others pulled his argument apart by showing how easily the use of small nuclear weapons on the battlefield would escalate to full thermonuclear exchange. But this wasn't enough to stop the generals from deploying tactical nuclear weapons in Europe. There are still about 100 American nuclear bombs in bases in Germany, Italy, Belgium and the Netherlands. Trump's deputy assistant secretary of defense, Elbridge Colby, architect of the 2018 National Defense Strategy, was an advocate of using tactical nuclear weapons in 'possible armed conflicts with both smaller hostile rogue states and with larger near peers'.[8]

Fear of a general thermonuclear war was at its peak in the late 1950s and early 1960s, but we now know that this was the period of US total nuclear dominance. At the time, American intelligence estimates exaggerated the number of Soviet ICBMs by a factor of ten (the mythical 'missile gap'), and greatly exaggerated the number of Soviet warheads and Soviet bombers – which in any case couldn't have reached the US without refuelling in vulnerable Arctic bases. In fact, until the mid 1960s, the Soviet Union wouldn't have been able to survive an American nuclear attack and couldn't be confident in its capacity to launch a large second-strike retaliation.

In this context it's worth considering the lectures of Herman Kahn, collected in 1960 as *On Thermonuclear War*.[9] Kahn believed that a cataclysmic nuclear war between the US and the Soviet Union was imminent. He differed from others, though, in arguing that nuclear war need not mean mutual destruction: with careful planning and the proper civil defence measures, America could win such a war. Would 20 million or 100 million die? The answer would affect postwar recuperation, but it wasn't necessarily true that 'the survivors will envy the dead'. The most discomfiting part of Kahn's argument was that subsequent records have shown he was probably right, though not for the reasons he gave. In 1960, mutual destruction was not assured. The US could have destroyed urban civilisation in the Soviet Union. The same was not true in reverse. The Soviet leadership could count on its weapons for retaliation against Western Europe but not the continental United States.

All nuclear strategy contains an element of madness, which Kahn seemed to personify. Much of the science of nuclear deterrence was, and still is, a matter of bluster. Kahn's analysis wasn't of the highest quality – there he sat, considering World War Eight (in 1973) – but he did make one useful contribution. He conceived the thought experiment of the 'doomsday machine', a device that would destroy the entire world population if any nuclear weapon were used. Although it would mean perfect deterrence, he argued that – because of the risk of accident – to build such a machine would be a great mistake.

Kahn didn't know it at the time, but as Daniel Ellsberg later revealed, the 'doomsday machine' was only a slight extension of US nuclear designs.[10] While the RAND intellectuals were theorising, the military continued to work on actual nuclear war plans, the details of which were kept secret even from US presidents. Strategic Air Command's Emergency War Plan 1-49 included a list of seventy cities on which thermonuclear bombs would be dropped, from Moscow and St Petersburg to Berlin, Potsdam, Warsaw and most of what is now Ukraine and Belarus. In 1960, the generals completed a comprehensive plan for a first-strike attack, the Single Integrated Operational Plan, or SIOP-62. In the case of non-nuclear conflict with the Soviet bloc, the US would drop 3,423 nuclear bombs on Soviet territory, Eastern Europe and China (the RAF was supposed to participate). Every city in the Soviet Union and China was to be destroyed. The power of the nuclear weapons to be used on Moscow alone was 4,000 times that of the bomb used on Hiroshima. Military analysts predicted that about 600 million people would be killed, including 100 million in Western Europe and 100 million in neutral countries adjacent to the Sino-Soviet bloc such as Afghanistan, India and Japan. It would be hard to argue that any document in history contains greater evil; there is nothing in the Nazi archives that approaches it.

In 1961, some of the defence intellectuals who had spent the previous decade working on nuclear strategy were brought into the Kennedy administration, where their ideas would be tested. Thanks to Ellsberg, SIOP-62 was unearthed by the new administration, which sought to improve on it. US nuclear strategy had developed towards the theory of 'counterforce': missiles and bombers should target enemy nuclear forces rather than cities. Counterforce may appear sane when compared with the lunatic destruction favoured by previous plans, but the new proposals were potentially no less deadly: should the negotiations that were supposed to accompany strikes on missile installations and airfields fail, the destruction of cities would still be threatened. Besides, military targets are often near cities. And once the Soviet Union had acquired nuclear forces capable of a second strike, the risk of uncontrollable escalation came into play. Counterforce provided the logic for the arms race, and nuclear stockpiles grew far beyond any practical consideration. When there are large numbers of nuclear weapons, it no longer matters what the nominal targets are.

The revised SIOP-63 didn't insist on the automatic destruction of China in response to a kerfuffle in Europe. But it too was a plan for a first strike. Nuclear historians speak of distinct eras in the nuclear period, but the shifts are either minor or illusory. SIOP-63 remained official doctrine until the early 1970s. Later administrations tinkered with nuclear guidance documents – the Carter administration added the summer dachas of Soviet leaders as targets – but actual planning was still the domain of Strategic Air Command. Politicians gave instructions on how nuclear war should be fought, and the generals in Omaha ignored them. In the event of a crisis, the US president would be given a binder, the 'Black Book', containing four or five options for nuclear war. Even the most restrained option would involve hundreds of strikes. The full details – which weapons would be used on which targets – were contained in the 'Blue Book', which no president or civilian leader was allowed to see until 1989. The last known equivalent to the SIOP is called OPLAN 8010-12. We know nothing about what it contains, but it's a fair guess there is new material on China.

Kaplan's new book, *The Bomb*, is both a sequel and an update to his Cold War history.[11] After 1991 it was no longer possible to pretend that Moscow was a serious competitor to American global power. But US missiles were still pointed at Russian cities, obscure factories and fields that might serve as improvised airstrips. Over the course of the next decade, however, both the US and Russia halved their nuclear stockpiles. The Non-Proliferation Treaty had been in force since 1970, to discourage non-nuclear states from acquiring nuclear weapons, but the existing powers had only paid lip service to disarmament. Now the US could focus on non-proliferation as a tool of power politics. It often failed. The Clinton administration sought to prevent North Korea getting the bomb, and with the 1994 Agreed Framework succeeded in temporarily hindering its weapons programme. But after the US refused to finance civilian reactors for North Korea under international safeguards the agreement came under strain, and the George W. Bush administration pulled out of the deal entirely. Pyongyang acquired its first nuclear weapon in 2006.

Advocating non-proliferation is a common hobby for retired American officials with time on their hands and a less than clean conscience. Were the US actually committed to limiting nuclear weapons, it would at the very least have to declare a 'no first use' policy for its own nuclear arsenal. The Soviet Union, China and India have all made such a pledge in the past (Britain and France have not). Kaplan takes seriously Obama's professed desire for 'a world without nuclear weapons', but the Obama administration refused to declare no first use. Its successes on nuclear matters – the Iran nuclear deal and the new START arms reduction treaty with Russia, signed in 2010 – were overshadowed by its commitments to build the next generation of US nuclear weapons systems. New 'Ground Based Strategic Deterrent' missiles will soon start replacing the Minuteman III. The US Navy is getting new W93 nuclear warheads. The US Air Force will have B-21 stealth bombers 'designed to overcome even an advanced adversary's air defences'.[12] In many respects Obama was a continuity president in matters of imperial management.

Ellsberg argued that every US president has used nuclear weapons 'in the precise way that a gun is used when it is pointed at someone in a confrontation, whether or not the trigger is pulled'.

Eisenhower threatened to use them in the Korean War and against China. Kennedy came close during the Cuban crisis. In 1969, Nixon threatened to use them in Vietnam. George H.W. Bush threatened Iraq with 'nuclear retaliation'.[13] The fact that none of these threats was carried out doesn't mean they weren't significant. Trump's threat in 2017 to 'totally destroy North Korea' with fire and fury was a rhetorically extreme example in a long record.[14] Eisenhower, Ford and Clinton all made similar threats.[15] In response to North Korean missile tests, the US twice fired conventional missiles from South Korea into the Sea of Japan. In 2019, it withdrew from the Intermediate-Range Nuclear Forces Treaty. The Trump administration also decided to acquire more tactical nuclear weapons, with yields quite similar to the Hiroshima bomb. As Kaplan says, discussion of US nuclear weapons describes them as a deterrent, but 'American policy has always been to strike first pre-emptively'.

Analysis of nuclear strategy is often approached from the perspective of one of the states involved, but it's possible to take the planetary view. Nuclear weapons have existed for three-quarters of a century. There are few international controls, and the weapons remain at the discretion of the nine states that possess them. Outside America, only four – Russia, China, India, and Pakistan – have sizeable arsenals and are in a position to use them without consultation with the US. The overall number of nuclear warheads has decreased since the 1980s, but the support systems and delivery mechanisms on which nuclear war would depend have become more sophisticated.

The balance of power among nuclear states has fluctuated. The US has sought nuclear superiority over other states at all times and has threatened to use nuclear weapons with dull regularity. It has no sustained appetite for arms control treaties and its war plans have included genocidal first strikes. Russia's nuclear forces decayed through the 1990s and the early 2000s. Its nuclear-armed submarines weren't even on patrol for much of that period. But over the past decade it has reversed some of the decay. It has maintained many smaller tactical nuclear weapons, ostensibly out of fear of a ground invasion from the West (and perhaps the south-east).

Since the 1960s, Britain's nuclear forces have been based on submarine-launched ballistic missiles. The missiles are leased from the US and stored at a naval base in coastal Georgia. Britain is now replacing its Vanguard submarines with four bigger Dreadnought-class boats, which are due to arrive in the early 2030s. The government has also ordered new warheads, which must closely adhere to American designs so that they remain compatible with the Trident missile and its aeroshell. British politicians like to talk of Britain's 'independent nuclear deterrent' but in practice its nuclear weapons are an appurtenance to US power (see 'Green Bamboo, Red Snow', above). There is no chance they would ever be used without approval from Washington. Nor would those of Israel or France, despite the unwillingness of their leaders to look like American lackeys.

China is the only thermonuclear power committed to a policy of no first use. Its stockpile is much smaller than that of the US or Russia. It has about 100 ICBMs, which can be kept concealed and on the move. For decades there were only a small number of ICBM silos in China, but satellite images show it is now building more than 200 in Gansu and Xinjiang provinces. The discovery added to the scaremongering about its nuclear capacities. The anglophone media is full of stories presenting minor developments as revolutionary advances. Fanciful 'hypersonic' technology and outmoded 'fractional orbital' systems of dubious utility are described as shocking new weapons. General Mark Milley, chairman of the Joint Chiefs of Staff, has said Chinese tests of these technologies constitute a

'Sputnik moment'. They are more likely to be a sign that China is trying to keep up with American advances in ballistic missile defence. The imperative is to ensure that its nuclear forces can survive a first strike. China's Type 094 nuclear-armed submarines, of which there are now six, are more capable than previous generations. Together with more siloed ICBMs they may soon provide a reliable second-strike capability. This would remove the US option of threatening a first strike on Chinese territory. The current ambiguity in the US-China nuclear balance may well represent a dangerous moment of transition similar to the one experienced between the US and the Soviet Union in the early 1960s.

There is a widespread belief that nuclear weapons can be thanked for the fact that there has been no total war between major powers since 1945. The most prominent exponent of this view, Robert Jervis of Columbia University's Institute of War and Peace Studies, argued that such wars can no longer occur if statesmen are rational.[16] In *The Myth of the Nuclear Revolution*, Keir Lieber and Daryl Press suggest that these grand claims are mistaken.[17] There have indeed been no large-scale wars, but in all other respects international politics resemble the pre-nuclear age. States with nuclear weapons don't act as if they are immune from external attack, and they still engage in reckless expeditionary wars and sometimes scuffles with one another. The main argument Lieber and Press put forward is that this is not just a legacy of old behaviour but a consequence of the nature of nuclear weapons.

Nuclear weapons are too powerful for most conceivable scenarios: in Edward Luttwak's unimproved-on phrase, they 'exceed the culminating point of military utility'.[18] The only benefit they have had for the states that possess them is protection against all-out conquest of the homeland. But conventional armies are still required. Lieber and Press show that stalemate between nuclear powers doesn't happen automatically. It takes effort to build and maintain a nuclear force that can survive a first strike and retaliate. Once states have reached stalemate with second-strike forces – the Soviet Union in the 1960s, China now – they must monitor their adversaries for signs of technological breakthrough that might allow for an attack that would disarm them.

Developments in weapons technology have made it harder to secure nuclear forces. ICBMs have become easier to find and silos easier to destroy. Ballistic missiles – especially submarine-launched ballistic missiles – are much more accurate than they were at the end of the Cold War, and new 'super-fuses' allow for greater control over detonation of their warheads. Lieber and Press think a US submarine-launched strike could have a greater than 96 per cent destruction rate against ICBM silos. They hold the conventional American view of the US as a relatively benign power, but the implications of their argument are clear. How confident can we be that the seventy-year gap isn't just a lull?

The *Myth of the Nuclear Revolution* contains one glaring omission. Since the detonation of the first nuclear bomb there has been much discussion of the climatic effects of nuclear war. The main fear is of 'nuclear winter', the notion that firestorms would emit enough black carbon into the stratosphere to cause global temperature drops, mass crop failure and famine. The hypothesis has been dismissed in the past, but American researchers – Alan Robock, Brian Toon and others at the National Centre for Atmospheric Research in Colorado – have persisted with it.[19] The hypothesis is contested, but the projected devastation is so severe that it would be unwise to dismiss it. The risk of climate catastrophe, as well as perhaps hundreds of millions of immediate deaths, must be accounted for in any totting up of the dangers of nuclear weapons. Yet Lieber and Press don't mention it at all.

In March, the National Intelligence Council delivered its latest 'global trends' briefing to President Biden.[20] It included the judgement that the use of nuclear weapons is 'more likely in this competitive geopolitical environment'. Efforts to find a role for nuclear weapons in conflict have so far fallen at the feet of Luttwak's maxim. But intentional use is not the only danger. Nuclear strategists systematically underestimate the chances of nuclear accident: it has no place in the logic of strategy. But there have been too many close calls for accidental use to be discounted. The stakes may be anthropogenic extirpation.

Lieber and Press argue that nuclear weapons 'have made the world a better place' and that abolishing them would lead to more conventional wars. But the assumption that nuclear weapons will indefinitely prevent large wars rests on unjustified optimism. The stronger argument against abolition is practical. Nuclear weapons can be renounced but nuclear capability can't: our energy needs won't allow it. And once you have that capability, the silos can always be refilled. When the only rule is the rule of force, agreements between states are always provisional. Solutions to these problems have been proposed. New treaties, such as the Treaty on the Prohibition of Nuclear Weapons, which many non-nuclear states have signed, are one approach. A reworking of the IAEA or the placement of fuel cycle facilities into international control are another. But such proposals rarely get far. Instead, the stockpiles are growing.

10
Astrostrategy

In December 2019, the US Space Force was established as the sixth branch of the US armed forces. Though founded by the Trump administration, the Space Force was not a Trump invention. Its precursor, Air Force Space Command, was set up in 1982. In 2001, a commission chaired by Donald Rumsfeld concluded that it was being neglected, and recommended setting up a separate 'military department for space', something that has remained a goal of American generals ever since.[1] But even some military space enthusiasts thought the 2019 announcement was premature. For the first four months of its existence the Space Force had an official staff of two: thousands of its personnel were technically still working for the Air Force.[2] It has since added more than eighty Air Force Academy lieutenants, and plans to have a permanent staff of 16,000 within a few years. The old Air Force wings – a wing is a unit incorporating a number of squadrons – have been reorganised into space deltas and garrisons, which have attracted plenty of bored volunteers from the terrestrial military branches. In part, this is an organisational drive, designed to bring US government space organisations under one roof. But the Space Force has a planned annual budget of $15.4 billion (and an official motto – 'Semper Supra'). It's not yet clear what equipment it will have at its disposal. It will operate systems that can jam communications satellites, and there is much speculation about new tests of the Boeing X-37 robotic spacecraft. When asked about this, the second in command of the Space Force, David Thompson, said: 'We don't need to tell the world everything we're doing.'[3] The US hasn't yet made what aerospace analysts call the transition from 'space operators to space warfighters'. But the vice chairman of the US Joint Chiefs of Staff, John E. Hyten, has described space war as 'inevitable'.[4]

The American *strategeion* sees itself as waging a constant battle against complacency. To ward this off, the political class periodically conjures up imminent threats to US superiority. In the 1990s the 'threat' was Japanese corporate power. The new millennium saw the (never convincing) rise of transnational 'terrorism'. The latest existential phantom is the 'malign influence' of China on the Indo-Pacific and beyond.[5] But it was the old Soviet Union that fitted the part best – and never better than in 1957, when Sputnik was launched into orbit from a test range on the Kazakh steppe. As a satellite, Sputnik was unimpressive: a beach ball with antennae that maintained orbit for just three months. As a catalyst for military development, however, it was unmatched. The US already had the technology needed to build an artificial satellite but had refused to fund one. Sputnik provoked a frenzy among the American political establishment. In January 1958, Lyndon Johnson, then Senate majority leader, convened a series of hearings that occupied the front pages of newspapers every day. The first hydrogen bomb test had taken place five years earlier. 'But there is something more important than any ultimate weapon,' Johnson told the Senate. 'That is the ultimate position – the position of total control over Earth.'[6] As Johnson saw it, it was in space that decisive power over humanity's future would be won or lost:

> Control of space means control of the world, far more certainly, far more totally than any control that has ever or could ever be achieved by weapons, or by troops of occupation . . . From space, the masters of infinity would have the power to control the Earth's weather, to cause drought and flood, to change the tides and raise the levels of the sea, to divert the Gulf Stream and change temperate climates to frigid.[7]

A state that controlled space would have the ability to refashion the Earth itself according to its will. Johnson argued that if it didn't seize mastery of space the US would be just as helpless as a post–Second World War state without an air force. It was in these Senate hearings that the US doctrine of space superiority, or space supremacy, was born. Sputnik launched the space race, which led to the Apollo programme, conceived – despite being a civilian undertaking – as part of a new era in which space was at the forefront of strategic thought. Wernher von Braun, the Nazis' chief aerospace engineer, had been brought to America on account of his experience on the V2 programme (the fact that his rockets had been built using slave labour was overlooked). He appeared regularly on American television, where he spoke of plans for the Moon, and imagined advanced bases in orbit with nuclear power plants for refuelling spacecraft. Before the development of good satellite reconnaissance cameras, the military believed human spies would have to be in orbit at all times. The US Air Force was planning to train astronauts before Nasa was even founded.

The militarisation of space proceeded at a measured pace, in part because the early practical military uses of satellites were limited: electro-optical imagery, radar, radio frequency sensing and targeting for ground weapons. These systems were integrated into the American military machine, and to a lesser extent into those of other armies. The first push to build orbital weaponry, the 'Star Wars'

Strategic Defense Initiative of the Reagan years, was cast as no more than a missile defence system, but recently declassified reports show that, just as the Soviets believed, the SDI was always intended to be used for 'space control'. These early efforts at space war planning faced the objection that the US military was already so far superior to any competitor as to make unnecessary any grand investments in revolutionary systems. The end of the Soviet Union meant that the US had command of space without the need for weapons. Military space development stalled. The parts of the defence budget intended for space were spent instead on tweaks to planes and ships.

The US still possessed the most advanced communications and spy satellites, which over the years enabled it to carry out global surveillance and the drone assassination programme. But satellites are inherently vulnerable, and the US's heavy reliance on its orbital machinery is connected with its fear of space war. Being straightforward to track and predictable in their trajectories, satellites can in principle be easily taken out by anti-satellite weapons, or ASATs, which can be simple ground-based missiles. The 2017 National Security Strategy claimed that America's adversaries possessed 'an asymmetric advantage': they were capable, at modest cost, of attacking the satellites on which US power now depended. As a result, US policy would now be to meet 'any interference with critical components of our space architecture . . . with a deliberate response at a time, place, manner and domain of our choosing'.[8] Trump revived Johnson's phrasing when he spoke of the need to secure 'the ultimate high ground' and declared space 'the world's newest war fighting domain'.

In August 2020, the Space Force published its 'capstone doctrine', *Spacepower*, which lays out a vision of a military apparatus the equal of the Army, Navy, and Air Force.[9] Given that war in space is likely, what is needed is 'a cadre of military space forces' to protect, defend and project US power there. Much of the document deals with the threat of anti-satellite weapons, but offensive operations against America's adversaries are also envisaged. Space itself is to be 'a source and conduit of national power'. The document outlines seven areas in which the US will seek to dominate: 'orbital warfare, space electromagnetic warfare, space battle management, space access and sustainment, military intelligence and engineering/acquisitions'. Plans for apocalyptic space weaponry are announced in the language of an accountancy firm.

The idea that US space power is a national military imperative presupposes the existence of competitors. A slew of small states have established space programmes in recent years, many of them farces (the 'UAE Mars probe' was built in the US and launched on a Japanese rocket). South Korea's first military satellite was launched in July 2020 by Elon Musk's firm SpaceX. The Indian Space Research Organisation now has a Mars orbiter. The EU uses its Copernicus satellite network for border surveillance, though *in extremis* it could also be used to direct missile strikes. The US National Air and Space Intelligence Centre records that the number of non-US reconnaissance and remote sensing satellites has tripled over the past ten years; only half of them were controlled by Europe, Japan or another US ally. American planners are forecasting 'a new competition for space beyond Earth's orbit', but not through concern about the Egyptian Space Agency or the Hellenic Space Centre but because they have cast the current space race as a struggle against Russia and China. Russia does have the ability to shoot down satellites, but Roscosmos is a shadow of its Soviet predecessors. Many of its satellites are no longer operating. Until just a few years ago some were still equipped with film cameras rather than digital imaging systems. It didn't help that the planned replacement for the Soyuz rocket, versions of which have been sending payloads and cosmonauts into space since 1966, was being developed in Ukraine when the Soviet Union was dissolved and so Moscow lost some of its more advanced facilities to Kiev.

The father of the Chinese space programme was a scientist on the Manhattan Project. Qian Xuesen went to America on a scholarship programme in 1935 and studied at MIT and Caltech before being recruited to work on jet propulsion and the atomic bomb. He would probably have remained in California, had he not been swept up in the red scare. After being questioned by the FBI and put under house arrest, Xuesen was traded to China in 1955 in return for eleven pilots captured during the Korean War.[10] He was put in charge of the Chinese nuclear weapons programme and the programme that produced the Dongfeng series of ballistic missiles. China launched its first satellite, Dongfanhong-1, in 1970, using a rocket based on Xuesen's missile designs. In hindsight the Xuesen affair was a remarkable blunder by the Americans. China made its first lunar landing in 2013. In June last year, it launched the final satellite in its geolocation network, BeiDou – its equivalent of the US government's GPS, Russia's Glonass and the EU's Galileo. Like NASA, the China National Space Administration has a rover on its way to Mars. Excluded by the US from co-operating on the International Space Station, it is now starting to build its own equivalent, the Large Modular Space Station.

In January 2019, the Chang'e-4 lunar mission landed on the far side of the Moon, something that had never been done before. In a follow-up mission launched in November 2020 Chang'e-5 collected and brought back samples from the Moon's surface, which no country had done since the 1970s. The Chinese lunar programme, like NASA's Artemis programme, has declared the long-term goal of establishing a Moon base. These are impressive endeavours, achieved with a space budget about a sixth the size of America's. In the US, Chinese space activities are spoken of as though they were inherently threatening, and different from America's in some fundamental way. US officials complain about China's hacking of NASA's Jet Propulsion Laboratory, for which two Chinese nationals were indicted by a grand jury in 2018. There is a latent fear that, while hopelessly outclassed by American military power on Earth, China may find an advantage in space. Chinese officials, too, see their efforts in strategic terms. The head of the Chinese lunar programme, Ye Peijian, has described the Moon as being like the Senkaku Islands, the ownership of which is disputed between China and Japan: 'If we don't go there now, even though we are capable of doing so, then we will be blamed by our descendants. If others go there, then they will take over and you won't be able to go even if you want to.'[11]

What form would strategic competition in space take? As well as an orbital infrastructure of satellites, space enthusiasts have imagined outposts on the Moon, habitats on Mars and spaceports in the asteroid belt. The first is the most straightforward. In the orbital plane shared by the Earth and the Moon, there are five Lagrange points, where the combined gravity of the two bodies allows for objects to be suspended, relative to both, without using thrusters (which otherwise maintain a spacecraft or satellite's position in space). China found the L2 Lagrange point useful for its Queqiao satellite, which provides continuous relay communications between Earth and the lander on the far side of the Moon. The L4 and L5 Lagrange points, along the route of the Moon's orbit of the Earth, are more stable and may be just as valuable to occupy. The same is true of Lagrange points between the Earth and the Sun. Building a Moon base would involve overcoming some severe logistical challenges: the Moon is dusty, Sun-beaten, dark for two weeks a month and has low surface gravity. But at least it has water ice at its poles. Controlling the mineral and energy resources of asteroids may also be an attractive prospect. The entire mass of the asteroid belt is only about one thousandth of the mass of the Earth, but about half of that is contained in just four large asteroids: Ceres, Vesta, Pallas and Hygiea.[12] Unlike planets, asteroids have no atmosphere and much less energy is needed to lift materials off their surfaces. In December, a Japanese mission returned to Earth with the first samples taken from below an asteroid's surface. Nations have fought plenty of wars over shitty little islands. Fighting over shitty little asteroids is not implausible.

The present age of astrostrategy remains for the most part concerned with satellites. More than 2,700 are active and in orbit around the Earth. About 70 per cent of them are in low Earth orbit – often at an altitude of just a few hundred kilometres – and are used for communications, navigation or reconnaissance. A further 20 per cent, including the major weather satellites, are in geostationary orbit, circling above the equator in the direction of the Earth's rotation at an altitude of 36,000 kilometres. There is no questioning the value of possessing parts of Earth's orbital infrastructure. The US government and US companies control more satellites than the rest of the world combined, and four times as many as China. But there is a strong argument that many satellites, at least at their current altitudes, aren't really in space at all. Conventional definitions, such as the Kármán line, say that space begins about 100 kilometres above sea level. But this is quite arbitrary: at eighty kilometres there are still wispy clouds. The Kármán distance is less than 2 per cent of the radius of the Earth. Compared with the scale of outer space it is Earth's epidermis. Theodore von Kármán, who helped found the Jet Propulsion Laboratory in 1944, thought of the line as no more than a 'jurisdictional boundary': the area within it could be said to belong to nation-states. Satellites in low Earth orbit follow a trajectory just above the lower layers of the Earth's atmosphere.

The International Space Station orbits at an altitude of about 400 kilometres, or less than 1 per cent of the distance to the Moon. The Earth's thermosphere extends to 600 kilometres, and the exosphere is visible, using a spectrometer, up to 10,000 kilometres from Earth. High-orbiting satellites, such as Galileo and GPS, are indisputably in space, but there are far fewer of them. The Outer Space Treaty (1967), which underpins international space law, didn't attempt to define where space begins.

A small coterie of military and aerospace analysts have considered the possibilities of space strategy and space war far beyond the Earth's immediate periphery. In 2001, Everett Dolman, professor of strategy at the US Air Force Air Command and Staff College, published *Astropolitik: Classical Geopolitics in the Space Age*, which has become the central text on the subject.[13] Dolman and others such as Jim Oberg and John Klein began by applying the theories of late nineteenth- and early twentieth-century geopolitics to space.[14] Considering space as analogous to the oceans, they turned to theorists of naval power such as Antoine-Henri Jomini and Alfred Thayer Mahan. Classical geopolitical writers such as Mahan are out of fashion, but they got some things right: he predicted war between Japan and the US over their imperial possessions in the Pacific forty years before it happened. Dolman's main insight was that the effects of gravity mean that even the vacuum of outer space has a topography, providing the equivalents of naval chokepoints such as the straits of Hormuz and Malacca. In space, linear distance is less important than the energy required to travel between two points. Thanks to the gravity wells formed by the planets, far more energy is required to travel from the Earth to the Moon than from the Moon to Mars – a distance 150 times greater. The mass of the Earth and other celestial bodies effectively create a terrain in the ostensibly featureless void, determining routes as surely as shipping lanes. Radiation belts (bands of charged particles caught in a planet's magnetic field), which damage spacecraft and kill humans, further define the topography of outer space transit.

Dolman attempted to provide what he called a 'blueprint for space control' in which the topography of outer space informs strategic decisions. In his schema, the space theatre was subdivided into Earth Realm, Earth Space (extending as far as the geostationary belt), Lunar Space, and Solar Space. Being ahead in the number of satellites in low Earth orbit does not equate to control of Lunar and Solar Space. But it must be given priority because everything that enters space must pass through low Earth orbit. For this reason, Dolman recommended that the US, as a unique and benign hegemon, seize military control of low Earth orbit while it can. This view is not unusual in elite circles and Dolman at least has a sense of irony about it: on the internet he goes by the moniker 'DrDethray'. In the grandest of grand strategies, war for control of near Earth space is a distinct possibility. It isn't hard to see the logic of these designs at work in the US Space Force.

No terrestrial conflict has yet ascended into space. In 1996, a dispute began between Tonga and Indonesia over the same segment of the geostationary belt.[15] The Tongan government contracted for its national communications satellite to be placed in orbit before the Indonesians. The Indonesian armed forces responded by jamming it. Among minor states the furthest such disagreements can go is old-fashioned terrestrial war, but states with space forces could fight it out in the heavens. War in space would not look like war on Earth. There are unlikely to be dogfights between spaceships or marines dropped on to dusty regolith surfaces far away. There would be disadvantages to crewing spacecraft at all – humans have to breathe and eat, and that comes at a cost – but remote control from Earth has disadvantages too, since over the distances of space it is subject to communications delays. Battles may well be resolved by careful positioning rather than by speed. It isn't helpful for military planning in space to model fleet combat on naval battles or fighter jet combat. And while submarines may approximate space movement better than ships, they can't adequately capture the strangeness of space.

Bleddyn Bowen's *War in Space* takes up the strategic questions posed by Dolman and considers the tactical problems of space warfare.[16] As is to be expected in this sort of study, there are nods to such military theorists as Jomini, Mahan and Julian Corbett, as well as Sun Tzu (for worldly flavour). Bowen offers a number of revisions to the usual accounts of space war. He too favours maritime metaphors but argues that for current purposes space is better thought of as a coastline than an ocean. This idea, reminiscent of Carl Sagan's concept of the 'shores of the cosmic ocean', suggests a reduction in scale. Rather than becoming preoccupied with the vastness of interplanetary space, it is better to recognise that contests in space will take place closer to the human societies of Earth than to the distant reaches of the solar system. (Sallies further into space require far better forms of power generation than currently exist.) 'Satellites, their infrastructure, methods of attacking them, and their influence on modern warfare and strategy' will be the focus of inter-state competition in space for the foreseeable future. Battles will be over satellite constellations and their terrestrial hubs and launch facilities. US space strategy has so far limited itself to enhancing the capabilities of its terrestrial forces. Anti-satellite weapons threaten those enhancements.

Destroying a satellite in low Earth orbit brings the risk that the resulting debris, travelling at 30,000 kilometres an hour, will destroy or damage other satellites in orbit. There is a danger that this could lead to a cascade, endangering all human activity in space, an eventuality known as the Kessler effect. As the number of satellites increases so does the risk. The US military is concerned with this possibility – which could be brought about by an accidental collision between satellites as well as by an attack – because it would pose a greater threat to US military power than to the forces of other nations. In 2007, China tested an anti-satellite (ASAT) missile against an old weather satellite in high orbit. A large amount of debris was produced that is still a threat to satellites today. The US condemned the test as an unacceptable step towards space militarisation, but a year later destroyed one of its own military satellites as a reminder of its capacities. In 2019, an Indian ASAT test caused debris to pass above the International Space Station. The first US ASAT test took place in 1959 and there have been others: in 1985, an American ASAT created a ring of debris that remained in orbit for years. Other anti-satellite weapons seek to block operations rather than to destroy and don't risk causing a Kessler effect. The US has experimented with using its ship-based anti-missile system, Aegis, against satellites, along with ground-based launches, but has not seen the need for extensive ASAT development. When you have most of the satellites there is little incentive to research anti-satellite weapons.

All analogies have their perils, but Bowen's notion of space as coastline works when it comes to space weapons: ASATs have more in common with shore defences than broadside cannons. The weaponisation of space is banned under the Outer Space Treaty, but the ban has never been properly observed. The Soviet Almaz space station was mounted with a machine gun. Space weapons tests seem to be on the increase, and states keep a watchful eye on one another. In July 2020, the US claimed that Russia had fired a projectile from an orbiting satellite; the Russian government says it was an inspection probe. Darpa, the US Defense Department's research agency, has launched tiny satellites – CubeSats, just ten centimetres across – from larger ones. More exotic kinds of weaponry are for the most part untested fantasies, but one particular dream refuses to die: the space laser. Demonstrations have been rumoured to be imminent since the 1980s but have been put back and back: the Pentagon's latest target test date is 2023. All the calculations suggest that such a weapon is unlikely to be effective. A laser powered by hydrogen fluoride or deuterium fluoride would use up two to three kilograms of fuel per second per megawatt of laser power. Even assuming it can be pointed at the right target, and avoid jamming efforts, such a laser would be too large to be practical in space. More serious technical problems confound partisans of 'directed energy weapons', particle beams and so on. For some reason the space weapons systems envisioned by the SDI and its predecessor programmes all had lithic names: 'smart rocks', 'brilliant pebbles', 'Excalibur'. Perhaps the futuristic can never escape the archaic imagination.

Bowen criticises space analysts for their US-centric perspective, but he doesn't really resist the imperial tractor beam. The scenario *du jour* in Washington is a conflict with China over Taiwan, and Bowen devotes a chapter to showing the way space power might affect the course of such a conflict. He discusses what would happen if the People's Liberation Army attempted to disable American space infrastructure, or to disrupt parts of it, in advance of an attack on the island. US aircraft carriers and other naval forces stationed at bases around China rely on satellites for navigation and targeting. With enough ASATs, China might be able to knock out American systems and take advantage of the ensuing confusion, but Bowen notes problems with this scenario: an attack on American military satellites would lead to reprisals against China's satellites; using jammers would reveal the locations of jamming facilities and invite their destruction. A Chinese invasion of Taiwan would rely to some extent on surprise, and attacking or interfering with satellites would serve as advance warning. The overriding problem is that even a limited attack on US satellites would force American involvement in the conflict: it would be a terrible strategic blunder. Bowen doesn't believe that satellite warfare means 'certain doom and destruction', but this is meagre comfort.

Most of the orbital infrastructure built by the United States isn't for war but for spying. The first images of the Earth taken from space, or at least from low Earth orbit, were produced in 1959 by a US reconnaissance satellite, codenamed Corona. The Geospatial Intelligence Agency, which interprets satellite imagery, has a staff as large as the Defense Intelligence Agency and occupies one of the largest headquarters buildings of any military or intelligence agency in the world, second only to the Pentagon. It was the GIA, along with the CIA, that provided funding for Google Earth. US reconnaissance satellites are essentially giant telescopes, but instead of being pointed out at quasars or searching for the universe's origins, they look down on Earth. In the sky-blue office complexes of the National Reconnaissance Office in Chantilly, Virginia, information gathered by US satellites is fed into an algorithm called Sentient. In 2013, when the NRO launched its reconnaissance satellite USA-247, it produced a logo for the launch that depicted an octopus embracing the globe; the tagline read: 'Nothing is beyond our reach.' It was a moment beyond the imaginative capacities even of hippie satellite conspiracy theorists.

The question of what the face of the Earth looks like, and what is moving across it, has become central to the global surveillance state America has constructed. While the national space agencies are brewing coffee in low gravity, the security state wields the global surveillance system for its own purposes. Not all of the ten million lidless eyes of the NSA and GCHQ surveillance network look down from space – the hacking of transcontinental and subsea internet cables, along with phone and location tracking, is at least as important – but satellite Earth observation is critical to global surveillance, and the capacities available to states are increasing. There is a sense in which the US drone assassination programme, and its concomitant policy of treating all adult males as combatants, shows ideology evolving to meet technology. At the same time, the scientific possibilities of satellites are being squandered: the two satellites responsible for monitoring the extent of polar ice, CryoSat-2 and IceSat-2, are set to expire years before any replacements are launched.

Daniel Deudney's *Dark Skies: Space Expansionism, Planetary Geopolitics, and the Ends of Humanity* makes a sustained argument against the militarisation of space and indeed the Promethean excitements of space itself.[17] To those who believe that space contains the possibility for transforming the human condition, *Dark Skies* will be anathema. Deudney dismantles the idea that space exploration will lead to a transcendence of the Earth's natural constraints: more likely, he thinks, is total surveillance and an increased risk of 'planetary scope technological catastrophe'. Though he doesn't mention it, the idea that humanity must escape the confines of Earth owes a debt to the 'Limits to Growth' models that came out of the MIT School of Management in the 1970s, and which served as part of the inspiration for China's one child policy. Deudney makes much of the fact that the technology of space exploration has its roots in the development of ballistic missiles and nuclear weapons, and calls military expansionism 'the von Braun programme', pushing the beginning of the space age back to German rocket research in the 1940s.

Ballistic missiles travel well into low Earth orbit in the course of their flights. Deudney says that for this reason they are space weapons, an argument that is wrong for the same reason mortars are not classed as bomber aircraft. It's no secret that the rockets that launch satellites and Mars probes are the cousins of ICBMs, but it all depends on the payload: space enthusiasts hope that they will carry the components for the first human outposts on other celestial bodies. Private space companies, SpaceX first among them, have succeeded in generating popular support for such enterprises, even as their corporate activities resemble those of any government contractor with good PR. There is a plausible argument that plans for space settlement – which is impractical and in the near future extremely unlikely – have provided cover for a really existing military expansionism concerned with Earth's orbit rather than grander projects. At great expense, military powers may be able to support outposts with potential strategic value, but the notion that flourishing habitats can be created on the frozen wastes of other planets as the Earth's ecosystems are destroyed is fanciful. Most are just too dark and cold. In the Islamic tradition, hell has rivers of boiling water to be drunk by the damned. On Saturn's moon Titan there is a 400-kilometre river of liquid methane at −180°C. Deudney compares the dream of civilian space settlements to the sky religions of ancient man and is against them in principle. Human societies struggle to unite lowlanders and highlanders in a single polity. Imagine the possibilities for violence between denizens of separate worlds.

In 1908, an asteroid struck Siberia with enough destructive force to flatten a 2,000 square kilometre area of forest. Had it instead struck a population centre it would have altered human history forever. Had it struck the same spot fifty years later it might have started a nuclear war. Asteroid strikes are not rare occurrences: they happen regularly. An international space effort would make asteroids a priority; national space programmes have not. One of the arguments for space settlements on Mars or elsewhere has been that they may ensure the survival of the species in the case of a large asteroid strike on Earth. Deudney rejects this idea, but he is also sceptical of the alternative approach of asteroid deflection. There is a famous paradox, raised by Carl Sagan and Steven Ostro, that developing the ability to deflect asteroids might increase the probability of an asteroid striking the earth, because deflection could be used as easily to direct an asteroid towards an enemy state as away from the earth.[18] Using an asteroid in this way might have the destructive power of a nuclear warhead with the added advantage of some degree of deniability. Deudney is in favour of planetary defence against asteroid strikes but argues that asteroid cartography and diversion should be the preserve of a consortium of 'the leading states on earth'. His ideological comrades would define 'leading states' as the US and its allies, which presents its own risks. In September 2022, NASA successfully diverted the course of a moon of the asteroid Didymos.

Deudney claims to support an Earth-oriented space programme for planetary security and habitability, and accepts the benefits of communication, navigation, and monitoring satellites. But he wants more international co-operation. He is – quite reasonably – sceptical about private space development and calls for a strengthening of the Outer Space Treaty. His aims are laudable, but not realistic: he doesn't really reckon with the role of national – particularly American – military power. Sitting in an office in Virginia or Beijing, one can now view the workings of power grids in California, monitor the front lines in a border war in the Caucasus, get ahead of the weather, observe with great precision the course of ships from São Paulo to Singapore, or count the number of trees in the boreal forest. This is not a power that will be relinquished voluntarily, and states will go to war for it. To attribute the danger more to the meagre support given to space exploration than to the configuration of the military state is a curious perspective. A more radical form of political opposition than any that someone like Deudney envisages will be needed to avert the militarist tendency represented by the US Space Force.

There is a temptation to view the prospect of space warfare as a product of inexorable technological advance. But there is a sense in which this view is itself outdated. Compare the rate of technological advance during the five decades between 1920 and 1970 with that of the fifty-year period that ended in 2020. The great and terrible scientific and technological inventions we associate with the present are almost all more than half a century old. The terrible pace of the mid-twentieth century has long since slowed. The Saturn V, built in 1967, is still the most impressive rocket ever made. During that axial age, humanity dreamed of ecumenopolises, of heavy industry and its by-products removed off-planet, of giant cylindrical worlds in orbit, of towers stretching into the heavens, of Dyson swarms of man-made infrastructure harvesting the full power of the Sun, of a Kardashev II civilisation capable of re-engineering the solar system. These dreams already seem absurd. In the great stagnation through which we are now living, comparatively modest projects to collect solar power in space or deposit nuclear waste into the Sun seem like grand schemes. Where are the space arks in orbit? The exploration of exoplanets in the circumstellar habitable zone? Satellite wars over the tiny layer of space immediately above the atmosphere are evidence of a fear of decline rather than of expansionary apotheosis. If, as Deudney and others believe, the project of space exploration, and not the military state, is an irredeemable danger to human survival, then the stagnation of modernity is a form of salvation.

III. A Prize from Fairyland

11
What Are We There For?

It is a cliché that the United States and Britain are obsessed with Middle East oil, but the reason for the obsession is often misdiagnosed. Anglo-American interest in the enormous hydrocarbon reserves of the Persian Gulf does not derive from a need to fuel Western consumption. Britain used to import considerable quantities of Saudi oil, but currently gets most of what it needs from the North Sea and hasn't imported much from the Gulf since the 1980s; Saudi oil currently represents around 3 per cent of UK imports. The US has never imported more than a token amount from the Gulf and for much of the postwar period has been a net oil exporter. Anglo-American involvement in the Middle East has always been principally about the strategic advantage gained from controlling Persian Gulf hydrocarbons, not Western oil needs. In 1945, Gordon Merriam, the head of the State Department's Near Eastern Affairs division, made this clear: the Saudi oilfields, he said, were first and foremost 'a stupendous source of strategic power'.[1] For Churchill, Persian Gulf oil had been 'a prize from fairyland far beyond our brightest hopes', because it had enabled the switch from a coal to an oil fuelled navy before the First World War.[2] The assistant US secretary of state, Adolf Berle, sketched out what remains US strategy: the US and Britain would provide Saudi Arabia and other key Gulf monarchies with 'sufficient military supplies to preserve internal security' and ensure that they were permanently guarded by Western navies.[3]

Other parts of the world – the US, Russia, Canada – have large deposits of crude oil, and current estimates suggest Venezuela has more proven reserves than Saudi Arabia. But Gulf oil lies close to the surface, where it is easy to get at by drilling; it is cheap to extract, and is unusually 'light' and 'sweet' (industry terms for high purity and richness). It is also located near the middle of the Eurasian landmass, yet outside the territory of any global power. Western Middle East policy, as explained by Jimmy Carter's national security adviser, Zbigniew Brzezinski, was to control the Gulf and stop any Soviet influence over 'that vital energy resource upon which the economic and political stability both of Western Europe and of Japan depend', or else the 'geopolitical balance of power would be tipped'.[4] In a piece for the *Atlantic* a few months after 9/11, Benjamin Schwarz and Christopher Layne explained that Washington 'assumes responsibility for stabilizing the region' because China, Japan and Europe will be dependent on its resources for the foreseeable future: 'America wants to discourage those powers from developing the means to protect that resource for themselves.'[5] Much of US power is built on the back of the most profitable protection racket in modern history.

The developed Asian economies are heavily reliant on Persian Gulf oil and Qatari natural gas. Three-quarters of Gulf oil exports go to Asian economies, and the five largest importers of gas from Qatar are Japan, South Korea, India, China and Singapore. US dominance in the Gulf gives it decisive strategic influence over any potential Asian rival. The US has a huge military presence in the region: United States Central Command is based at al-Udeid airbase in Qatar, the largest air force base in the world, with more than 10,000

US troops. Bahrain is the permanent dock of the Fifth Fleet, as well as having a US airbase and 7,000 US military personnel. The US has 5,000 permanent troops, two naval bases and an airbase in the United Arab Emirates. In Kuwait, it has access to three army bases and an air force base. In Oman, it has four airbases and two naval bases. In Iraq, the US still has troops stationed at al-Asad airbase north-west of Baghdad (once nicknamed 'Camp Cupcake' for its luxuries). In Saudi Arabia itself, the US operates a military training mission based in Eskan village. Only Iran, which broke away from the US system in 1979, houses no American military bases.

An agreement signed by British representatives and the Omani sultan in 1798 made Oman the British Empire's first satrapy in the Middle East (it was also Britain's last colonial possession in the Gulf). The East India Company had in 1763 established a trading post in Bushehr, now in Iran, from which the empire's growing Gulf business was managed. In 1819, to subdue the coastal Arab sheikhdoms and establish a protectorate over the Trucial States – now the United Arab Emirates – the British Navy bombarded and laid siege to Ras al-Khaimah. By 1917, Britain had established dependencies in Kuwait, Bahrain, Qatar, Iraq, and parts of Iran. Thousands died during Ibn Saud's conquest of the central Arabian peninsula in the first decades of the twentieth century; he received a monthly stipend from the British government throughout. When the new Saudi regime was threatened by a rebellion in 1929, British troops helped put down the mutineers. Britain bankrolled the Saudi monarchy (after 1943 with the help of the US) until the oil industry ended the need for subsidies.

The Suez crisis is generally treated as the decisive moment in the transition from British to US dominance in the region, but in *AngloArabia: Why Gulf Wealth Matters to Britain*, David Wearing shows that, in spite of Suez and other setbacks for Britain on the periphery (the 1958 coup in Iraq, the civil war in Yemen in the 1960s), British influence in fact increased in the core Gulf states over the next fifteen years, with successful palace coups backed by the British government in Saudi Arabia in 1964 and Sharjah, one of the Trucial States, in 1965.[6] Qatar, the Trucial States and Oman remained British protectorates, their currencies pegged to sterling. Wearing makes a strong case that it was the cost of the military 'protection' of the Gulf that forced the end of Britain's formal empire there in 1971, and the beginning of US hegemony.

Before withdrawing from its dependencies, the British government placed retired military officers as advisers to Gulf monarchs it had for the most part installed in order to protect 'oil and other interests' and a 'very profitable market in military equipment', in the words of the then foreign secretary, Michael Stewart.[7] Even now, a striking number of Middle East rulers are graduates of Sandhurst, including the kings of Bahrain and Jordan, the crown prince of Dubai, the emir of Abu Dhabi, the emir of Qatar, and the late emir of Kuwait. Most Saudi leaders are educated in the US but the former heads of the Saudi National Guard and the General Intelligence Service, as well as members of the Allegiance Council and a former defence minister, also attended Sandhurst. A skeleton British military presence remained behind in the Gulf. In 2016, Theresa May pledged to increase Britain's military commitments there, 'with more British warships, aircraft and personnel deployed on operations than in any other part of the world'. In April 2018, the Royal Navy reopened HMS *Jufair* in Bahrain – the base had been taken over by the US after Bahrain became independent in 1971. Another military base opened in Oman in 2019.

Britain's residual influence in Saudi Arabia meant that during the oil crises of the 1970s the kingdom secretly broke its own embargo to supply Britain. Saudi Arabia also continued to pump much of the massive surplus generated by oil sales into British financial institutions. It finances about a fifth of the UK current account deficit. A ten-person team in Whitehall, known as Project Falcon, manages the UAE's investments in Britain. During the financial crisis in 2008, Gordon Brown appealed to the Gulf to provide private bailouts for British banks. A Serious Fraud Office investigation into the deal, which saw Barclays receive £4.6 billion from Qatar and £3.5 billion from the UAE and helped it to avoid nationalisation, resulted in a £50 million fine in 2022. Qatar's investments in the UK are many and conspicuous: Harrods, the Shard, the London Stock Exchange, Heathrow Airport. Saudi Arabia and the UAE's portfolios of UK bonds and equities are exceeded only by their US investments.

The US's inherited mastery of the Gulf has given it a degree of leverage over both rivals and allies probably unparalleled in the history of empire. Washington has established a highly conservative regional order through alliances with successive military dictatorships in Egypt and an ethno-nationalist Israel. Its overwhelming military control of the region ensures that Japan, South Korea, India and even China must deal with the US in the knowledge that it could, if it wished, cut them off from their main source of energy. It is difficult to overstate the role of the Gulf in the way the world is currently run. Without control of Gulf oil, it is doubtful that relations between the US and its main Asian ally, Japan, would be so firm. Both Obama and Trump talked of plans for a US withdrawal from the Middle East and a 'pivot' to Asia. If there are indeed such plans, it would suggest that recent US administrations are ignorant of the way the system over which they preside works.

The Arab Gulf states have proved well suited to their status as US client states, in part because their populations are small and their subjugated working class comes from Egypt and South Asia. The

1973 oil embargo is probably the only example of a backlash from the periphery to the imperial centre, although it was a dispute over profit-share rather than an example of Jacquerie: Western oil companies had been extracting huge profits while the Gulf states received little more than an allowance. These companies have less power now, except in Oman, where Royal Dutch Shell still owns a third of the main oil company. There are occasional disagreements between Gulf rulers and their Western counterparts over oil prices, but they never become serious. Even on the subject of Israel, Saudi Arabia follows the US line. Saudi Arabia's helotry to the West was one of al-Qaida's preoccupations but the US–Saudi alliance has if anything strengthened since the group's founding. The extreme conservatism of the Gulf monarchies, in which there is in principle no consultation with the citizenry, means that the use of oil sales to prop up Western economies – rather than to finance, say, domestic development – is met with little objection. Wearing describes the modern relationship between Western governments and the Gulf monarchs as 'asymmetric interdependence', which makes clear that both get plenty from the bargain. Since the West installed the monarchs, and its behaviour is essentially extractive, I see no reason to avoid describing the continued Anglo-American domination of the Gulf as colonial.

Saudi Arabia and the other five members of the Gulf Co-operation Council are collectively the world's largest buyer of military equipment by a big margin. Most of their arms are supplied by the US, but both Britain and France make substantial contributions. In 2017, the US and Saudi Arabia signed the largest arms deal in history, estimated to be worth $350 billion. Between 1985 and 2006 Britain signed a series of contracts (the Al Yamamah deal) worth tens of billions. Sales stepped up dramatically when the war in Yemen began: Britain sold Saudi Arabia arms worth £3.3 billion in 2015, compared with £107 million the year before. The deals are highly profitable for Western arms companies (Middle East governments account for about half of all British arms sales), but the charge that Western governments are in thrall to the arms companies is based on a misconception. Arms sales are useful principally as a way of bonding the Gulf monarchies to the Anglo-American military. Proprietary systems – from fighter jets to tanks and surveillance equipment – ensure lasting dependence, because training, maintenance and spare parts can be supplied only by the source country. Western governments are at least as keen on these deals as the arms industry, and much keener than the Gulf states themselves. While speaking publicly of the importance of fiscal responsibility, the US, Britain and France have competed with each other to bribe Gulf officials into signing unnecessary arms deals.

Control of the Gulf also yields less obvious benefits. Until 1971 the Gulf states pegged their currencies to sterling, which competed with the dollar as an international reserve currency. After the loss of its Gulf protectorates, Britain had to concede to the global hegemony of the dollar. There were mixed feelings about this in Washington. Under the Bretton Woods agreement the US dollar was pegged to gold and economists feared that even the US gold reserves would prove insufficient as a base for the world's financial system. The gold standard was finally abandoned, and in 1974, the US Treasury secretary, William Simon, secretly travelled to Saudi Arabia to secure an agreement that would help contribute to the dollar's dominance. As David Spiro documented in *The Hidden Hand of American Hegemony*, the US made its guarantees of Saudi and Arab Gulf security conditional on the use of oil sales to shore up the dollar.[8] Under Simon's deal, Saudi Arabia agreed to buy massive tranches of US Treasury bonds in secret off-market transactions. In addition, the US compelled Saudi Arabia and the other Opec countries to set oil prices in dollars, and for many years Gulf oil shipments could be paid for only in dollars.

෴

For the people of the region, the effects of a century of AngloArabia have been less satisfactory. Since the start of the war in Yemen in 2015 some 150,000 people have been killed, not counting those who have died of disease or starvation. In that time Britain has supplied arms worth nearly £5 billion to the Saudi coalition fighting the Yemeni Houthis. The British army has supplied and maintained aircraft throughout the campaign; British and American military personnel are stationed in the command rooms in Riyadh; British special forces have trained Saudi soldiers fighting inside Yemen; and Saudi pilots continue to be trained at RAF Valley on Anglesey. The US is even more deeply involved: the US Air Force has provided mid-air refuelling for Saudi and Emirati aircraft – at no cost, it emerged in November 2018. Britain and the US have also funnelled weapons via the UAE to militias in Yemen. If the Western powers wished, they could stop the conflict overnight by ending their involvement. Instead the British government has committed to the Saudi position. As foreign secretary, Philip Hammond pledged that Britain would continue to 'support the Saudis in every practical way short of engaging in combat'. This is not only complicity but direct participation in a war that is as much the West's as it is Saudi Arabia's.

The Gulf monarchies are family dictatorships kept in power by external design, and it shows. The Gulf principalities may not match the extremes of Saudi repression but are no less authoritarian. Yet until the assassination of Jamal Khashoggi at the Saudi consulate in Istanbul in October 2018, Crown Prince Mohammed Bin Salman, the de facto ruler of the kingdom, was widely talked about as an enlightened reformer. When Germany suspended arms sales over the incident, the UK foreign secretary, Jeremy Hunt, urged them to reverse the decision. The main threat to Western interests is internal: a rising reminiscent of Iran's in 1979. To forestall such an event, Britain equips and trains the Saudi police force, has military advisers permanently attached to the internal Saudi security forces, and operates a strategic communications programme for the Saudi National Guard (called Sangcom). In Bahrain, described in 2013 by the Royal United Services Institute as Britain's closest Gulf ally and 'the equivalent of an aircraft carrier permanently in the Gulf', demonstrators inspired by the Arab Spring were forcibly dispersed from the Pearl roundabout in Manama in 2011. The crackdown began in earnest two days after the US secretary of defence, Robert Gates, had visited the country. Saudi and Emirati security forces crossed into Bahrain over the King Fahd causeway in British-made Tacticas armoured personnel carriers to support Bahrain's security apparatus.

As Wearing argues, 'Britain could choose to swap its support for Washington's global hegemony for a more neutral and peaceful position.' It would be more difficult for the US to extricate itself. Contrary to much of the commentary in Washington, the strategic importance of the Middle East is increasing, not decreasing. The US may now be exporting hydrocarbons again, thanks to state-subsidised shale, but this has no effect on the leverage it gains from control of the Gulf. And impending climate catastrophe shows no sign of weaning any nation from fossil fuels, least of all the developing East Asian states.[9] US planners seem confused about their own intentions in the Middle East. In 2017, the National Intelligence Council described the sense of neglect felt by the Gulf monarchies when they heard talk of the phantasmagorical Asia pivot. The report's authors were profoundly negative about the region's future, predicting 'large-scale violence, civil wars, authority vacuums and humanitarian crises persisting for many years'.[10] The causes, in the authors' view, were 'entrenched elites' and 'low oil prices'. They didn't mention that maintenance of both these things is US policy.

12
The Benefits of Lawlessness

'Honourable was the swift and timely aid offered to them in their struggle by the West,' *The Times* said of the Libyan rebels who rose up against Gaddafi during the Arab Spring in 2011; Western military intervention on behalf of the rebellion was 'a good deed in a weary world'. Today, more than five years after Gaddafi's fall in October 2011, Libya has been relegated to that class of countries (Afghanistan, Somalia) from which we hear occasional news of US drone strikes but little else. Gaddafi's overthrow was quickly followed by a national implosion. The historical divide between Tripolitania in the west and the cities of Cyrenaica to the east reopened; disparate bands of militias hacked up the country; arms dealers enjoyed a surge in business unmatched since the collapse of the Soviet Union; paramilitary forces took control of the oil infrastructure. By 2014 two competing governments had emerged, neither of which was in a position to govern. Algerian and Tunisian jihadists found a haven free from French-trained counter-insurgency units. Islamic State established its most powerful satellite in Gaddafi's ancestral seat of Sirte, where it named the city's mosque after Abu Musab al-Zarqawi and carried out public executions for witchcraft. Feuds which had lain dormant or been actively discouraged in Gaddafi's time resurfaced and still persist, with varying degrees of severity, between at least a dozen tribal groups and rival towns. The small town of Tawergha, for example, devastated in 2011 by rebel forces from its large industrial neighbour Misrata, remains an empty ruin, its former residents scattered in four refugee camps around the country.

Western-led regime change has produced a catastrophic breakdown: 400,000 people are internally displaced out of a population of six million; more than a million have fled abroad. Many layers of conflict – tribal, regional, ethnic, religious, for and against the old regime – are now superimposed, one on top of another. Libya is now a country of several governments and none, where rival entities with grand titles – the Government of National Accord, the Government of National Salvation, the House of Representatives – fight for the right to claim authority over a state that no longer exists. The real forces in Tripoli are the militias that roam the city. In the country as a whole, there are two increasingly hostile power blocs: one consisting of old army units under an ageing general in the east, the other an alliance of the tribal merchant elites of the city-state of Misrata in the west. Both blocs have their eyes fixed on Libya's capital in anticipation of another round of brutal fighting.

Tripoli itself has an unmistakable air of decay. The cranes above the grey edifice of what was supposed to become the Intercontinental Hotel haven't moved in six years. The crumbling, unfinished tower blocks on the edge of town loom beside the remains of others burned out or bombed in the war. Many still bear slogans from the time of the revolt. There are oases of wealth, tidy streets that could be in some dull part of urban France, but turn a corner and you encounter others as squalid as anything in the poorest quarters of Niamey. Countless posters of martyrs plastered on to roadside billboards in the heady afterglow of victory are faded now, nearly to white.

In the shabbier areas of Tripoli long lines of people queue for bread each night. For the past six months markets which were once regulated by the state have been closed and the price of food has tripled. Even in affluent areas many of the streets are either unpaved or so broken and covered in mud that they look unpaved. Roads and drainage systems are in disrepair. Even a shower of rain leaves narrower streets flooded and beaches dozens of cars along the ring road. When I was there, power cuts lasted fourteen hours a day. In mid-January 2017 the whole country from the Tunisian border to Benghazi was without power for more than twenty-four hours after a militia stopped up the gas pipeline to the al-Harsha powerplant west of Tripoli. Outside the nearby city of Khoms I saw more than 100 people queueing in single file along a desolate road to refill small gas cylinders. Every morning hundreds of people queue, usually in vain, in the hope of withdrawing the equivalent of $50 from their banks, which are desperate for hard currency. Those with access to euros or dollars are better off with the black market pedlars, who stand in suspicious-looking huddles in Essaah Square in the Medina, up beyond the gold merchants and the cafés with Italian names.

Wealthier people talk of migration ('Believe me, if someone has a way out they take it') and admit to a sense of regret ('It's a mess that will take decades to fix'; 'Gaddafi was no angel, but . . .'). I spoke to a bomb disposal expert who had taken many risks as an underground activist in 2011, hanging 'Free Libya' flags by night and later joining the uprising. Now he was riddled with guilt. 'They were different times, but when I look back I ask myself: if I had stayed home, would Gaddafi have stayed in power, and would all of this never have happened?'

The only police in Tripoli are traffic cops. They don't even flinch when a gun is fired at the other end of the street. At the Interior Ministry's administrative headquarters, the front gate was guarded by a lone man wearing a T-shirt and beret and carrying a Kalashnikov. Told that I was there to meet the director of protocol he asked, 'Who is the director of protocol?' – not as a challenge but with genuine curiosity. Inside, two deserted storeys up, a captain in a smart grey wool coat sat behind a big desk in a corner office watching John Travolta in *Be Cool*. At least he had turned up for work; much of the Libyan police force now exists only on paper. A colonel in the internal intelligence service told me that he, and every other high-ranking officer he knows, shows up once a week to pick up his paycheck – Libya's oil has ensured a trickle of money to the Interior Ministry even through the worst of the fighting – and spends the rest of the time at home. 'It's too dangerous: there's no security whatsoever. There's no police, no army, no discipline, just flip-flops and Kalashnikovs,' he said, before listing the names of convicted criminals who had been released during the 2011 uprisings and were now active in the militias.

The superficial appearance of order in Tripoli depends on a fragile understanding between the four militia bosses who run the city. Haitham Tajouri, a former prison guard who drafted in many of his former charges, controls the largest militia. The Salafist sheikh Abdulraouf Kara's Special Deterrence Force (Radaa) has a sprawling base at the airport to the east of the city. The Nawasi brigade, headed by Mustafa Gadour, an old associate of Kara, is quartered in a former riding school. Abdul Ghani al-Kikli (also known by the nom de guerre 'Ghneiwa') is based in the Abu Sleem area, just south of the disused zoo. These militias have formed a tentative alliance against armed outsiders trying to muscle in on Tripoli. Underneath the big four are many smaller groups. Tripoli University, for example, is under the 'protection' of the Saadawi militia; the west of the city is Fursan militia territory; the remnants of al-Qaida-linked militias control the Nasr forest behind the Rixos Hotel, along with a string of other jihadist groups, including the Muqatilah (commonly known as the Libyan Islamic Fighting Group), which operates across the whole city.

The streets are mostly clear of the arbitrary checkpoints that crop up in Libya's more stable neighbourhoods. You can move around Tripoli without much trouble, but militiamen of various persuasions are everywhere, wearing fake Barbour jackets over US Navy combat trousers and carrying rifles. In the immediate aftermath of Gaddafi's fall the National Transitional Council, which took charge with the backing of the Western powers, was compelled to dip into the state coffers – ample at the time – to pay off the militiamen who had done the spadework for the rebellion. The kinds of salary they were offering produced a dramatic increase in the number of 'revolutionaries'. The majority of militiamen today are young men, often high on tramadol, who signed up after the fall of the regime for the sake of a gun and a new pair of trousers. The militias seized government offices and took over the businesses and villas of notables, going on to colonise the shells of the Defence and Interior Ministries and draw state salaries. Most of the larger militias are nominally under the command of government ministries but in practice take orders from no one.

Some of the militia leaders claim they uphold order in lieu of the police out of a sense of civic duty, but it doesn't take long to see how they really work. Haitham Tajouri's men spend much of their time steaming around in armoured vehicles and four-by-fours with rocket-launchers bolted to their flatbeds. On the Gurgi Street roundabout Radaa and Nawasi fighters are regularly posted in Toyotas mounted with anti-aircraft guns or huge machine guns ripped off combat helicopters. I saw one of Radaa's men wearing a tan *jelabiya* and white *taqiyah* casually sitting in the driver's seat of a vehicle that had been modified to carry what looked like a 16-foot naval artillery cannon – all the better for deterring pickpockets, no doubt. The cannon formed the rearguard of a column of Radaa's Canadian Terradyne armoured vehicles, which was returning from a drug bust in the residential district of Gergarish. The bust had gone wrong and turned into a street fight with a Nigerian criminal gang. Driving through the area afterwards you could see buildings with their fronts ripped away; there was a strong smell of gunpowder and something like flint.

Sheikh Kara's Radaa force in particular moves around the city with a conquering air. In January I visited their base at the rear of the airport, where one of the militia's commanders told me at length of Radaa's popularity and general saintliness. 'We conduct operations to find escaped convicts and counter drugs and alcohol trafficking because the police are too weak to do so and because the spread of crime and drugs is very dangerous,' he said. It was hard to take him seriously, especially given Radaa's alliance with Tajouri, who is universally known as a foul-mouthed, blasphemous cocaine-snorter. 'There are Africans on our soil feeding our children drugs and alcohol,' he went on. 'They are illegal immigrants in many cases and they run brothels and spread lethal diseases.' Anti-African sentiment has become widespread since the uprising, when black Libyan towns and tribes were accused of siding with the loyalist forces and rumours spread that Gaddafi employed African mercenaries. During the bust in Gergarish, Radaa rounded up 700 sub-Saharan Africans. Most of them were bussed to immigration detention centres, but sixty were kept behind in the Radaa's own private prisons.

Countless people are held in militia prisons across Libya; Radaa alone holds more than 2,000. They are said to be dismal places, but I wasn't permitted to see one. Instead I was shown a rehabilitation centre – another contract extorted from the Justice Ministry – which had a carpentry shop, a spotless bakery, a small assembly line for making doors and a Quranic school. Unlike many militias, Radaa is not driven chiefly by self-enrichment: Kara's Salafism – a non-jihadist variety – is relatively apolitical, pious and conservative, and Radaa is respected since it represents a semblance of order. A commander at the base said they would disband if a real state emerged, but there's no one who could make them.

Most of the other Libyan militias don't pretend to have an ideology; they appear trapped in the logic of armed revolt, eternal revolutionaries, but they don't really need a pretext for going about their business of smuggling, extortion, murder, and kidnapping. (I never went two days in Tripoli without meeting someone whose neighbour or friend had been kidnapped, not at some point over the past few years but that very morning.) Nuri, a former militiaman I met recently on the outskirts of Tripoli, said car-jackings were the latest craze: even clapped-out cars are appropriated for hit-and-run jobs. He lamented the lack of order and was particularly scathing about his former comrades in Quwwat al-Mutaharika, the militia he left at the start of the last battle for Tripoli in 2014. He said they had descended into thuggery and hoped General Khalifa Haftar would come from the east and lay down the law.

Khalifa Haftar is a Gaddafi-era general turned CIA asset who reappeared in Libya after twenty years in exile in Virginia to take part in the revolt in 2011. He then returned to the US, but cropped up again in February 2014, when he delivered a traditional coup-style broadcast on national television, claiming to have seized power on behalf of the 'Supreme Council of the Armed Forces in Libya', the precise wording used by Egypt's junta. His claim was laughed off in the following days when nothing seemed to happen. But Haftar stuck at it and by July, with the former heads of the air force, navy, air defence forces, and military police at his side, he had succeeded in starting a war in Tripoli. Militias and army units under his command – he remained at a distance – fought Tripoli's militia bosses, and forces from nearby Misrata, for control of the capital, destroying Tripoli International Airport in the mêlée. He failed to win power, but his Libyan National Army, which is made up of old army brigades, tribal militias and scriptural Salafists, survived. Haftar claims to have 50,000 men under his command, a figure that's difficult to verify but if accurate would make the LNA the most powerful single force in the country.

Haftar's line is that 'Libyans had no idea what democracy meant'; the country, he says, needs a military man in charge. The CIA appears to have cut him off some time ago, but for eighteen months he openly appealed for Western backing. Western diplomats told me he was considered 'a strongman who just isn't strong enough' and 'a less charismatic Gaddafi' (though French intelligence is now working with him, and Boris Johnson has been pushing for Britain to revisit the matter). Spurned by the US, he has turned to Russia for backing and was recently photographed in Moscow wearing a ushanka. A classic war on terror rhetorician, he has been taking on Islamic State, non-IS jihadists, and anyone else who stands up to him in Cyrenaica from his base in the eastern city of Marj. His followers now control much of Benghazi and the Gulf of Sirte oilfields. Allegations that he has targeted civilians and ordered extra-judicial killings have done little to discourage support for him among those who hope that he can push through a solution.

If and when Haftar moves on Tripoli the strongest resistance will come from Misrata. Two hours by road from the capital, Misrata is, in effect, a well-organised city state; it is also an industrial-commercial hub, with the country's major iron and steel complex and a range of businesses. Misrata's industrial and merchant elites have a major stake in Tripoli: it is their consumer base. The city's detractors, Haftar among them, claim that its leaders are too close to the Libyan Muslim Brotherhood and too hungry for power. Misrata's militias comprise 40,000 well-armed men, a loose coalition of mainstream Islamists, Salafists and pragmatists who do not always see eye to eye. Despite its divisions this is probably the most coherent bloc in the country, and the old merchant families who dominate the city have made it clear that they have no interest in living under Haftar.

The Misratans can properly claim to have risked much in the rebellion against Gaddafi and did well in the battle against Islamic State in Sirte, where they lost hundreds of men but were beaten by Haftar to the surrounding oilfields. Italian intelligence is working ever more closely with Misratan forces (the partly state-owned Italian multinational ENI has extensive oil interests in Libya), just as Russia, Egypt and the United Arab Emirates are increasing their support for Haftar. International involvement is doing nothing to lower tensions. An airstrike by Haftar's LNA on 3 January badly injured the chief of the Misratan Military Council, Ibrahim Beit al-Mal, as he visited a southern airbase in Jufra. Mohamed al-Ghasri, the main military spokesman for the Misratan forces, claimed two weeks later that a 'war in the south is imminent' and that the Misratans were already clashing with Haftar's soldiers in the surrounding desert.

The remnants of the Government of National Accord, meanwhile, are desperately clinging to power. Formed by the UN under the 2015 Libyan Political Agreement, it was intended to reconcile the two governments that had emerged by 2014: the Government of National Salvation in Tripoli, and the House of Representatives government based 1,000 kilometres away in the eastern cities of Tobruq and Bayda (for a time its 'parliament' met on a Greek cruise ship in the port of Tobruq). Uniting Libya under a single government was seen as a first step to rebuilding the country, but in the event the GNA simply became the third government in a triad of pretenders.

From the outset it was plagued by accusations that it was a sham, installed by the West to legitimise a new military intervention: the first request the US made to the GNA was that it authorise US airstrikes on IS in Sirte. The impression that it was a tool of the West gained ground when the GNA's Presidential Council arrived in Tripoli – three months late and already two members down after internal squabbling – having been ferried from Tunis by the Italian Navy. (By then the previous UN special envoy to Libya, Bernardino Leon, had been found bartering the authority of his office to the UAE for a highly paid directorship, which he took, and moved to Abu Dhabi.) During its first months in Tripoli the GNA had to hold its meetings in the naval base where it had disembarked. It now has control of the Presidential Council building, a glass construction put up on the site of a medical clinic that Gaddafi demolished in 2006 when he discovered its staff had celebrated Saddam's hanging.

Half of the windows of the council headquarters have been shot out, and when I went there in January it was surrounded by a moat of dirty water. Inside I met Ahmed Maiteeq, the urbane deputy prime minister. Days earlier one of the council's remaining deputies, Fathi Majburi, had burst into a meeting between the Presidential Council's prime minister, Fayez Serraj, and UN officials, accompanied by armed bodyguards. A third member of the council, Moussa Kouni, had resigned the week before. Maiteeq insisted that the GNA's inability to govern was the fault of the two other pretender governments, and that they were orchestrating the power outages and hard-currency shortages in the banks in an attempt to undermine it. Haftar, he said, was merely a militiaman with propaganda skills who posed no serious threat. All the militias would be reabsorbed into an official security hierarchy and many problems would simply dissolve now that the GNA had its own budget. The 2017 budget is certainly an improvement: before it was agreed in December, the

Central Bank had supplied only enough funding to the GNA to allow it to keep the lights on. 'Always when you have a new state there are problems,' Maiteeq said, 'but can you imagine what it would be like without the GNA? What would the future of the country be then?'

This is crackpot optimism. There is no state, and although the GNA claims that it rid Sirte of Islamic State, its only contribution to that effort was to sign off on US airstrikes. On 3 February, the GNA set up a Turkey-style EU migrant deal for Libya in exchange for €200 million; Médecins Sans Frontières correctly described the announcement as 'delusional' and the GNA has no authority to make the deal stick. The GNA can stay in Tripoli only with the backing of the Misratan militias operating in the city and because it has made pay-offs to other militia bosses, including Tajouri. One high-ranking official in the Interior Ministry, now technically under the control of the GNA, told me he had been in the room when GNA officials agreed to slip Tajouri millions of dollars in return for his co-operation. The current UN envoy, Martin Kobler, agrees with Maiteeq that the only alternative to the Libyan Political Agreement is chaos, but the two already co-exist. It's difficult to find anyone who takes the GNA seriously. Invoking its UN backing, as it does, makes matters worse. Anything associated with the UN is vilified in Tripoli. In any case the Libyan Political Agreement, a two-year arrangement, expires at the end of this year and there is no sign of a plan for its replacement. There are capable officials untarnished by the suspicion of foreign influence, like the mayor, Abdulrauf Beitelmal, and his chief of staff, Salem Mokadmy, who are trying to clean up the city centre and could govern the country if the opportunity arose, but they can only work in the lee of the militias. The presence of men with rocket launchers tearing around the main junction in front of the town hall makes it difficult to maintain the roads and collect the rubbish.

The Western powers are half-heartedly attempting to prop up the UN-backed authorities, but that's not all they're up to. US drones regularly fly over the country and the US ticks names off its kill lists with the help of F15s based in Britain. Contingents of US, Italian and British special forces operate in Libya under scant cover. They fought side by side with the Misratan militias against Islamic State in the battle for Sirte last year. The Italian army has even set up what it calls a field hospital in Misrata but it is really a military base: it has just 12 beds but 300 army officers. By the same token the support of Russia, Egypt and France is emboldening Haftar. The landscape is so fractured and messy that British and Italian special forces have ended up on what looks increasingly like the opposite side to their French counterparts without realising how it happened. Yet again the Western powers are stoking a civil war they don't understand and for which they haven't planned.

For the capital of a supposedly post-revolutionary country, Tripoli is woefully short of political vision. 'Here it was only ever "Let's get rid of Gaddafi" – there was no idea beyond that,' one activist told me. Public discussion is minimal, stale and usually reducible to factional posturing; there is a deep, apolitical emptiness. What kind of society Libya should be and how the country might be run are questions that cannot be formulated, let alone discussed. The main priorities are personal security, food and warmth, and the struggle to secure them encourages narrow factionalism. Lawlessness has its benefits – there is no oppressive regime – but they're wearing thin. Tripoli is no longer the capital of an authoritarian state. There is no fear of being overheard by an informant or of imminent arrest by the secret police. Instead there is the worry of not knowing who controls which streets on any given day, the constant threat of kidnap, rumours of an impending fight, and the knowledge that violence could break out at any moment.

A common refrain among the now extinct species of Libyan revolution optimists used to be that the collapse was a result only of the iniquities of the Gaddafi era. The bizarre system Gaddafi created (on top of a backwater economy: until oil was discovered in 1959 the country's main exports were cuttlefish bone, esparto grass, and battlefield scrap) certainly bequeathed a legacy that one would not expect to produce an abundance of fresh thought. Gaddafi was so personally critical to the Libyan regime that merely killing him really was most of the way to overthrowing it. The old regime had a long shadow and a lot to answer for. But why did Gaddafi's fall not present opportunities for the fundamental political and economic structures to be overhauled?

Part of the problem was the state of the opposition. In Egypt and Tunisia a political opposition had organised for years through the trade unions and civil rights groups but a comparably organised Libyan opposition had barely formed at all. When the popular uprising took Benghazi and spread to the western cities the regime retained enough support to survive the initial protests and respond with massive force. With Gaddafi quashing the revolt the stage was then set for a show of European heroism. In the end it was British, French, and US military action that brought the regime down. Just months earlier, Britain and France had been supplying the old regime with equipment designed for quelling rebellions, including 'wall and door breaching projectile launchers' and armoured crowd-control vehicles. But the Western powers sought regime change under the cover of what Robert Gates would later call the 'fiction' that NATO forces were only disabling Gaddafi's military command centres. It was US Predator drones and French fighter aircraft that attacked Gaddafi's convoy as it fled Sirte and French intelligence that sent Gaddafi's coordinates to the Misratan rebel militias who pulled him from a drainpipe in the desert and executed him. (The

Western-backed rebel leadership would later claim it was an agent of French intelligence who pulled the trigger.) Air strikes, British and French special forces, and an illegal circumvention of the UN arms embargo by the US helped to overthrow Gaddafi and there was little planning for what would come next.

After a couple of meetings with Mahmoud Jibril the Western powers threw their weight behind his group of regime defectors and ageing exiles, charging them with bringing the fighting opposition under their wing. Jibril had been Gaddafi's head of national planning and Mustafa Abdul Jalil, who chaired the National Transitional Council, was the former minister of justice who had personally approved the death sentences in the Bulgarian nurses affair in 2007.[1] They never put forward much of a political programme, nor did they create a base of political support within the country. The armed rebels put up with the NTC for a year in exchange for massive cash transfers but then tired of the game and initiated the dangerous chaos that continues to the present day. Most of the old NTC figures then fled the scene.

The situation quickly became so bad that according to the US envoy Jonathan Winer the major powers briefly considered passing Libya into an 'international trusteeship' with a technocratic leadership, a dubious idea which the US, Britain and France eventually rejected.[2] They didn't want to take that level of responsibility. The Libyan state had been dismantled before opposition forces could gather expertise or cohesion, the Western powers effectively withdrew, and the country was now an ungovernable mess.

On 15 April 2019 US president Donald Trump made an unexpected phone call to Khalifa Haftar, in the midst of his long awaited attack on Tripoli, aimed at overthrowing Libya's nominal ruling authority, the UN-backed Government of National Accord. According to a White House statement, Trump 'recognized Field Marshal

Haftar's significant role in fighting terrorism and securing Libya's oil resources', and the two men discussed their 'shared vision for Libya's transition'. Only the week before Trump called him, the State Department had condemned Haftar's assault on Tripoli as a dangerous escalation. The US has since joined Russia and France in blocking a UN Security Council censuring him. The GNA was embattled, a government in name only in a state without a state. Why was the White House supporting an obviously reckless act of aggression? Parts of the story are becoming clear. Haftar visited Riyadh shortly before launching his assault on Tripoli, and the Saudis pledged generous financial backing. On 14 April, as his forces were struggling to advance, Haftar flew to Cairo for an audience with Trump's favourite Middle East ally, Abdel Fattah el-Sisi. Trump made his intervention the following day.

Haftar amassed power in eastern and southern Libya for four years with the support of Egypt, the UAE and France. A putchist officer in Gaddafi's 1969 coup, Haftar fell out of favour in 1987 during the ill conceived Toyota wars in Chad, where he was taken prisoner. Abandoned by Gaddafi, he was recruited by the CIA for its half-hearted effort to build a Libyan opposition and flown first to Zaire then Virginia. He seems to have lived there, on the CIA payroll, until 2011 when he cropped up in Benghazi during the uprising against Gaddafi. In February 2014, Haftar appeared on Libyan television, declaring another coup in the name of a Supreme Council of the Armed Forces. In May 2014 he launched Operation Dignity, a campaign he has been fighting ever since.

Haftar's forces met resistance and have not been able to reach the city centre proper. A friend in southern Tripoli told me he has moved his family out of the city. There have been air and artillery strikes on residential areas. The World Health Organization estimates that at least 350 people have died. Haftar's forces call themselves the Libyan

National Army but they are made up of the rump of Gaddafi's gutted army, tribal militias and mercenaries. Human Rights Watch notes 'a well-documented record of indiscriminate attacks on civilians' and 'summary executions of captured fighters'. Haftar has been clear about his intentions should he succeed in taking control of the country: military rule, in the Egyptian mode, with himself in charge.

Haftar's bid for Tripoli poses some odd questions. Why was it launched on the day the UN secretary-general, António Guterres, was visiting the city? Why didn't Haftar secure the support of one of the major militias controlling Tripoli? And why didn't Washington see it through to the end?

13
In Egypt's Prisons

It's no secret that Hosni Mubarak's regime was repressive. Yet although in its treatment of prisoners and many other ways besides, Abdel Fattah el-Sisi's is worse, statesmen around the world praise its role in Egypt's 'democratic transition'. When John Kerry visited Cairo last year he reported that Sisi had given him 'a very strong sense of his commitment to human rights'. These issues, he said, were 'very much' on Sisi's mind. For more than thirty years it was US policy to support autocratic government in Egypt as a route to 'regional security'. The US backed Mubarak's regime until its very last days; even during the mass protests of January 2011, the US hoped Mubarak could survive if he made political concessions. Mubarak is gone, but the US Defense Department's links with the Egyptian military – long-standing and solid – have remained. Officials are steadily restoring the flow of aid and equipment that was temporarily suspended in the wake of the coup: there is no serious 'human rights' issue for Washington.

The US is not alone in this. When Shinzo Abe visited Cairo in January 2015 he spoke of the 'high esteem' in which the Japanese government holds its relationship with Sisi, and pledged hundreds of millions of dollars in development loans. Diplomatic support from Europe, which suffered minor interruptions when the repression peaked late in the summer of 2013, has largely been restored. In addition to visiting the UN General Assembly, Sisi has been received on official visits to the Vatican, Davos, Rome, and Paris: little or nothing has been said about routine human rights abuses, let alone the Rabaa massacre or the mass imprisonment and torture of dissidents.

When David Cameron held a meeting with Sisi in New York in September 2014 he spoke of 'Egypt's pivotal role in the region' and its importance to British policy. 'Both economically and in the fight against Islamist extremism', he said, Egypt was a crucial ally and the UK was 'keen to expand practical partnerships'. Cameron urged the president 'to ensure human rights are respected'; he was much more specific on the point that Egyptian state debts to Britain's international oil companies should be promptly repaid. The British embassy issued reports with titles like 'Egypt: Open for Business?' and the UK investment delegation to Cairo was the biggest in a decade. Western leaders – as Sisi well knows – have very little interest in upsetting Egypt, strategically located as it is between the world's major energy-producing region and the developed world. The West appears to see no contradiction in supporting the 'stability' of the Sisi regime at a time when the Egyptian population is suffering from the extreme instability that comes with mass arrests and torture.

Mohammed B., a twenty-eight-year-old postgraduate student, was arrested on 6 October 2013. He was taking part in one of the many anti-coup marches held across Cairo that day. The intended destination was Tahrir Square, but as the march reached the neighbourhood of Dokki, it was attacked by various branches of the security services: dozens of demonstrators were killed and scores arrested. Along with hundreds of others Mohammed tried to flee by taking a series of side streets, but was surrounded and arrested. He was taken to a police station and held, along with two doctors, an engineer and two academics from Cairo University, for seven or eight hours without water. At midnight they were moved, but not – as they had expected – to one of Cairo's many prisons.

The prison system in Egypt is the legacy of a long period of British control, followed by the successive autocracies of Nasser, Sadat and Mubarak. It was in a British prison during the Second World War that some of the torture techniques now employed by Egyptian intelligence were refined. The Combined Services Detailed Interrogation Centre was annexed to a British army camp in the Cairo suburb of Maadi. The camp had a cinema, boxing ring and ice-cream parlour for the soldiers, but a few hundred metres away British interrogators were experimenting on as many as sixty prisoners at a time, attempting to induce hallucinations with thyroxine, or trying to break them psychologically by forcing them to dig their own graves.

The Interior Ministry operates forty-two official prisons authorised to house civilian detainees. Information about them is relatively easy to come by and they are sometimes even inspected. Yet abuse and torture are rife, encouraged by a legal system which in many cases relies on confessions. Some of the worst prisons are well known: Wadi Natrun, Abu Zaabal and Tora Liman, believed to have been one of the earliest CIA black sites under Mubarak. There is also the Borg al-Arab, where the former president, Mohamed Morsi, was held, and the Sijn al-Aqrab, or 'Scorpion Prison', the most famous maximum-security prison in Egypt.

The law requires that the police refer a case to a prosecutor and begin an investigation within 24 hours of an arrest. Detainees must then be transferred to one of the forty-two registered institutions while awaiting trial. But that isn't what is happening today. There is overwhelming evidence that military and paramilitary police forces are operating a parallel system of detention outside official channels, and outside the law, partly in order to deal with the sheer number of people arrested since the coup. Egypt has experienced a spike in the number of citizens in detention unlike any in its history. At the beginning of 2013 Egypt's official prison population stood at somewhere between 60,000 and 66,000. According to the Interior Ministry's own figures 16,000 Egyptians were arrested in the nine months following Morsi's removal in July 2013. A more plausible independent estimate by the Egyptian Centre for Economic and Social Rights put the number for the same period at more than 41,000. Sisi has waved away such figures: the official prisons do not, he claims, have the space to accommodate tens of thousands of people. He may be right. Yet imprisoned they have been. So where are they?

Having interviewed lawyers, psychologists and former detainees, I have learned the names of sites where torture and ill-treatment are far worse than anything in the official prisons. Inside facilities like Maskar Zaqaziq, a base in Sharqiyah run by Amn al-Markezi, the central security forces, there are unacknowledged prisons which make the official jails look humane. In Interior Ministry buildings in Lazoughli Square and Gabar ibn Hayan, suspected political dissidents are tortured and interrogated at length by the national intelligence service. And in the Al-Azouly and Agroot military prisons in Ismailia and Suez, prisoners are held incommunicado, sometimes blindfolded, for months on end.

Mohammed B. and his cellmates were transferred from their police station to Maskar Ashra-Nus, 'Camp 10.5', a barracks outside Cairo belonging to Amn al-Markezi. His account of their reception at the camp is like many others I've heard from former detainees in Egypt. They were beaten relentlessly by groups of officers, verbally humiliated, stamped on with boots with metal heels and lashed with leather straps. They were then stripped, hung from the ceiling, beaten with sticks, subjected to stress positions, and beaten on the soles of their feet; some were given electric shocks. Mohammed was stripped and forced to crawl on the floor on his forearms and stomach for more than an hour in a method of torture that appears to have been inspired by military training exercises. Eventually, and without any attempt to extract information from them, the men were bundled into makeshift cells inside the barracks. Mohammed's measured three metres by six and contained fifty-nine other men: so crowded that he had to stand on one leg for periods of up to two hours. There was no toilet, and no one left the room save for short rounds of recreational torture at the hands of the guards.

Crammed into a concrete box, the inmates tried to devise a system that would allow them to sleep. They divided themselves into groups of four on rotating shifts – standing and sleeping – with each group assigned a certain number of floor tiles. This soon failed. Then they tried lying on their sides, head to tail. That didn't work either. A third system, which involved pairing the men up in lines, one standing with his legs apart as the other crouched between them, proved the least onerous. Mohammed said that the guards would mock their thirst and the stench of the cell from the other side of an iron door. He was held in Camp 10.5 for four days before being removed to a registered prison. Others, he learned, remained locked in the cell for weeks.

The cells in Wadi Natrun prison, where he spent the next six months, were bigger – five by ten metres for thirty prisoners – and in comparison with Camp 10.5 the conditions were bearable. Crucially, the cell had what could be loosely described as a toilet. But detainees were still regularly taken out of their cells, stripped naked and tortured. Mohammed was twice put in solitary confinement. 'The room had no windows and inside there was nothing', he told me, 'except thousands of cockroaches – they crawled all over me for hours.' The people he met there had come into the official detention system by a variety of routes. Some had been held in police stations for weeks; others had been in the custody of Amn al-Markezi, as he had been; one claimed to have been taken first to a secret prison in the Sinai peninsula, where he said he'd been held in an underground dungeon for seventy days. Mohammed was eventually tried before a court and cleared on every fantastic charge the state had laid against him. Most were not so lucky. Of the 125 men tried on the same day just seven were released.

There is nothing out of the way about Mohammed's case. Letters smuggled out of prison by the Egyptian journalist Ahmed Ziada, who was arrested while covering protests at Al-Azhar university in December 2013, describe his time in Nasr City Two police station, where he was beaten and given electric shocks before being taken to Abu Zaabal prison. In another letter, dated 19 February 2014, a detainee named Kareem al-Beheiry details the unbearable conditions of an Amn al-Markezi base where officers assault, mock and humiliate detainees as a way of alleviating boredom. Descriptions of improvised cells packed with inmates are frequent. The Egyptian climate adds to the horrors of overcrowding. In a letter smuggled out of Helwan police station in July 2014 the authors, who refer to themselves as 'the prisoners in cell number three', describe temperatures of 50°C in a room four metres by six containing sixty people. According to standards set by the European Committee for the Prevention of Torture, prison authorities should plan for seven square metres of cell space per detainee and observe an absolute minimum of four square metres. In cell number three, sixty detainees were held in a space suitable for between three and six people; in Mohammed B.'s case, a space suitable for between two and four people.

Islam A., a digital marketing professional, was pulled from an anti-government demonstration in late 2013 by *baltagiya* (civilians hired, and armed, by the state and most often deployed against protesters), who dragged him into a nearby block of flats. 'I tried to reason with them,' he said. 'I told them you support the government and I don't, but we have brains in our heads and tongues in our mouths and we can discuss this like human beings. They didn't even reply, they just beat me.' Islam was beaten and cut about with a long knife until he fainted – he has extensive scarring on his shoulders and chest. He was semi-conscious when a plainclothes officer arrived to make a formal arrest. 'A sea' of Amn al-Markezi officers was waiting for him outside the flats. He, too, ended up in Camp 10.5 – 'living hell', he called it – and held for five weeks in a cell of four metres by six with sixty-one other prisoners. He was repeatedly interrogated by intelligence staff from Amn al-Watany, the national security agency, who appeared to believe he was one of the leaders of the protest he had attended. On one occasion he was questioned by a senior officer while eight other Amn al-Markezi men formed a circle around him and beat him. On another he was stripped and laid face down on the floor with a dozen other inmates while officers threw freezing water over them. Sometimes detainees were taken out of the cells and subjected to a stress position known as the *falaka*, in which the victim's feet are tied to a wooden pole and the soles beaten. Again, Islam's experiences are far from unusual. Dozens of detainees have described police and Amn al-Markezi officers bursting into cells and beating them with clubs, or burning their blankets and clothes in front of them. Others describe having a rope put around their necks and being dragged from their cells to be given electric shocks.

Torture 'in all its forms' is prohibited under Egyptian law, and ministerial decree 668 formally abolished flogging as a punishment in 2002. Article 27 of the prison regulations mandates that a physician examine prisoners when they arrive, or on the morning of the next day, and document their state of health. Yet the law is seldom applied, conditions are appalling and the consequences are plain: by collating statistics from the Justice Ministry's own Forensic Medical Authority with those of NGOs and including the thirty-seven prisoners who died in a police van inside Abu Zaabal prison in August 2013, we can safely say that at least 150 people have died in official custody in Egypt since the coup – it is impossible to say how many may have died in non-registered jails. Amnesty International has documented countless cases of torture; prisoners are regularly interrogated while blindfolded or given electric shocks to the testicles to elicit confessions; in one case a woman was made to give birth while handcuffed.

Amn al-Markezi is almost entirely free from public scrutiny. But the Egyptian army is even less accountable, and it is from military facilities such as Azouly prison in Ismailia, Agroot prison in Suez and the headquarters of Battalion 101 in Arish that the worst testimonies come. One man detained at Azouly claimed in a letter dated 24 March 2014 that access to the toilet was permitted once a day, before dawn, that inmates were tortured with boiling water and even boiling oil, and that he frequently heard women screaming somewhere inside the facility. Letters and survivors' accounts describe three distinct layers inside these army camps. The first floor is for military prisoners who are lawfully detained. The second is known as the 'prosecutions floor' and holds civilians who have been given a military trial. The third floor – the 'investigations floor' – houses people who have been 'disappeared'.

Third-floor detainees are known to have been held for up to six months and are sometimes blindfolded throughout their incarceration. They are later sent to an official prison – often with serious injuries – wearing the same clothes they had on when they were arrested and bearing papers with forged arrest dates. Holding civilian detainees inside a military prison is illegal, but proceedings would in any case be difficult given that the very existence of Azouly and Agroot is not officially acknowledged. Unknown numbers of prisoners are being held. They are subject to punitive sexual assault; suspension from ceilings, doors and windows; waterboarding; and being burned with cigarettes. Research by Human Rights Watch shows that between the beginning of November and the end of December last year, 820 new civilian cases were referred to military prosecutors.

It is arguably no surprise that repression has reached these levels. In the past four years a revolution was attempted, failed and gave way to a reconstituted regime, headed by the most energetic and efficient figures among the old guard; a military council arrested the president, suspended the constitution, rounded up writers, chased out human rights groups and massacred demonstrators. Any regime with a profile of this kind is likely to abuse its prisoners. But what has happened at the higher levels of the Egyptian state indicates that a particular agenda has been systematically pursued.

One of the first things Sisi did after the Supreme Council of the Armed Forces reclaimed the presidency in July 2013 was to appoint a serving general as head of the Mukhabarat intelligence service. Mohamed Farid al-Tohamy was well known for his hatred of the Muslim Brotherhood, his sympathy for and contacts with Israeli military intelligence, and as a Sisi and SCAF loyalist. Although Tohamy has since been retired, his appointment presaged a series of promotions for other loyalists and military intelligence veterans that enabled Sisi – himself a former head of military intelligence – to consolidate his control over first the military and then the other organs of the security state. Sisi has concentrated the power of the regime in the presidency and a small entourage of senior generals. It has become popular outside Egypt to describe his regime as a return to the days of Mubarak, but Sisi isn't content to revert to the *status quo ante*: he has sought the greater prize of restoring the army's place as the central institution of state power, with himself as its undisputed head.

Recently leaked recordings of telephone exchanges last February between General Mamdouh Shahin, a senior SCAF figure with a broad mandate, and General Abbas Kamel, the director of Sisi's office, suggest the extent of military influence even over the corrupt fiefdom of the Interior Ministry.[1] The recordings reveal that Shahin had contacted Mohammed Ibrahim, the interior minister, to discuss reclassifying the military building in which Morsi was being held (probably Abu Qir naval base): he wanted it to be designated an official prison in order to avoid potential problems at Morsi's trial. The minister complied, with Shahin supplying an official declaration for Ibrahim to sign. Which isn't to say that the ministry has been thoroughly suborned: there is still a rivalry between the ministry and the army, but the latter is in the ascendant.

Sisi has extended his own form of military organisation, management and logic to almost every aspect of the Egyptian state. A range of senior posts are now occupied or controlled by serving or retired generals: a supervisor building roads or compiling government statistics is scarcely less likely than a soldier to answer to a ranking general. Even the universities, which harbour the last vestiges of dissent, have been turned into guarded compounds in which professors accused of 'participating in political activity' are removed, and students are monitored by intelligence officers and security forces. At the same time the Zuwar al-Leil (literally, 'night visitors') have re-emerged: intelligence officers who harass dissidents and others with midnight raids. Highly centralised and unresponsive to public opinion, the administration is more repressive than Mubarak's was at the height of its excesses.

Men, women and even children who find themselves under arrest – whether they're Muslim Brothers, students, labour activists, socialists, or just unemployed people protesting about their situation – are regarded as an army would regard captured combatants in a world without Geneva protocols. This is the essence of military dictatorship: a vision of the state and the population it rules as two opposing armies, the first better equipped but smaller than the second, which makes brutality an indispensable tactic. That this is how Sisi and his circle see matters does much to explain the surge in the use of torture. As Aida Seif al-Dawla, a professor of psychiatry at Ain Shams University and the head of a rehabilitation centre, puts it:

> Detainees are tortured when they are arrested, then tortured at the police station, sometimes tortured by the intelligence service, and when they arrive at a prison, official or otherwise, they are tortured. While they're inside the prisons they're tortured, and if there is a hunger strike planned, or officers believe prisoners are plotting something for the next round of prison visits, they torture them.

'At this point,' one veteran activist has remarked, 'all Egypt's a prison with soldiers as guards.'

Diana Eltahawy, a former member of the Egyptian Initiative for Personal Rights, observes that Egypt's prisons 'are very much a microcosm of the wider society'. Poorer detainees suffer some of the worst abuse and often work for richer prisoners in order to buy access to slight improvements, just as they might if they were at liberty. Women, who face endemic sexual harassment and assault in the big cities, find these conditions replicated – and intensified – in police or Amn al-Markezi custody. Wealthy, well-connected or high-profile prisoners generally receive better treatment from the guards, as well as better food and access to healthcare. Much attention has been paid to the plight of the three Al Jazeera journalists sentenced last June, one of whom, Peter Greste, has just been released. A recent *Daily Telegraph* leader argued that 'of all the events that have shamed Egypt's rulers, the farcical trial and conviction' of these journalists 'was among the most egregious'. But worse happens every day to people whose names we will never know. The Egyptian state demands compliance: 'security' is all that counts. Anyone thought to be a threat to civil order is extracted from the population, locked up and imaginatively punished, terrifying those who remain outside the cage. And of those who four years ago dreamed of a new society and are not themselves behind bars, most are now succumbing to the lethargy of defeat.

In November 2020, Egypt's National Security Agency made a series of arrests targeting the country's leading human rights organisation, the Egyptian Initiative for Personal Rights. On 15 November, there was a night raid on the home of the EIPR's administrative director, Mohamed El Basheer. On 18 November, Karim Ennarah, a researcher, was taken from the beach-front in the town of Dahab, where he was on holiday. EIPR's director, Gasser Abdel Razek, was arrested the following day at his home in Cairo. His lawyers say his head was shaved and he was kept in solitary confinement with only a metal bed to sleep on.

EIPR occupies a central position in Egypt's dissident movement. It publishes research on every aspect of the Egyptian state's repressive practices. It documents the activities of the national security state, the executions of prisoners, and the government's dealings with the IMF. It campaigns on behalf of victims of state violence.

The arrests appeared to stem from a meeting held on 3 November at EIPR's offices, attended by a group of European diplomats. Such meetings are not unusual: EIPR holds them from time to time and does so openly. But the arrest and torture of the regime's political opponents are not unusual either. The importance of EIPR's work has led the state to take an interest in its international reputation. The organisation's profile has in the past afforded it some limited protection. But given the military junta's attitude to opposition, EIPR's continued existence has been something of a contradiction, which Egypt's leaders would like to resolve.

EIPR is known and admired internationally, and there has been an outpouring of support for the detained men. The United Nations, the UK Foreign Office, representatives of European governments and international human rights organisations have condemned the arrests. So has Bernie Sanders. Political prisoners in Egypt are caught in endlessly renewed bouts of remand detention. International expressions of solidarity are important in trying to break the cycle.

An initial hearing for EIPR's director was held before the supreme state security prosecutor in November 2020. It had been brought forward; there were hopes the expedited hearing was a sign the government was having second thoughts and the cases might be dismissed. That isn't what happened. After the hearing, Gasser was returned to prison. Egypt's Foreign Ministry has claimed the arrests are a procedural matter, but this clearly isn't a question of not having the right permits. The charges against EIPR's staff are the usual ones in political cases: 'spreading fake news' and 'membership of a terrorist organisation'.

The accusations are absurd. The Egyptian government began to put additional pressure on EIPR, including surveillance, in October 2019. In February, Patrick Zaki, a young researcher who had worked for the organisation but was then studying in Italy, was arrested at Cairo airport and later tortured in detention because of a forged arrest report, which claimed he was arrested in his hometown and includes charges of 'incitement to protest'. He was only released from prison in December 2021.

The arrests coincided with a smear campaign against EIPR in the parts of the Egyptian press owned by the General Intelligence Service. The current head of intelligence is General Abbas Kamel, President Sisi's right hand man. The arrests were no error by an overreaching police chief. The order came from the top. Sisi has calculated that international expressions of sympathy for EIPR will be fleeting.

Sisi and the military junta have done what they can to ingratiate themselves with their international backers. They have invited energy companies to exploit oil and gas resources. They have signed arms deals that have turned a small state, in global terms, into the world's third largest buyer of weapons. And they have made Egypt a home for yield-seeking international capital: the state's expenses are now increasingly financed by dollar denominated loans sensitive to currency fluctuation. Egypt's external debt has more than tripled in the past ten years.

It's easy to see why the country's rulers have trouble pre-empting the reactions of foreign governments that provide weapons, training and surveillance equipment to the repressive apparatus and then occasionally complain about their use. A military state laden with French fighter jets, Italian frigates, German submarines and British assault rifles finds itself reprimanded by its providers for arresting principled troublemakers. In the contorted logic of European governments, this is a form of influence. To their authoritarian collaborators it looks like caprice.

The last time I met with Gasser Abdel Razek he told me he wanted to quit, go to culinary school and open a restaurant. But the work of a committed activist is never done. He always knew he could be arrested at any moment. He didn't hide the fact that the prospect of imprisonment, and especially solitary confinement, frightened him. Beyond statements of concern, the campaign for the release of EIPR's staff is demanding action, at least from the states whose representatives were at the meeting on 3 November.

There used to be a joke in Cairo that Egyptian presidents had two stock responses to an emergency: close the central Sadat metro station and arrest Alaa Abd El-Fattah. An activist in the Tahrir Square movement in 2011 (as well as the son of an important communist dissident), Alaa first experienced Egypt's prison system in 2006 as a result of his street activism. After the 2011 uprising he was arrested again. Since the military coup in 2013 he has spent most of his time behind bars. In December 2021 he was sentenced to a further five years for 'spreading false news'.

Egypt has thousands of political prisoners, but Alaa has become something of a symbol of the popular uprising. One measure of his importance is that the state prosecutor used to issue warrants for his arrest through the national media rather than over normal channels. Yet despite near constant incarceration, over the past decade Alaa has been a prolific writer. Fitzcarraldo Editions recently published a new collection of his work.[2]

Alaa's writing is a record of radical thought from the Tahrir occupation, through the violent counterrevolution of the Supreme Council of the Armed Forces ('a revolution so fragile a stray bullet could end it'), the brief collaboration between the Egyptian army and the Muslim Brotherhood in 2012, the 2013 military coup and its attendant massacres, and the extrajudicial executions of the Sisi regime. There is cutting criticism of the state written from prison cells with 'record breaking cockroach density'. His speeches in court display the rare bravery of a man putting the state on trial at his own hearings.

The Tahrir movement was quickly outflanked by the army. It was the generals who jettisoned Hosni Mubarak in 2011, ruled after his resignation, and continue to rule with such brutality today. An essay entitled 'Graffiti for Two' combines Alaa's political analysis with poetry by another high-profile political prisoner, Ahmed Douma. The two men composed it by shouting between their prison cells. Alaa reflects on the defeat of a movement that believed in a myth of youth salvation by 'young officers'. All revolutionaries, he writes, 'attempt and fail to return to a time of innocence and childhood, and end up in a state of late adolescence'.

In an influential book on the Arab Spring, Asef Bayat observed that the movements took the form of reformist uprisings rather than revolutions in the twentieth-century sense.[3] Most of the demonstrators set their sights short of an attempt to seize power. Instead they demanded that the state 'carry out meaningful reforms on behalf of the revolution'. A class-based political movement did not develop in Egypt. The landlords were not deposed. The uprising created a revolutionary experience among committed activists, but it did not produce even thwarted revolutionary outcomes. Bayat also argued that 'no visionary intellectual current seemed to accompany the Arab Spring.' But Alaa's writing is clear evidence of such a current. He regrets that the revolutionaries, and he himself, were guilty of 'the crime of lack of rigour' at the critical moment. But it was the Egyptian military regime and its international supporters that suppressed radical political formations wherever it found them. While President Sisi hosts royal visits from Britain, and Western weapons companies continue to arm the junta, the work of Alaa and other Egyptian dissidents remains an example of intellectual creativity and moral integrity.

14
Successors on the Earth

On 29 June 2014, the group that until then had been called ISIL or ISIS renamed itself Islamic State and declared that it had established a caliphate under its leader, Abu Bakr al-Baghdadi. Using modern tactics and archaic violence it expanded the territory under its control at spectacular speed, seemingly unstoppably. Its ranks swelled and swelled with new recruits impressed by the scale of its victories. Supporters travelled in large numbers from North Africa and Europe to become part of the society it had pledged to create. Strict justice, revolutionary energy, old prophecies fulfilled: its millenarian ideology included plenty that appealed to young men of a certain type. Sweeping across Upper Mesopotamia, its fighters summoned up memories in the European mind of Timur and the Golden Horde. But these weren't primitive rebels. They came – echoing American claims in Iraq – as builders of a state.

At its height IS controlled a territory larger than Hungary with a population of eight million. It operated two administrative capital cities: Mosul in Iraq and Raqqa in Syria. It held Fallujah and for a time Ramadi, sixty miles from Baghdad, as well as innumerable small towns and villages, much desert and a good deal of irrigated countryside. The horrors of IS rule are well known: the killings of Shia; the choice offered to the Christians of Mosul (conversion, ruinous taxation or expulsion); the slaughter of polytheists; the revival of slavery; the massacre of Yazidis on Mount Sinjar. Less well known are the thousands of mundane regulations instituted by the caliphal bureaucracy. The claim to be a state, not just another band of zealous militiamen, was central to what IS stood for. In support of its statehood it operated marriage offices, a telecommunications agency, a department of minerals and a central birth registry. Its motor vehicle authority issued licence plates carrying the IS logo. Its department of alms and social solidarity redistributed wealth to the poor. Its department of health brought in sanitation regulations that stipulated more frequent bin collections than in New York. It wasn't that everything worked smoothly: the caliphate struggled to provide electricity, particularly in Mosul, which had been cut off from Iraq's main grid. But that is true of many governments in the Middle East.

Like any state, the caliphate produced mountains of paperwork. Since its collapse under the weight of US military power some of the records of its rule have come to light. The IS files show that the caliphate was concerned with more than just scripturally correct governance. Its main temporal concern was orderliness. IS operated a sprawling network of police stations, prisons and courts. More than one might imagine was written on repaving and cleaning streets. There are records of police arrests, treatises on the maintenance of hair, the proper pricing for Caesarean births and pamphlets of sumptuary laws. There are notices limiting the profits of pharmacists and others setting the price of satsumas. A document from Raqqa detailed driving regulations: 'It is absolutely forbidden for cars to go about without a comprehensive repair toolkit.' Another from Deir Ez Zor sets out new fishing regulations in light of 'the greed and ambition of some of the fishermen'. The files reflect the history of the caliphate's wars. In October 2014 the central bureaucracy announced the opening of a prosthetics factory in Ninawa. A proclamation bans the use of GPS on phones, along with all Apple products. The central religious authority published an edict banning the sale of knock-off clothing unless the word 'imitation' was printed next to the brand name in lettering of the same size. Rooftop pigeon-rearing was prohibited for fear that fanciers might abuse their perches to look at women in their homes. In December 2014 the religious establishment issued a judgement declaring that billiards was permitted but only if there was no blasphemy or cursing during play.

IS drew inspiration from Al Siyasat al-Sharia, a treatise on Islamic governance by the thirteenth-century jurist Taqī Al Dīn Ahmad ibn Taymiyyah. Ibn Taymiyyah, who had lived through the Mongol invasions of Syria, wrote judgements justifying waging war against professing Muslims; he was also a theorist of caliphate politics. His influence is visible throughout the IS files, but nowhere more so than in a paper obtained by Aymen Jawad Tamimi entitled 'Principles in the Administration of the Islamic State'. Written in 2013 by an IS member called Abu Abdullah al-Masri, it tells its own story of the creation of Islamic State, from the group's emergence in Iraq to 'the blessed uprising of Syria'. The control of the Islamic world by the West using pliant autocrats, Masri explains, has led to irreligious behaviour. This must be remedied by erasing modern borders and establishing a state run in accordance with Islamic law. The document lays down guidelines for managing natural resources, establishing a system of provinces, the reception and integration of migrants, and running a central media institution. It also justifies the employment of civil servants who had held office under prior governments. This subject has received some attention in early studies of IS: most books note that in Iraq the old Baath public sector was used as an organisational template, and former Baathist regime figures were co-opted for its military and civilian bureaucracies. But IS did more than maintain the existing bureaucratic structures: by issuing decrees and threatening violence, it made them more efficient. In December 2014 the IS administrators of Anbar province issued a message to civil servants commanding them to work regular hours or suffer the consequences.

After capturing Mosul in June 2014, IS issued a fourteen-point city charter. Smoking, alcohol and drugs were all banned. Women should stay at home or go veiled. Flags other than the caliphate's were outlawed. Apostates who refused to repent would be killed. But the charter also codified the state's duties: armed factions would be disbanded, rotten laws overturned. In October 2014 the authorities closed a number of departments of Mosul University on the grounds that they had been judged illegitimate under Sharia. They included the college of political science, human rights and fine arts, the archaeology department and the school of English translation. The department of hotel management was also shut down – though this was less of a loss given that all the hotels were closed. Elsewhere IS gave a great deal of thought to schools and colleges: in Raqqa it opened a new college of medicine. The subject of education comes up a great deal in the files. Teachers were told not to focus on 'glorifying and eternalising the leaders', as the Baathists had done in Iraq, but aim instead to raise a pious generation with the practical skills to run the state 'without needing the expertise of the West'. The caliphate was designing a society that would be more independent than any other modern Middle Eastern state.

One of the larger tranches of documents was recovered from a provincial office of the IS department of agriculture. Papers of this kind offer an insight into the way the caliphate ruled in rural areas. In the countryside, IS simplified and speeded up land rental applications. A notice from Deir Ez Zor notes the declining level of the Euphrates and orders that 30 per cent of the land be sowed with summer crops and 70 per cent kept for single irrigation crops such as melon and sesame. There are records of an elaborate tax structure for agricultural products (reaping a barley harvest required one form, selling it another). This was a state of taxmen and rate-paying farmers. Land confiscated from Shia and Christians was let out to Sunnis, ensuring that money kept coming in, and tax revenue may well have exceeded revenue generated from black market oil sales. IS was not weighed down by religious strictures about markets. On the contrary, the 'Principles in Administration' declare the need for 'a comprehensive administration of collective expenses and collective production'. Some of what it offered the population it ruled was based on the benefits of a high taxation economy and central planning.

There was, of course, another way of ensuring orderliness. A document left behind in Aleppo presents a spreadsheet of punishments for various offences. Blasphemy was punishable by a death sentence, as was homosexual sex (both parties). Drinking wine would incur eighty lashes. Engaging in espionage was a capital crime. The penalty for adultery depended on the 'chasteness' of the accused. A married adulterer would be stoned to death but the unmarried could escape with 100 lashes and a year's banishment. 'Highway criminality' was more complex, with punishments ranging from crucifixion (for bandits who have committed murder) to the severing of the right hand and left foot (for highway robbery alone). But violence too required planning and bureaucracy. A religious police force on a similar model to Saudi Arabia's maintained order across the caliphate. Other Sunni militias in Iraq and Syria were absorbed into the formal security apparatus through loyalty oaths. The files show that soldiers were paid a basic salary of $50 a month, with supplements of another $50 for each wife and $35 for each dependent child. Wages fell when constant warring caused the state's finances to suffer.

Retributive justice was important, but the caliphate also encouraged loyalty by other means. Tamimi has translated the lyrics of dozens of *anasheed* – patriotic anthems written and recorded by the state's Ajnad Foundation for Media Production. They vary in quality. Removing the 'stain of humiliation' is a common theme, as are the glories and strengths of the caliphate. Some are battle songs. In 'Soon, Soon' the might of the IS armies is driven home with the beat of war drums: 'We will come to you with slaughter and death, with fright and silence we will tear the bonds.' In February 2015 the foundation released 'We Have Come as Soldiers of God', which describes the caliphate's growth as apotheosis: 'We know religion, we live by it; we build an edifice, we ascend it.' The caliphate ('earnest in its affairs, strict in its tongue' in the 2016 anthem 'The State Has Arisen') is contrasted with the hypocrisies of Western or Westward-looking nation-states. The anasheed continually assert that IS is a project made to endure. The most famous IS anthem was 'My Ummah, Dawn Has Appeared', released at the end of 2013: the 'blood of the righteous' has been spilled, but the efforts of the martyrs have now brought a new dawn, 'eternal glory that will not perish or disappear'.

To bring an end to the caliphate the United States fought what it called a 'war of annihilation'; together with its allies it carried out 34,000 air and artillery strikes. Amnesty International has estimated that more than 1,600 civilians were killed in the bombardment of Raqqa alone (the coalition has accepted responsibility for a tenth of these deaths); the figure for the coalition assault on Mosul was more than 5,800. Washington declared victory over IS on 22 March this year, but airstrikes continue in both Syria and Iraq. IS has not been obliterated: having been smashed with a hammer, the shards and tektites of its presence remain. In the central Syrian desert and rural areas in northern Iraq, its fighters still engage in car bombings and kidnappings. On 29 April Abu Bakr al-Baghdadi, who had not been heard from for many months, released a video in which he declared that the battle would continue until the day of judgement. IS's defeat has inevitably led to discussions among its sympathisers and ex-sympathisers over what went wrong. Defectors blamed Baghdadi and the leadership either for failing to adhere to the group's principles or for intransigence in upholding them. Above all else they charge that the caliph failed to defend the IS project in attracting US wrath on such a scale. Its current leaders see the collapse as a temporary setback and think in terms of the caliphate's return while seeking to redefine it as a global entity, within which Iraq and Syria are merely two provinces – alongside Libya, Yemen, Sinai, Somalia and other countries yet to be absorbed. In this new conception, territorial contiguity and statehood are less important than long-term survival and international appeal. If all else fails, there is always the option of traditional jihadist tactics, as the Sri Lanka Easter bombings demonstrate.

IS's deep origins were in the transnational jihadist movement that emerged in the 1970s from the confluence of the Iranian revolution, the Soviet invasion of Afghanistan, the Camp David Accords and the 1979 siege of Makkah. Like al-Qaida before it, IS sought the eventual destruction of the Saudi monarchy. But IS and the Sauds have things in common. Both were determined to act against apostasy and heresy; both insisted on the dangers of innovation. Papers written by IS intellectuals praise Wahhabi scholars and Muhammad ibn Abd al-Wahhab himself. But they also deviate from the Wahhabis – most significantly in the declaration of a caliphate, an act that was antithetical to Wahhabism, which arose in opposition to the Ottoman caliphate. In an audio message in November 2014, Baghdadi said that IS was pursuing the reverse of bin Laden's strategy. Al-Qaida had been determined to combat the 'far enemy', the crusader West, as a first step towards securing the fall of corrupt Middle Eastern dictatorships. No, Baghdadi said. Deal with the Shia first, wherever you find them, then the Sauds. IS saw present-day Saudi Arabia as a debauched tyranny that had corrupted Wahhabi ideals. But it also modelled itself on the original Saudi state (1744–1818), a viciously anti-Shia emirate founded by Wahhab and Muhammad bin Saud. Like IS, that state was destroyed by outside forces when Ibrahim Pasha of Egypt crossed the Nile and sacked its capital, Diriyah, on behalf of the Ottoman Empire. Six years later it returned in an altered form.

The Islamic State had more proximate origins in the destruction of the two states in which it established itself. The catastrophic Anglo-American invasion of Iraq provided for the first part of that story. The second was a result of the course of the war in Syria. The Syrian branch of the Arab Spring movement quickly turned into an armed rebellion against the state and eventually a civil war. Activist networks committed to non-violent organisation were overtaken by the brutal logic of the stand-off. It was clear from the earliest days of the uprising that the nature of the Syrian regime made sectarian conflict a distinct possibility. The government's configuration – in particular its denominational power base, alliance with Iran, and penchant for brutal militarised repression – made a large portion of the opposition see armed overthrow as the only way forward. But any such uprising would have been impossible without external sponsorship. Support came in the form of financial backing: arms (and later, direction) from Saudi Arabia, Qatar, Kuwait, and the United Arab Emirates, all regimes keen to see Assad fall.

The course of the Syrian civil war, which was without doubt the worst and most brutal conflict in the world at its height, a generational war without real historical comparisons, was critical. A government that had survived primarily through force and external contrivance found itself fighting disparate militias across the country for control of the state. Contrary to claims that the world ignored the conflict, there was constant intervention by regional powers and the west. The US and UK intervened consistently on the side of the armed opposition until 2015, and contributed to the perpetuation of the conflict as a bloody stalemate. The Gulf sponsors bear the brunt of responsibility for encouraging the jihadist turn. But the United States, Britain, and France knew exactly what was happening and went along with it.

Believing the anti-Assad proxies could succeed, Western powers, which were set on regime change, went so far as to sabotage efforts, including those made by UN envoys, to find a political resolution to the crisis. Hugh Roberts has termed this a 'hijacking' of the original popular movement, a notion with much merit.[1] It was the extent of the jihadist rise – both in conjunction with and exemplified by the Islamic State and Libya's descent into chaos – that gave the United States second thoughts. As it stalled its support for the rebels, Russia exploited this opening to decide the matter in the regime's favour. The successes that the armed Syrian opposition enjoyed from late 2011–15 were dependent on continued support across the open border with Turkey (in the south of the country, proxy forces set up by the US and Jordan proved ineffective). This was effectively ended by the territorial advances of Islamic State and the Russian intervention in October 2015, after which it became clear that the US would not proceed with efforts against Assad. It is fortunate that Syria was not considered strategically important enough to US power to risk an even more dangerous escalation.

But by 2016 the armed opposition was clearly flagging. The regime's capture of Aleppo was a significant victory and the armed opposition in the area predictably fell apart. Extreme religious conservative militias – many of them led by veterans of the Jihadist insurgency against the US in Iraq – had long since taken over as the main bulk of the rebel forces. Rebel positions near Damascus, including the critical stronghold in the Eastern Ghouta oasis, were forced into an ignominious surrender. The remaining Sunni Arab armed opposition generally had little to no understanding of the parallel fight of the Kurdish militias led by the Syrian Democratic Forces (SDF) in the North and even less sympathy for their cause. In some cases they were openly contemptuous of historical Kurdish grievances and current Kurdish ambitions and clung, like the regime, to a statist insistence on the integrity of Syria's existing borders. The Kurdish militias trusted the main of the Arab opposition even less than the regime and essentially refused to co-operate on their project of overthrowing it. What was left was a rump rebel force in Idlib which has remained isolated and the precedent IS itself had built in the Levant.

IS was born of the wars in Iraq and Syria, countries which are fundamentally broken. Its message played to a sinned-against and vengeful Iraqi and Syrian peasantry, feeding on and fuelling all the Sunni grievances: the corruption of Middle Eastern leaders, complaints of constant Western incursions. These conditions remain. IS files show that dismissing its adherents as irrational or, worse, nihilist, would be an error. They had a vision. Whether it would have survived its own militarism and aggression is impossible to know. For the most part, the remains of the caliphate have been reabsorbed by the wider jihadist movement and its grand ambitions have been put aside. But there is no guarantee this will be permanent. The immediate predecessor to IS, the Islamic State in Iraq, was crushed and driven underground in 2008. It re-emerged energised and more dangerous.

15
The Revolutionary Decade

Until recently Tunisia was seen as the lone success story of the Arab Spring. But on 25 July 2021, President Kais Saied summoned the prime minister to the presidential palace in Carthage and dismissed him, declared a state of emergency, suspended parliament and sent the army to block the entrances to the building. Over the next 48 hours, a nationwide curfew was imposed, the head of the national television station was replaced and elected officials were stripped of legal immunity. Saied suspended the much-praised post-revolution constitution, dissolved parliament and imposed rule by personal decree. Since then, regional governors have been removed, civilians have been tried in military courts, several opposition politicians have been imprisoned and others have been sentenced to jail in absentia.

Some fled, or tried to. Nabil Karoui, the runner-up in the 2019 presidential election, escaped through mountain passes but was arrested in Algeria. That the president himself was responsible for the coup, rather than its object, isn't historically unusual. The *autogolpe* has many precedents, but what was remarkable this time was that, two months before the coup took place, a plan describing almost the exact course of events was leaked to the press. The plot had been rumbled, but it succeeded anyway.

Where was the civil and political opposition? The religious conservative Ennahda Party, still the best organised political movement in Tunisia, didn't offer much of a challenge. Scattered protests against the coup were too little, too late. Mutual rancour prevented unified opposition. The trade unions seemed ambivalent and called for a national dialogue, which never happened. The internal security forces backed the president's position, as did the army. It can't have hurt that a former army chief of staff and a retired chief of the navy were Saied's national security advisers.

This summer, on the anniversary of the coup, a referendum was held on a new constitution designed to consolidate Saied's gains. In contrast to its post-revolutionary predecessor, the document was cobbled together by the president's office, and granted Saied the right to dictate the powers of a new parliament. The ostensible head of the drafting committee, Sadok Belaïd, publicly said that the constitution would lead to 'a disgraceful dictatorial regime'. The referendum was boycotted by most of the opposition parties and most of the electorate. Turnout barely exceeded 30 per cent and the published breakdown of figures looked suspicious. The 95 per cent vote recorded for 'yes' allowed Saied to claim a resounding victory, but since local and international monitors hadn't been able to observe the voting, it's impossible to trust the result. Saied had prepared the ground by filling the Independent High Authority for Elections with his own supporters, dissolving the High Judicial Council, and firing an entire generation of judges (fifty-seven in all).

The principal achievements of the Tunisian revolution of 2011 – ending twenty-three years of dictatorship under Ben Ali and bringing in parliamentary politics – seem to have lasted only a decade. Saied's new order is upheld by force. In central Tunis security forces are present in higher numbers than ever before. Fences restrict access to Kasbah Square, the symbolic heart of the revolution, and police positions and metal barricades are fixtures in the streets. The two armoured vehicles that used to guard the statue of Ibn Khaldun on Avenue Habib Bourguiba have returned. The battered police truck that once sat under the Sea Gate arch at the entrance to the old city is back too. When I visited in September there were long queues at the markets: there is a shortage of cooking oil. Economic malaise is visible in all but the smartest neighbourhoods.

Tunis doesn't have the extreme privation visible in the slums of Cairo. The closest equivalents are semi-slums with a reputation for being dangerous after dark. These areas have been hit hardest by the rise in the price of basic goods. In Douar Hicher, north-west of the city centre, I saw residents marching through the streets and burning tyres. In Mornag, another working-class neighbourhood, similar actions have been repressed with tear gas. When I travelled north through the city from Bab al-Khadra to Bab Saadoun, street sellers were hawking scavenged electronics, cables and second-hand belts from carts lined with cardboard. In Djebel Lahmar, a collection of narrow streets lined with shacks where roofs are patched together out of old pieces of furniture, shopkeepers told me they were worried about a shortage of sugar. That day the news agency Tunis Afrique Presse reported that a Maltese ship loaded with Brazilian cane had docked in Bizerte. This was good news for the sugar shortage but an unpropitious subject for the country's main newswire to have to cover. Since the coup, independent sources of information have become harder to come by. In August, a military court sentenced Salah Attia, editor of a news website, to three months in jail for criticising the president on television. In September, Saied announced a new law imposing prison terms for 'spreading false information'. The editor in chief of the independent news outlet Inhiyez was arrested after police raided his house and confiscated his computers. There has been an increase in random police brutality, and in arrests of activists who have been documenting police violence.

Before he was a putschist, Saied was a constitutional lawyer. In the years after the revolution he made regular appearances on TV as a commentator on constitutional matters; one of his observations was that constitutions tend to become tools of executive power. He won the presidency in 2019 by presenting himself as an outsider. There was some truth in this: before the revolution he had been a minor academic in the capital. But it was also a simplification: he attended the same school in Tunis as three former presidents. His brand of conservative nationalism, paired with an outward asceticism, proved popular. As did his promise to remove venal political contaminants and to restore *haybat al dawla*, the prestige of the state. Enemies ascribe to Saied the arrogance and intransigence of an apostle. By positioning himself against Islamists he has found favour in Egypt and the Gulf states. In the media, he speaks out about the depredations of the rich and the need for direct democracy. This veneer of revolutionary rhetoric is helpful against political opponents but never seems to come to anything.

The council of advisers Saied has assembled are for the most part inaccessible. His first chief of staff, Nadia Akacha, another constitutional lawyer, spoke for the new regime, but in January the two had a very public split – Akacha is now in exile in Paris. The other members of the presidential council rarely appear in public. In La Marsa, an affluent coastal neighbourhood on the edge of Tunis, I met Hamadi Redissi, a political scientist who has conducted a detailed study of Saied's rise. He told me that the coup has been sustained by two forces. First, the network of partisans and propagandists who have capitalised on public frustration with the crises of the revolutionary decade. Second, members of the bourgeoisie who support Saied's moves against Tunisia's trade unions and religious conservatives. 'Supporters of the president and the coup care a great deal about taking on the Islamists,' Redissi said. But another factor has been the brute fact of state intimidation. 'People are afraid of Kais Saied, and I understand why.'

The Saied project is to shift the country away from the representative democracy won during the revolution and towards autocratic presidentialism, combined – or so it was claimed – with a form of municipal democracy. Predictably, the autocracy has materialised and the municipal democracy has failed to show. The new order is enforced by traditional means. Saied's director general of security is a secret policeman from the Ben Ali era. The head of national intelligence is said to be close to the Egyptian junta. A personalised presidential system backed by a police state: the obvious conclusion is that Tunisia has reverted to the kind of dictatorship overturned in 2011. But whatever else he may be, Saied is a product of the revolutionary decade, a period that was unambiguously more positive in Tunisia than in any other Arab state. How could that decade have led to this?

Tunisia followed the familiar post-independence path from anti-colonialism under one long-term leader to neoliberalism under the next. The country's first president, Habib Bourguiba, who took office in 1957, commanded respect thanks to his experience in the independence struggle against France. He ruled without serious challenge until his dotage and the effective regency of his second wife, Wassila Ben Ammar. The man who replaced him, Zine al-Abidine Ben Ali, was a creature of the security state. After seizing power in a palace coup in 1987, Ben Ali made extending that state one of his central projects. He also pioneered the evolution of the Arab republic into a state characterised by crony capitalism, a course Mubarak would also follow in Egypt. Under Ben Ali, Tunisia was run as something close to a family concern. The extended Ben Ali family controlled a remarkable proportion of the economy. Relatives of Ben Ali or of his wife, Leïla Trabelsi, headed the central bank, the largest private financial institutions, ministries of state and the national airline. By some estimates, the presidential clan received as much as a fifth of all private sector profits. The archetypal figure was Belhassen Trabelsi, the first lady's brother, who combined mafia-style intimidation with spectacular wealth and control over an impressive network of companies and ventures. One obvious goal of the revolt that began in December 2010 was to pull up the marble and the leopard skin rugs from the palaces.

Plenty of countries have corrupt leaders and oppressive police; that doesn't explain why the Arab Spring uprisings began in Tunisia. Unemployment had been high for two decades, but that could also be said of many other places. Anglophone commentators reached for explanations based on education and technology (the 'Facebook revolution' thesis). But they won't do. For one thing, they don't account for the fact that the uprisings began in the underdeveloped interior and not in Tunis. And tech theories ignore Tunisia's history of effective traditional activism. In 2008 there was a mass revolt in the Gafsa mining basin, involving nearly six months of strikes and sit-ins. The protesters included not only phosphate and iron miners but unemployed workers, the widows of men killed in industrial accidents, and disaffected university graduates from the north. What began as a series of riots against local corruption soon spread, taking aim at the state itself. Teachers occupied schools and much of the public sector was brought to a halt. This class rebellion was put down by the national guard, but not before a degree of fragility had been revealed in the Ben Ali system. What the regime didn't realise was that the situation in the interior had become a genuine crisis. It could be contained for a time, but not finally repressed.

That crisis reached a head on 17 December 2010 with the self-immolation of Mohamed Bouazizi in the small provincial city of Sidi Bouzid. Harassed by local police for selling fruit from a cart, Bouazizi experienced the common tribulation of the Tunisian underclass, best described by the Maghrebian term *hogra* – degrading administrative contempt. Partly spontaneous, partly organised by trade unions and disaffected elites of a loosely socialist or religious-conservative bent, demonstrations spread to the capital, where privation converged with labour activism and widespread unemployment. Bouazizi's death served as a symbol of general brutality and desperation, much like the death in police custody of Khaled Saeed in Egypt.

Outrage at police excesses was soon combined with a demand for the end of the Ben Ali regime. The national trade union organisation, the UGTT, and opposition political parties led demonstrations in Tunis, and the unions organised a general strike in the industrial port city of Sfax. In a televised address on 13 January 2011, Ben Ali tried in vain to reassert his authority. The next morning he fled by plane to Saudi Arabia (where he died in 2019). Belhassen Trabelsi set off for Sicily, by yacht.

The ruling party, the Rassemblement Constitutionnel Démocratique (RCD), backed by the business elite, briefly tried to keep the show on the road. But demonstrations continued at the RCD headquarters on Avenue Mohamed V, and the party was dissolved by the courts in March. Unlike Mubarak's National Democratic Party, the RCD was a functional tool of the regime, so its abolition was a major achievement. (The old party HQ, a glass tower opposite the central bank and the 'museum of money', now contains a lesser ministry of state.) The sit-in at Kasbah Square was kept up until the prime minister, Mohamed Ghannouchi, resigned on 27 February. In many other Arab states, a military coup would have been inevitable at this point. But among the circumstances in favour of the Tunisian revolutionaries was the weakness of the military, and its relatively small size as a proportion of the population – the army had been gutted in the early 1990s after a false coup scare.

Temporary control of the country passed to the Higher Authority for the Realisation of the Objectives of the Revolution, Political Reform and Democratic Transition, a council of opposition figures and union leaders which oversaw elections in October 2011. The question that dominated the immediate aftermath of the uprising was the role of religious conservatives in national politics. Since independence, they had largely been exiled from public life – Bourguiba had once appeared on television during Ramadan drinking orange juice, something that would be inconceivable in other predominantly Muslim countries. In Morocco and Turkey, political parties influenced by the Muslim Brotherhood were promising 'justice' and 'development'. In Egypt the nominal offering was 'freedom and justice'. In Tunisia the equivalent Islamist party was Ennahda, or 'renaissance', a name that signalled a more abstract rediscovery of lost values. Some of its members had been allowed to run as independents in the parliamentary elections held under Ben Ali in 1989, and were successful enough that the state then arrested 25,000 party members. The movement survived, however, and in the 2011 elections it won a clear plurality of seats in the national constituent assembly.

The first government of the revolutionary period was a coalition between Ennahda and two secular centrist parties, Ettakatol and the Congress for the Republic. Ennahda held much of the power, and the prime ministership. Balancing the tensions between the post-revolution factions wasn't easy, and the economic situation was dire. It was never clear that Ennahda was capable of dealing with either problem. In a bid to placate disgruntled members of the middle class, the government hired tens of thousands of civil servants, most of them in public health or agriculture. But unemployment among the working class couldn't be brought down. The governing troika was failing to hold things together. I was in Tunis in 2013 when two prominent left-wing politicians were murdered. The unions staged general strikes and the country was approaching terminal crisis. In Egypt at the same time, the army was dispensing with the façade of civilian rule and brutally repressing religious conservatives. Partly from fear that a similar spectacle would ensue, Ennahda agreed to step down from government and give way to a technocratic cabinet.

The national dialogue held in late 2013, which drew together the principal political and civil society organisations, seemed to offer some hope. By January 2014 a post-revolutionary constitution had been agreed in a negotiated compromise between the main factions. Orderly parliamentary and presidential elections were held that autumn. Ennahda's leaders accepted the loss of their parliamentary plurality to a new formation, Nidaa Tounes, behind which the business elite had thrown its weight. Rached Ghannouchi, Ennadha's founder and president, agreed that the party wouldn't take on any major ministries, or field a candidate in the presidential election against Nidaa's soon to be nonagenarian leader, Beji Caid Essebsi. Essebsi was the face of the establishment that had maintained its position from the early days of independence. After winning the presidency he returned a statue of Bourguiba on horseback to the place du 14 Janvier. But Ennahda was still powerful enough to have a say in the formation of the new government. Ghannouchi and Essebsi had met in Paris during the dialogue, and Nidaa Tounes agreed to make minor concessions to the religious conservatives.

Compared with the brutal developments in Egypt and the civil wars in Syria, Libya and Yemen, the situation in Tunisia seemed promising enough. But the dominant narrative was still of a 'transition' to democracy. Ban Ki-moon praised Tunisia as 'a model to other peoples seeking reforms'. It didn't look that way to the majority of the population, who experienced economic stagnation and little else. None of this registered in the world at large. What the Anglosphere and Europe wanted was a revolution of democratic liberalism catalysed by Western technology companies. Leave out social media, and this was much the same story that was told about Eastern Europe in 1989, when the idea of a pure democratic liberalism obscured any ethnonationalist blemishes. What was it covering up this time? The Essebsi presidency certainly didn't fit the story. It was hardly a revolutionary achievement to raise a man who had been minister of interior in 1965 to the presidency. The revolution hadn't produced a new generation of political leaders: it had brought back the marginalised elites of the Ben Ali era.

In his final years, Essebsi started to blame the constitution for political stalemate and to suggest revising it. After the revolution there had been much talk of reforming the police state, and the political police were partly cleansed. But a jihadist movement was running rearguard actions in the Chaambi mountains on the border with Algeria, providing a ready justification for maintaining the security apparatus. Attacks resulting in mass casualties at the Bardo National Museum and the coastal city of Sousse added further impetus. The military budget doubled between 2012 and 2016, with all the focus on internal security. Tunisia, unlike other Arab Spring countries, was for the most part blessed by the neglect of the great powers, which saw it as marginal to developments in Egypt and Syria. Their major concerns as far as Tunisia was concerned were irregular migration and the terrorist threat. The US increased military aid and John Kerry paid a visit to praise the dedication of the security forces. In 2014, a new internal electronic surveillance body was set up, modelled on the NSA, with support from the EU and other Western embassies. Well-equipped anti-terror police based in the Ministry of Interior's offices in western Tunis stepped up their activities. By 2018, security officials were threatening to stop protecting MPs unless they passed a law criminalising criticism of the police.

The revolution had unseated a president and dismantled a ruling party without a military coup or civil war. Those were its successes. But the economic system remained almost entirely untouched. Tunisia's elite were patient, and under the Essebsi settlement regrouped without their more egregious extremities. Ben Ali cronies like the Mabrouk brothers, one of them his son-in-law, still owned the country's largest private bank. This was the landscape when Essebsi died on 25 July 2019. The elections to replace him were an opening. Many of the presidential candidates – twenty-six in all – had held office before, including four former prime ministers and one former president. Some voters found Saied's promise to cleanse the system convincing; others just saw him as the least of twenty-six evils. In the end, there was a second-round run-off between Saied and the businessman Nabil Karoui. A familiar and powerful public figure, the owner of the TV station Nessma, Karoui was the closest thing Tunisia had to a natural successor to Essebsi. By contrast, Saied was such a minor player in the establishment that he could pose as an outsider willing to take it on.

Much was made of the fact that Saied won the presidency without the machinery of a political party behind him. But no one else had an effective party, except Ennahda, which backed Saied in the second round. That decision was contentious. In the modest office above a dental surgery to which he has since confined himself, Abdelhamid Jelassi, who was number three in the Ennahda hierarchy before he broke with the movement in 2020, told me he had opposed the decision to support Saied's presidency but was overruled. He said that Ghannouchi 'behaved like a tribal chief' and ran Ennahda like the underground organisation it had been in the 1990s. But others in the party favoured Saied merely because they thought he was a better choice than Karoui, a slick double-dealer. They believed they could control Saied if they had a strong majority in parliament. In the parliamentary elections Ennahda did win the most seats, but it incurred significant losses in the south to a breakaway Islamist party and elsewhere to social democrats. Even so, the party took control of several government ministries and Ghannouchi himself became parliamentary speaker.

Once again, the balance both within parliament and between it and the presidency was unstable. One of the principal victories of the revolution had been the transfer of power from president to parliament, but now this seemed at risk. The central battlefield was the delay in setting up a constitutional court, which would have provided a route for parliament to remove the president. It became clear that Saied wouldn't accept such a court. But to the public, the power struggles between political institutions seemed like squabbling in the face of general economic distress. By the spring of 2021, Saied was asserting rights to extra-constitutional presidential powers. A coup seemed possible even before the blueprint for its execution was leaked.

Ennahda put up the most vocal resistance to Saied's suppression of parliament. The consequences for the party may be severe. Most of its leaders have been called in by the security services or detained by the counterterror department. On 20 September, Ghannouchi was summoned for questioning and not released until the following morning. When I visited Ennahda's headquarters in the Montplaisir district of the city centre, the party was holding a press conference on the arrests. In a room with walls covered in photographs of martyred supporters, party leaders said that the counter-terror investigation – nominally into members who had left the country to join Islamic State – was spurious: cover for a straightforward attack on the most organised element of the opposition. The former prime minister Ali Laarayedh, who had recently been released from detention, received me in an office on the fourth floor. He said that the security services were operating under 'phone orders' – meaning that they were acting on the basis of a call from the top rather than due process. 'I am certain that if he thinks he can get away with it, Kais Saied will prevent all opposition political parties from operating,' he told me. He said that while Saied remained in power there was no route back to constitutional government.

Ennahda has called for an escalation of protests against Saied. But the party's opponents often dislike the idea of joining with its efforts even when they agree with their aims. On the streets of the capital, it's common to hear people accuse Ennahda of practising *siyaset al qatiyaa*, or 'herd politics'. Another of the party's leaders, Ajmi Lourimi, told me he believed Saied wanted to draw Ennahda into a violent confrontation; their task, he said, was to use the streets in collaboration with other opposition forces to return the country to democracy. At present, that seems a remote possibility. The problem is that the only other national organisation with the capacity to challenge the state, the UGTT union, has chosen to negotiate in private with the presidency. In June, a general strike was held to protest at the economic crisis and union leaders talked of the government's 'repressive deviation'. But in September Saied and the unions seemed to have reached a deal in exchange for modest wage increases for public sector workers. I went to the UGTT's temporary headquarters in Lafayette, a building guarded by union toughs, but its leaders kept cancelling meetings with me. Nor did they show up at the offices of the union's newspaper, *Echaab*, the ground-floor depot of which was stacked with discarded air conditioners. Saied's main method of influencing the UGTT has been to threaten corruption charges arising from the length of time senior members have served on its executive board – a similar threat to the one that led to the sacking of the judges. At the moment, as a way of keeping them quiet, it seems to be working.

While the political class has been at war, the majority of Tunisians have been getting poorer. More than half the population now work in informal jobs, if they work at all. On 24 September an unemployed man in his forties set himself on fire on the rue de Londres. Passers-by helplessly threw dirt and water on him to put out the flames. This wasn't a repeat of Bouazizi so much as another reflection of economic desperation: self-immolations are common in Tunisia – there are as many as 100 a year. Many workers earn no more than 400 dinars a month – little more than £100. The situation is without obvious remedy. Tunisia doesn't have much oil; most of its exports go to the EU, but it's only a small offshore supplier. After the revolution, negotiations for a limited free trade agreement with the EU went nowhere. In the interior of the country, most people work on farms or mine phosphate; many move to the coast to make textiles for Europeans, in competition with factories in Turkey and Malaysia. Over the past decade, government debt has doubled as a proportion of GDP. International finance has become scarcer since Saied's coup. Neither the state nor the opposition parties seem to have any answers. Earlier this year a former British ambassador to Tunisia shopped around for ideas on the letters pages of the *Financial Times*.

Between 2012 and 2020 Tunisia was essentially under IMF tutelage. The IMF called for a reduction in subsidies for food, fuel and energy. Instead, it advocated targeted relief programmes – but those have a way of not getting to the poorest people. Over time, it became more forceful, moving from negotiating with Tunisian authorities to simply issuing orders. In 2017 and 2019 it effectively compelled the government to cut energy subsidies, in the face of strong public protest. According to the latest IMF programme, leaked in January, Tunisia should privatise some state-owned companies and 'contain' the cost of civil service wages. Now that the UGTT won't speak out, only the splintered left parties offer resistance. 'The only solution Saied has is another IMF loan, which we have tried before,' Hosni Hamadi of the Workers' Party told me. 'With the economic situation as it is, their measures will lead to an explosion.'

The international powers have offered little; the EU has hedged its bets. On 29 March, the day before Saied dissolved parliament, the European Commission sent an envoy to Tunis to finalise €450 million in budgetary support. European countries have maintained a rhetorical commitment to democracy, but in practice they have been more interested in Tunisia playing its part by maintaining a coastguard force to intercept migrants trying to make it to the EU, and by ensuring it is a stable transit country for gas pipelines. Anthony Blinken, the US secretary of state, has acknowledged Saied's 'alarming erosion of democratic norms', but in August an assistant secretary of state, Barbara Leaf, met Saied for a photo opportunity and a discussion about the 'ongoing military partnership'. The US recently began providing a command and control system to the Tunisian military. In March, Tunisia secured a deal for a supply of American surveillance aircraft. At the end of September, the ambassadors of the UK, France, Germany, and Japan met Saied's prime minister to urge Tunisia to sign on the IMF's dotted line. On 15 October, the fund agreed to lend $1.9 billion over four years, much less money than the Tunisian authorities had hoped.

Since the coup, Tunisian politics has been a matter of pronouncements from Carthage Palace. In some respects Saied's rise accords with a global trend towards centralising nationalists – evident from the Americas to Turkey, from India to Indonesia. But in no comparable country had recent history broken so drastically with the tradition of dictatorship. The current order may not represent a terminal state. Tunisia, like most of the non-oil exporting Arab states, faces financial drought, and it's not clear whether Saied can force through the deeply unpopular austerity programme the IMF demands. In mid-October, as bakeries began to shut down across the country because the state wasn't subsidising them, two separate anti-Saied demonstrations were held simultaneously in the centre of Tunis. The marches were big enough, but neither group wanted to be associated with the other. The parliamentary elections scheduled for 17 December, which have been designed to exclude real political participation, won't be mistaken for a return to constitutional government. Should the situation deteriorate, the push will come from the interior or the semi-slums, those parts of Tunisian society that are as distant as can be imagined from the political class.

The fate of the Tunisian revolution matters, both for the Arab Spring as a historical process and for the prospects of peripheral countries constrained by the international system. The revolution had an effect on every other country in the Middle East, but went deepest at its point of origin. For the Arab states closer to the world's major energy-producing region and neo-imperial protectorate, the interests of the great powers seemed to preclude an independent course. But what about small states on the region's edges? The question didn't only apply to Tunisia. There were significant uprisings in 2019 in Algeria and Sudan, in Sudan's case resulting in a traditional coup. The Hirak protests in Morocco in 2016 and 2017 applied similar pressure. For a time, the Tunisian revolution appeared to offer an encouraging answer. Saied's coup means it must now be treated as an autopsy rather than a retrospective.

16
Kinetic Strikes

A spate of recent conflicts are said to have been decided by the use of drones. In November 2021, Tigrayan forces were advancing on Addis Ababa. When Ethiopian security forces pushed them back, the Tigrayans credited the army's use of drones with turning the tide. In Libya, drones were used by the forces of the UN-backed Government of National Accord against Khalifa Haftar's 'Libyan National Army'. In Nagorno-Karabakh in the autumn of 2020, the Armenian side lost about half of its artillery and air defence systems to drone strikes in the first hours of the war. Videos of low-cost drones operated by Azerbaijan's armed forces destroying Armenian tanks and motorised infantry units impressed military analysts.

In 2018, a US Army major argued that the United States should use more small and expendable 'tactical drones' in its military operations. Something like this advice has been taken up by smaller states. Drones are popular because they offer air power on the cheap. Some armed drones can be bought for under $2 million. The American MQ-9 Reaper is much more expensive but still less than an F-16, even before you count the expense of training a pilot who might be killed. This is just as well, since drones get shot down all the time.

In 2011, Iranian forces downed an RQ-170 stealth drone operated by the CIA. In the Ukraine conflict between 2014 and 2016 so many OSCE reconnaissance drones were brought down over the Donbass that they were withdrawn entirely.

Far from disappearing as a vestige of a primitive culture of rebellion, in the twenty-first century assassination has radically expanded as a tool of modern states. The US military has used reconnaissance drones in wars since the 1960s. The armed drone is a more recent development. The first drone to fire a missile in flight was a Predator (tailfin no. 3034) on a test range in California in early 2001. The Hellfire missiles it carried were designed as anti-tank weapons to be fired from helicopters. Predator 3034 was also used in the first attempt at a drone assassination. The target was the Taliban leader Mullah Omar in October 2001. The attempt failed, but it marked the beginning of a drone boom. By 2016, the US was killing 4,000 people a year using drones, most of them away from traditional battlefields.[1]

The combination of the unprecedented global surveillance system built by the NSA and remotely piloted aircraft produced the most widespread assassination campaign in human history. A drone operator at a computer terminal in Creech Air Force base in Nevada can control a drone taking off from an airfield in Qatar or Djibouti that flies 1,000 miles to assassinate someone in Yemen, Pakistan or Syria. The process is full of euphemism. Drones are 'birds'. The people targeted for death are 'objectives'. Missile attacks are 'kinetic strikes'. They use the language of games: kills are 'touchdowns', target fact sheets are 'baseball cards', a successful assassination is a 'jackpot'. The US is not the only country to conduct drone assassinations. France has carried them out in Mali, the UK in Syria, and Israel has used drones to kill Palestinians in Gaza. But the US remains the only state to use drones in warfare at scale. In December 2021, a *New York Times* investigation based on a cache of Pentagon documents found that claims of precision in the US air war in Afghanistan, Iraq and Syria are delusional. Drone operators and airstrike targeters do not know what they are hitting. Decisions are made on the basis of a few seconds of footage captured from above. Misidentification is rampant: a cotton gin, say, mistaken for an explosives factory. And when drone operators and pilots can correctly identify someone they want to shoot at, their targets are usually close to bystanders.

A straight line can be drawn between celebrations of 'precision' air weaponry and airstrikes in civilian areas. The inability of US drone operators and targeters to find and identify individuals accurately has led to a strategy based on volume. Drop a lot of bombs, accept that many civilians will die, and occasionally you will kill someone you meant to. This has coincided with the re-emergence of assassination as a technological replacement for military action in the maintenance of imperial power. The US has been responsible for the vast majority of all targeted killings with drones, but the spread of drone warfare to minor states is likely to mean an extension of the basic cruelty of air campaigns.

Drones have no monopoly in the global assassination business. In October 2019, Abu Bakr al-Baghdadi, the former caliph of the Islamic State, was assassinated by US special forces. He was discovered in a compound in Barisha in the Idlib province of northern Syria a few miles from the Turkish border. The raiding party took off from an airbase in Anbar in Iraq in eight helicopters. The special forces team blew the side off the building in which Baghdadi had been staying (apparently for some time). The US claimed he killed himself by detonating an explosive vest. The soldiers brought back pieces of the corpse and confirmed it was him with biometric tests.

President Donald Trump announced many of the operational particulars of the Baghdadi assassination personally, including details of Baghdadi's last moments that Trump is unlikely to have known. He also thanked the Russian, Turkish, Syrian, Iraqi, and Syrian Kurdish governments for their co-operation. But there is no doubt that the extent of the US global surveillance system was critical. Baghdadi took great efforts to ensure his personal security; the task became more difficult after IS lost the ability to hold and govern territory in 2018. The CIA effort to track him down appears to have been aided by the capture of one or two of his deputies. Iraqi intelligence say that Ismail al-Ithawi gave them information about Baghdadi's habits. The capture of Abu Suleiman al-Khalidi by Hayat Tahrir al-Sham, the former al-Qaida affiliate in Syria, may also have helped lead to the Barisha raid.

Baghdadi was born in the Samarra countryside in Iraq to a family of pastoral farmers who claimed they could trace their ancestry back to the prophet Muhammad. As a young man he had been an aloof theology student and football coach. After the invasion and occupation of Iraq he was imprisoned for ten months in Abu Ghraib and Camp Bucca. He emerged a fanatic of the jihadist insurgency. In 2006 the US assassinated the former leader of al-Qaida in Iraq, Abu Musab al-Zarqawi. Zarqawi's successor was assassinated by the US in April 2010. Baghdadi took control of the group a month later. The assassination did not mean the end of Islamic State. In rural Iraq and eastern Syria it was still engaging in extortion, raiding and kidnapping. And one of Baghdadi's deputies soon took his place. In February 2022, Abu Ibrahim al-Hashimi al-Qurashi, the fourth leader of the Islamic State organisation, became the fourth to be killed in a US raid or airstrike. US intelligence found Qurashi by tracking a courier working for ISIS in Syria's Idlib province. Special forces flew in from Iraq in helicopters, surrounded the house that Qurashi had rented (apparently posing as a taxi driver), and ordered the residents out with loudspeakers. Qurashi and twelve others, mostly women and children, were killed.

The US claims that Qurashi, like Baghdadi, detonated the bomb that did the damage. The only people left alive who know exactly what happened are the special forces operatives involved, and they are unlikely to tell. Qurashi was born Muhammad Said Abdul Rahman al-Mawla (he also went by the name Abdullah Qardash, among others) in a majority Turkmen village near Mosul. He joined the jihadist movement after the invasion of Iraq in 2003 and, like his predecessor, spent time in American detention in Camp Bucca. He rose through the caliphal hierarchy to become overseer of the Islamic State's judges. His birthplace led to doubts about his ethnicity – Arab or Turkmen? – and hence his suitability to succeed Baghdadi as caliph. The caliphate no longer existed as a territorial state, but the question mattered to ISIS supporters. Iraqi intelligence thought Qurashi was in hiding somewhere east of the Euphrates, perhaps in the Samawah desert. That he was in fact in Idlib, less than two miles from the Turkish border, is no great surprise. Atmeh, the village where he was living, is near Barisha, where Baghdadi was killed. The area is under the control of Hayat Tahrir al-Sham, a former al-Qaida affiliate on poor terms with ISIS. But the mass displacements of the Syrian civil war make it easy to disappear. Villagers who in the past might have been suspicious of outsiders are used to new arrivals coming and going.

Some American news outlets reported that the goal of the Atmeh raid had been to capture Qurashi. But President Biden said the choice was between a special forces night raid and an airstrike. The reason they opted for the raid was to 'minimise civilian casualties' (without success, it would seem), not because it was a capture attempt. The results of these JSOC operations tend to be the same. Qurashi had claimed the title of caliph but the organisation he headed could no longer be called a state. The former territory of the caliphate is now divided up among the Syrian Kurds, the Turkish army and its proxies, Syrian government forces, and Iraqi Shia paramilitaries. ISIS has reverted to the organisational structure it had before its spectacular conquests in 2014: it is more a loose network run by committees than a coherent bureaucracy. Its main activities are guerrilla operations, much like those of its affiliate in the Sinai Peninsula, and it doesn't require much central direction.

The pattern of US assassinations in the Middle East is clear. The US regularly conducts drone assassinations in northern Syria, often with disregard for civilian casualties and without firm evidence of who it is shooting at. (The US claims to have killed an implausible number of 'senior al-Qaida leaders' in drone strikes.) When the US needs to be sure of its victims, it usually prefers to get up close. But there are exceptions. In January 2020, the assassination of IRGC leader Qassem Suleimani represented another transformation of the assassination policy. The killing of Suleimani was deemed illegal by the UN Special Rapporteur on extrajudicial, summary or arbitrary executions, Agnes Callamard. 'For the first time, in January 2020, a State armed drone targeted a high-level official of a foreign state on the territory of a third one – a significant development and an escalation,' Callamard said. But in general when certitude is needed the US has opted for a special forces raid; the chief advantage is that it's easier to confirm the identity of the victims.

In those parts of the Middle East where autocrats have not survived to stamp their authority, US policy has been substantially based on these assassinations. For Islamic State this has had mixed effects. The marginalised, predominantly rural Sunnis in Syria and Iraq who formed the base of support for the Islamic State have seen no real change in their material conditions. Many of the cities IS once held were all but destroyed by Western air power, and have been only partly rebuilt. Former footsoldiers remain in scattered prison camps. In January, hundreds escaped when the group launched an attack on a prison in Hasakah. The assassination policy against IS leaders did not prevent its rise, or cause its fall. There are plenty more veterans of the Iraq insurgency, plenty of former Camp Bucca detainees.

In stark contrast to the Levantine desert, the more stable regions of the neo-imperial Middle East have received very different treatment. Even in the south of the Arabian peninsula the policy has tended to be to support autocratic governments against state breakdown. In May 2021, there were daily demonstrations in towns and cities across Oman. Public protests are rare in the Persian Gulf monarchies. Some were held in Oman in 2019, when protesters demanded that the sultanate address rising unemployment. This was also a central concern of Omani protesters during the Arab Spring uprisings in 2011. But the main demonstrations in 2021 were in the two main port cities, Salalah and Sohar, where unemployment has historically been highest. Activists have shared photographs of British-made tear gas canisters used against them, similar to those used by police in Hong Kong.

The demonstrations began when protesters staged sit-ins in front of government buildings to demand a solution to rising living costs and a general lack of jobs. The crowds were modest, but in a country with a small population (about 4 million, only half of whom are nationals) they were significant. At first the response from the security forces was cautious. Then security forces began to take a harder line. Police fired CS canisters in Sohar and made arrests. The national newspapers published prominent reports of the sit-ins. It was the first major political crisis in Oman since the death of Sultan Qaboos in 2020 and the succession of his cousin Haitham. The dramatic fall in oil prices during 2020 caused by the coronavirus pandemic had a severe effect on Oman's economy. The sultanate sought financial aid from Qatar, but it wasn't enough. Sultan

Haitham adopted a standard package of austerity measures: utility subsidies were cut in January, a value added tax was introduced in April, and the salaries of government employees were cut in May. Military spending was untouched and remains the highest in the world as a percentage of GDP.

While assassinating designated enemy leaders in the Levant, the British and American governments have tried wherever possible to pre-empt more serious challenges to the Omani sultanate, and to the other Persian Gulf monarchies. Oman is arguably the closest British ally in the region. Muscat was the first and last British colonial possession in the Gulf. British intelligence agencies have influence in all the major organs of the Omani state. Royal Dutch Shell still owns a third of Petroleum Development Oman. The port of Salalah is managed by a British national. Oman has if anything become more central to UK military planning in recent years. In 2019, the UK Joint Logistics Support Base was opened in Duqm. It is one of the naval bases designed to service the UK's new aircraft carriers. Duqm is also the site of the largest British army training facility in the world. Part of the reason Oman's military budget is so inflated is to tie the country to its Anglo-American sponsors with long-term procurement contracts. Whatever protesters in Oman wanted to achieve, it was out of reach. To challenge the sultanate would be to challenge the extent of British influence in Oman and the billions the sultanate spends on British fighter jets.

In February 2021, the US government announced it was ending its support for 'offensive military operations' in Yemen. As an Interim National Security Strategic Guidance document released that year explained, the US decision was meant to signal a change of direction: under President Biden, America would no longer 'give our partners in the Middle East a blank cheque to pursue policies at odds with American interests and values'. But America has not withdrawn from the conflict entirely. On 8 February, the then head of US Central Command, General Kenneth McKenzie, said the US would continue to provide intelligence for Saudi and UAE forces. The cheques may not be blank, but they wouldn't be empty either. The Biden administration tried to give the appearance of a decisive break with the Trump era, but in the Middle East its policies have been more of the same. The secretary of state, Anthony Blinken (the epitome of the 'politics as smart law firm' faction of the Democratic Party), criticised the UN Human Rights council for 'unacceptable bias against Israel'. The administration conducted airstrikes in Syria, approved $200 million of arms sales to Egypt, and made plans to increase NATO troop deployments to Iraq. In the Arabian Peninsula, the US military is expanding its strategic infrastructure with plans to make use of the Red Sea port of Yanbu and air bases in Tabuk and Taif.

Unlike the US, the British government continued all of its military support for the war in Yemen. Government figures showed that the UK approved $1.4 billion of arms sales to Saudi Arabia between July and September 2020. (There had been a year's suspension of arms exports since June 2019, after the Campaign Against the Arms Trade took the government to court.) The UK has also cut its provision of humanitarian aid to Yemen by more than half, despite UN warnings that the country is facing 'the worst famine in decades'. The US and UK have not only provided the weapons; they have given direction at every operational level. British soldiers manned radar systems in support of the air war. US planes conducted mid-air refuelling for bombing sorties. Despite this support, the result has been a deadly stalemate.

Aside from the more than 10,000 civilian casualties caused directly by the air war, there is the incalculable body count of the resulting famines, cholera epidemic, and the ground fighting. The intervention has also not prevented Houthi attacks on Saudi oil infrastructure, meaning it has been a clear failure even on its own ignoble terms. The new US policy looked sane by comparison with Britain's. But it would be naive to view the UK's actions in isolation from American decisions. It is more likely that the ongoing British involvement was agreed in advance of Biden's announcement. With UK and US support, the war will continue indefinitely. The British government refuses even to investigate allegations of war crimes committed by its side in the conflict.

One of the few genuine foreign policy changes marked by the transition from Trump to Biden was a reduction in the use of assassination, partly because of revelations of its bluntness. But there is no telling how long it will last. In the unlikely case that more stable regimes can develop in the Levant, American and British policy will switch from remote assassinations to support for autocracy – so long as it accords with their interests.

Postscript: Reactive Management of the World Empire

The idea that the United States is an empire in decline has gained considerable support, some of it from quarters that until very recently would have denied it was ever an empire at all.[1] Yet the shadow American power still casts over the rest of the world is unmistakable. The US still has military superiority over all other states, control of the world's oceans via critical sea lanes, garrisons on every continent, a network of alliances that covers much of the industrial world, the ability to render individuals to secret prisons from Cuba to Morocco, Poland and Thailand, preponderant influence over the global financial system, about 30 per cent of the world's wealth, and a continental economy not dependent on international trade. To call this an empire is if anything to understate its range. Within the American security establishment what it amounted to was never in doubt. US power was to be exercised around the world using the 'conduits of national power': economic centrality, military scale, sole possession of a global navy, nuclear superiority, and global surveillance architecture that makes use of the preponderant American share of the earth's orbital infrastructure.[2]

If proponents of the end of the US global order do not assert a decrease in the potency of the instruments of American power, that is because there has been no such decrease. The share of global transactions conducted in dollars has been increasing, not declining.[3] No other state can affect political outcomes in other countries the way the US still does from Honduras to Japan. The reach of the contemporary US is so great that it tends to blend into the background of daily events. In January 2019, the US demanded that Germany ban Mahan Air from landing on its territory.[4] In September 2020, it sanctioned the chief prosecutor of the International Criminal Court for refusing to drop investigations in to American citizens.[5] In February 2022, at US request, Japan agreed to redirect liquefied natural gas, which is critical to Japanese industry, to Europe in the event of a conflict with Russia over Ukraine.[6] In 2022 the US found itself unable to force India to eschew Russian oil, but this was partly a result of the contradictions of a hydrocarbon blockade on Russia that exempted its principal European customers. At the height of that conflict, Secretary of State Anthony Blinken found the time to visit Algiers to negotiate the reopening of a natural gas pipeline to Spain via Morocco. These were all quotidian events, unremarkable daily instances of humdrum imperial activity. The practical operation of the empire remains poorly understood, not despite its ubiquity but because of it.

From this perspective, the menial adherence of Britain to the US global project is at least intelligible. Historically, American planners divided their approach to the rest of the world by region.[7] In Western Europe and Japan, American interests were usually pursued by cautious political management. In Latin America and the Middle East, constant interventions, coups, and invasions were needed. In East Asia and South-east Asia there was military exertion at scale.[8] As long as it lasted the Soviet Union was cordoned off and contained, against the wishes of the generals in the Strategic Air Command, which preferred to destroy it in a nuclear holocaust.[9] The major US allies were on the right side of this calculus and had less reason to begrudge it.

When dealing with the US, elites in the periphery still often behave as though they are dealing with the imperial centre. The US permits a variety of political systems in its subordinates. US clients include medieval monarchies, military juntas, personal presidential autocracies, apartheid parliamentary systems, and reasonably democratic systems with greater social equity and conditions than the US itself. What has been required is to keep reasonable accordance with American foreign policy goals. In Britain's case, this has been so consistent, both over time and between political factions, that one must wonder whether Britain retains an independent foreign policy at all. The Johnson government's stance on Ukraine, more Virginian than the Pentagon or the CIA, continued uninterrupted through the collapse of the Truss government and the troubled ascent of Rishi Sunak. The vision was straightforwardly that of Britain as airbase, provider of troops to the Baltic frontier, and advanced anti-tank weapons when needed. As prime minister, Sunak may have discovered the promises made by his two forebears to increase military spending to 2.5 or 3 per cent of GDP were beyond the capacity of the Treasury, but the decision to back away from those pledges was based on means, not a contrary prospectus.[10] British leaders may talk of a shifting world system, but the ensign-style in British foreign policy persists.

To its credit, the contemporary US foreign policy establishment has shown some candour about its world-ordering ambitions. Much of the discussion takes place in public between a nexus of think-tank and academic institutions.[11] Respectable pillars of the establishment such as Michael Mandelbaum have talked of the US acting as 'the

World's Government'.[12] By 2011, John G Ikenberry – the central figure in 'liberal international order' scholarship – was willing to entertain the idea of 'imperial tendencies in the unipolar distribution of power that stands behind American foreign policy'.[13] Some discussion has begun about the kinds of imperial activity in which the US should engage. In 2014, Barry Posen began to advocate for 'restraint' in the use of force in global affairs, if only for the ultimate goal of the empire's reinvigoration.[14] But whatever the merits of these contributions, traditional hegemonists and Neo-Cold Warriors have retained a plurality.

The *du jour* subject in international affairs commentary is the transition from a unipolar order to a multipolar or polycentric world. But this is easy to overstate. International affairs scholars have long predicted a return to a balance of power among the great states, as a correction to the enormous imbalance represented by the US. One problem is why it seems to have taken so long. Stephen Brooks and William Wohlforth persuasively argued that the extent of American power had to be reckoned with in a different way: the US had attained power preponderance – a degree of global power so great that its very extent served to disincentivise other states from challenging it.[15] One interpretation of the actions of the contemporary US military and security establishment is that they have been engaged in a concerted effort to prove power preponderance. Designated allies such as Britain have tended to see reconciling themselves to US might as the logical choice.

The election of Donald Trump in 2016 provided natural stimulation to omens of American decline.[16] Most of the US national security establishment did not welcome Trump's rise, and four years later would cheer his departure. In parts of the Holy Roman Empire, a new elector was obliged not just to attend the funeral of his predecessor but to bury the body. After Joe Biden's victory in 2020, many

Trump opponents appeared to desire the finality of interment. In the dark of election night, when early vote counts made Trump look ascendant, former State Department analyst Aaron David Miler wrote of 'champagne corks popping' in Moscow, Ankara, and Beijing. It was clear why Biden's victory was seen as a form of deliverance by many in the US. But among the elites in the core American allies a similar view was not uncommon.[17] In Britain there was more ambiguity: Rishi Sunak's future adviser James Forsyth wrote that the end of Trump was a 'mixed blessing' but would at least 'take the drama out of Anglo-American relations'.[18]

The Trump administration's foreign policy was in fact more orthodox than is generally admitted. While derided as an isolationist by the imperial bureaucracy, for whom the term is a stock insult, Trump was committed to America's 'unquestioned military dominance'.[19] Many of his appointees were old regime hands: his trade representative, Robert Lighthizer, was a Reagan-era official; the director of the CIA, Gina Haspel, ran a torture site under George W. Bush; Trump's fifth secretary of defence, Mark Esper, was formerly an adviser to Barack Obama's defence secretary Chuck Hagel. Having pledged to 'get out of foreign wars', in office Trump did nothing of the sort. He pursued the global assassination programme established under Obama and prosecuted the US-backed war in Yemen. Trump did not get along with the diplomats at the State Department, but his administration did very little that was out of the usual line of business. That Trump was disdainful of international co-operation on terms other than its own was nothing new, and disputes with the foreign policy intelligentsia were for the most part matters of style, not principle. In Latin America the US set up the Western Hemisphere Strategic Framework to increase its influence. In the Middle East, Trump overturned the minor accommodation the Obama administration had reached with Tehran and in doing so reverted to the traditional American strategy of strangling Iran while prevailing on the Gulf monarchies to recognise Israel. Trump criticised the costs of the US military's presence in the Middle East, but US troop levels there in fact increased during his time in office, as did military spending overall. His eccentricities were those of the modern Republican party, a reflection of the polity's right-wing shift rather than of a barbarian anomaly. Dismantling American hegemony would have been a historic act, but Trump never considered it.

The US withdrawal from Afghanistan in August 2021, which necessitated the simultaneous withdrawal of the forces of any remaining Western allies, was yet another death for American empire.[20] The clamour of the final exit partly drowned out the tawdry record of every US president in Afghanistan from Bush to Biden. That twenty years of occupation and state-building crumbled in weeks confirmed only that the Afghan government had been an artificial and corrupt dependent. Under both Trump and Biden, US planners had concluded that the US could no longer afford such exposed wards.[21] Biden could at least claim to have stuck the withdrawal, though not without a signature act of punitive sadism. By freezing the assets of the Afghan central bank during the latest humanitarian crisis, the humiliating condition of the exit could be paid with a flourish of parting malice.[22]

Enough of the US global order survived the withdrawal from Afghanistan that it could die again in February 2022 with the Russian invasion of Ukraine.[23] Contrary to unserious predictions before its outbreak, this was no 'hybrid war', 'cyberwar', or 'space war' but a traditional ground operation at scale that proved far more difficult than the Russian leadership imagined. In the event, expectations of a dash for Kyiv causing the quick capitulation of the Ukrainian government were frustrated. The US strategy of building up Ukrainian armed forces as a specific counter to Russian armoured invasion proved quite effective. The US, Britain, Poland, and other allies supplied key weapons and detailed intelligence, including satellite targeting, while seeking to inflict some economic damage on Russia with sanctions.[24] That US intelligence appeared to have had a source in the Kremlin with access to the war plans also ran counter to the narrative of the empire's demise.

That the US has, so far at least, held the line against Russia even at the extremity of eastern Ukraine tells somewhat of a different story. Russia's general strategy has since 2008 been to reassert influence in the former Soviet states around its borders. Yet between 1999 and 2009 NATO expanded into Poland, Hungary, the Czech Republic, the Baltic states, Romania, Bulgaria, Slovakia, Slovenia, Albania and Croatia. Perceiving this as a defeat, Russia had sought to bring it to a stop. Yet in Georgia, the Caucasus, Crimea, Belarus and Kazakhstan, recent Russian operations were small-scale. Why a completely different, and far more hubristic, strategy was adopted for Ukraine remains poorly understood. Part of the story must lie in the agreements signed between the US and Ukraine between September and November 2021.[25] Yet the US, Britain, and NATO itself had studiously kept to ambiguous ground about future Ukrainian accession. The decision to invade seemed set at the latest by the failure of US-Russia talks in January 2022. In any case the invasion itself was a grave gamble. It has been mirrored in the strategy of the US and its allies, which since April 2022 has shifted from a simple frustration of the initial invasion to the grander ambition of using the war to achieve strategic attrition of Russia.[26]

In large part, talk of the end of American dominance was a reaction to the concurrence of the global financial crisis and China's industrial rise. For some Western strategic planners, conflicts in

Afghanistan and even Ukraine have come to be seen as distractions from the China threat, which represents the only plausible challenge to American global hegemony. In its 2022 National Security Strategy the Biden administration declared that the 2020s were to be a decisive decade. Past military adventures in the Middle East were criticised as extravagances and distractions in the era of competition with China.[27] 'We do not seek conflict or a new Cold War,' the NSS said, but 'we must proactively shape the international order in line with our interests and values'. In order to prevail in competition with China, the US had to enhance its industrial capacity by 'investing in our people'. The present moment was said to represent 'a consequential new period of American foreign policy that will demand more of the United States in the Indo-Pacific than has been asked of us since the Second World War.'

What should be made of the fact that it is Biden, not Trump, who has overseen a major escalation of tension with Russia and a mercantilist escalation in the trade war with China?[28] At the time, the one ostensibly distinctive part of the Trump programme appeared to be the trade war. Trump was made to stand for an insular protectionist turn, but the same basic policies have been continued under Biden.[29] Still, Biden has proved to be just as unwilling to limit capital flows into dollar debt, which impoverish American workers but inflate the prices of assets owned by the rich, and maintain US power over the international financial system. Given that Biden supported the 2003 invasion of Iraq and spoke of his admiration for Dick Cheney, it was always unlikely that he would pursue a quietist strategy on China.[30]

The US political system as a whole appears at present to be opting for China containment. Under President Biden US strategy is to 'isolate and punish' China.[31] Encouraged by the US, Japan, like Britain, is engaged in a major arms build-up. American politicians make showy visits to Taipei. The US has threatened China with nuclear weapons in the past on the basis that it does not have a comparable nuclear arsenal. There is some debate over whether China's current nuclear armed submarines are quiet enough to avoid tracking by the US. China is also working to make its ICBMs more secure. It is possible that soon they will together constitute a reliable second-strike capability against the US. The most dangerous moment of the Cold War was in the early 1960s, when an aggressive and overwhelmingly dominant nuclear power saw itself in competition with an adversary that didn't yet have equivalent nuclear forces. The US and China may be approaching a similar point.

In November 2022, when Biden met Xi Jinping at the G20 in Indonesia, both appeared to strike a more conciliatory tone. Biden said the two had 'a responsibility to show that China and the US can manage our differences' and 'prevent competition from becoming conflict'. But the 2022 decision to ban Chinese access to the semiconductor trade was a straightforward escalation. Both Trump and Biden responded to the immediacy of their respective moments according to a general strategy that is longer lived than either of them. To some extent this is inevitable in great powers. Augustus's policy of restricting the Roman empire's eastward expansion was followed by the next eleven emperors. And US foreign policy has been quite stable for thirty years: a mode best characterised as reactive management of the world empire, with the strategic goal of pre-empting the emergence of any potential challengers to its primacy.

For all the talk of multipolar worlds, other poles of world power have been hard to find.[32] Russia has hardly proved itself a global power in its botched invasion of Ukraine. Fantasies of European strategic autonomy have shown themselves insubstantial. India's economic growth has been notable but it projects very little influence away from the sub-continent. The minor nationalisms exhibited in Turkey and Iran hardly qualify them as poles of global power, and the former still serves as a staging ground for American nuclear weapons. As the former Tsinghua professor Sun Zhe observed, developing countries are not co-operatively 'rising together' to 'challenge the current order' – the likes of Brazil and South Africa are if anything declining.[33] So where is the multiplicity in world politics? Even the non-alignment of the Cold War appears, for now, to be lacking.[34]

Much of the presaged systemic change reduces to the emergence of Sino-American competition, which multipolarity poorly describes. The strategic balance so far remains hugely in favour of the US. China does not militarily threaten the US. Chinese naval power is routinely exaggerated; the PLA navy is not predicted to rival the US Pacific fleet for another generation, and it still has no quiet nuclear submarines. It is not clear that China is capable of mounting an invasion even of Taiwan, and there are good reasons to think the standing committee knows this. For its part, China has not even made a serious effort to escape the dominance of the dollar in its trade with the rest of the world. It is the US that asserts a policy of isolation and punishment of China, not vice versa. So long as the US is maintaining a 'defense perimeter' in the East and South China seas that, unlike the 1950s original, extends to a few kilometres from mainland China, it is not dealing with a peer, it is threatening a recalcitrant.

Assertions of the inevitability of American imperial decline over the long term are fair enough; in their most abstract form and on a long enough time scale they must eventually obtain. And the US position does look shakier than it has for decades. But what is striking is how seldom the system said to be in decline is given even a cursory description, especially in the subordinate parts of the Anglosphere. Why the reticence to explain the nature of American power? And why ignore that so much of contemporary American grand strategy is oriented precisely to prevent its dissolution? As the 2022 National Security Strategy said, 'prophecies of American decline have repeatedly been disproven in the past'. This time the effort may be in vain. The risks of both a Sino-American confrontation and the Russo-American nuclear stand-off implied in the war in Ukraine are considerable. Whatever is to come, the fact remains that global power at present remains unipolar. The task for those not committed to its continuation is to understand it and, wherever possible, to challenge its assumptions.

Acknowledgements

Many of the chapters in this book began as essays for the *London Review of Books*. The original versions of Chapters 2, 3, and 4 of Part I appeared in the 1 July 2021, 6 October 2022, and 19 January 2023 issues respectively. Chapters 6–10 of Part II first appeared in the 24 March 2022, 8 September 2022, 22 October 2020, 24 February 2022, and 4 March 2021 issues in that order. Chapters 11–16 of Part III first appeared in the 9 May 2019, 2 March 2017, 19 February 2015, 20 June 2019, and 17 November 2022 issues in that order.

I thank Daniel Soar, Jeremy Harding, and the editors at the *LRB* for their support and contributions.

Notes

Introduction

1 The consensus view is best represented by G. John Ikenberry, Richard Haas, and Jessica T. Mathews. Peter Gowan, Susan Watkins, and Perry Anderson are valuable foils.

2 The bulk contributed of course by Joseph Nye, but see also G. John Ikenberry's emphasis on 'institutions, ideas, alliances, and partnerships' in 'Why American Power Endures', *Foreign Affairs,* November/December 2022.

3 For a full description of tripolarity in the world economy see Silvia Miranda-Agrippino and Hélène Rey, 'The Global Financial Cycle', in *Handbook of International Economics*, Vol. 6, 2022, pp. 1–43. (Anders Stephenson has noted the trouble with polarity in international relations, but it has proved too useful to be discarded without replacement. The global nuclear balance of course remains polar *sensu stricto*.)

4 National Security Council Defense Planning: Guidance FY 1994–1999, 16 April, 1992.

5 NATO 2022 Strategic Concept, Adopted by the Heads of State and Government at the NATO summit in Madrid, 29 June 2022. The National Security Strategy of the United States of America, December 2017 asserted that the US had 'stood by while countries exploited the international institutions we helped to build'.

6 David McCourt, 'Has Britain Found Its Role?', *Survival*, Vol. 56, 2014.

7 In Michael Smith, *The Real Special Relationship: The True Story of How the British and US Secret Services Work Together*, Simon and Schuster, 2022.

8 Susan Strange, 'Sterling and British Policy: A Political View', *International Affairs*, Vol. 47, No. 2 (April 1971), pp. 302–15.

9 The phrase was used in Joe Biden's 2022 State of the Union address and then chosen as the theme of Liz Truss's UN General Assembly speech in September 2022.

10 In *The Virtual American Empire: On War, Faith and Power*, Routledge, 2009, Edward Luttwak writes that 'American diplomacy quite suddenly had to function without much of its former economic leverage'.

11 For the relevant figures on global trade see data.worldbank.org/indicator/NE.TRD.GNFS.ZS. For discussion of dollar funding in international commerce see Committee on the Global Financial System CGFS Papers No 65, 'US Dollar Funding: An International Perspective', prepared by a working group chaired by Sally Davies (Board of Governors of the Federal Reserve System) and Christopher Kent (Reserve Bank of Australia), June 2020.

12 'Brazil discussing with US sanctions on Teheran to help liberate Iranian fertilizers', *Mercosur*, 11 April 2022.

13 A stand-out example was Robert Vitalis's *Oilcraft: The Myths of Scarcity and Security That Haunt US Energy Policy*, Stanford University Press, 2020. The Quincy Institute's July 2020 paper 'A New US Paradigm for the Middle East: Ending America's Misguided Policy of Domination', and 2021 paper 'Nothing Much to Do: Why America Can Bring All Troops Home From the Middle East' ran with the same theme.

14 For a thorough discussion see Micah Zenko, 'US Military Policy in the Middle East: An Appraisal', Chatham House, October 2018.

15 In November 2021, the United Nations Development Programme estimated 377,000 deaths since the start of the war.

1. Eternal Allies

1 In September 2021, for example, then National Security Adviser Stephen Lovegrove insisted in a speech at the 'Council on Geostrategy' that 'the UK is, and will remain, a global power'.

2 'Memorandum on the Present State of British Relations with France and Germany', Eyre Crowe to Foreign Secretary Sir Edward Grey, 1 January 1907.

3 Churchill at Fulton, Missouri, 5 March 1946.

4 See Jon Meacham, *Franklin and Winston: An Intimate Portrait of an Epic Friendship*, Random House, 2003, p. 29.

5 'Position Paper Prepared in the Bureau of European Affairs', February 1957, Department of State BNA Files: Lot 64 D 241, 5A.

6 The context, a speech at the United States Military Academy West Point, is important.

7 From a speech given at the Lord Mayor of London's Banquet, 22 November 1999.

8 Dean Acheson to Robert J. Schaetzel, 1 April 1963, Box 28, Dean Acheson Papers, Yale University Library, New Haven.

9 A full account is given in P. L. Pham, *Ending 'East of Suez': The British Decision to Withdraw from Malaysia and Singapore 1964–1968*, Oxford University Press, 2010.

10 O'Neill to Rab Butler, July 1964, in Helen Parr, *Britain's Policy Towards the European Community: Harold Wilson and Britain's World Role, 1964–1967*, Routledge, 2005, p. 17.

11 Paul Cheeseright, 'Involvement without engagement: The British Advisory Mission in South Vietnam', *Asian Affairs*, Vol. 42, No. 2, 261–75.

12 Hansard, Vol. 690, Tuesday 3 March 1964.

13 Priscilla Roberts, *The British Royal Air Force: Operations over Laos against the Ho Chi Minh Trail, 1962*, Wilson Center, December 2018.

14 Harold Wilson to Lyndon Johnson, February 1967, National Archives PREM 13/1788.

15 Henderson, Nicholas, 'Britain's Decline; Its Causes and Consequences', March 1979 (published in *Economist*, 2 June 1979).

16 As far as we know, the relevant Foreign Office records of relations between Britain and Argentina from this period having been shredded, as Grace Livingstone discussed in the *London Review of Books* blog 'Search and Destroy', 10 February 2022.

17 Cited in George Boyce's *The Falklands War*, Bloomsbury Publishing, June 2005, p. 221.

18 Lehman Jr, John F., 'Reflections on the Special Relationship' in *Naval History Magazine*, Vol. 26, Number 5, September 2012.

19 Cited in 'Surveillance secrecy: The legacy of GCHQ's years under cover', *Guardian*, 21 Aug 2013.

20 The House of Commons Foreign Affairs Committee report of 23 May 2000 touched on all of these consequences. The long-lasting perceptions of the bombing of the Chinese embassy are described in 'The night the US bombed a Chinese embassy', BBC, 7 May 2019.

21 On 17 March 2002 Tony Blair wrote to Jonathan Powell that the case for being 'gung-ho on Saddam' should be obvious for a 'political philosophy that does

care about other nations e.g. Kosovo, Afghanistan, Sierra Leone'. (See The Report of the Iraq Inquiry, Section 3.2, article 429.)

22 Charles Maechling Jr., 'Too Special a Relationship Makes Britain a Feeble Ally', *International Herald Tribune*, 18 December 1997.

23 John Mearsheimer to the King's College, Cambridge Politics Society, 15 February 2022.

24 Lawrence Freedman, *Foreign Affairs,* May/June 2006.

25 As the former head of MI6 John Scarlett put it in the foreword to Smith, *The Real Special Relationship*, 'there is a widespread view that the relationship is more appreciated and talked up by the British as a means of promoting their global role', p. ix.

26 It took more than a decade for the BBC to unearth information on SAS executions of detainees in Helmand: 'SAS Unit Repeatedly Killed Afghan Detainees, BBC Finds', BBC, 12 July 2022.

27 'US Air Force Deployment in Britain is Third Largest in World', Matt Kenard, Declassified UK, 10 May 2022.

28 Peter Ricketts, *Hard Choices: What Britain Does Next*, Atlantic Books, 2022.

29 This is a version of the declinist view of American empire in which, instead of being elbowed aside, 'the US itself is losing interest in leading the system it was instrumental in creating'.

30 Cabinet Office 129/100, FP(60)1, 'Future Policy Study 1960–70', 24 February 1960.

31 On 11 January 2023, the UK and Japan signed a reciprocal access agreement, allowing military forces to be stationed on one another's territory.

32 'UK doubles money to Saudi Arabia and Bahrain through "secretive" fund', *Middle East Eye*, 25 August 2022.

33 As an MoD press release put it on 29 May 2022, 'Qatar remains the only partner with whom the RAF operates joint squadrons'.

34 'Navy has made great strides but must rise to future challenges', Royal Navy, 29 July 2021.

35 'Britain needs a post-Brexit foreign policy', *Economist*, 2 January 2021.

36 'UK PM Liz Truss commits to raise defence spending to 3% of GDP by 2030', Reuters, 18 October 2022.

37 A speech at DSEI, 13 September 2017, in London.

38 National Security Council Defense Planning: Guidance FY 1994–1999, 16 April 1992.

39 Ricketts, *Hard Choices*.

40 'The return of geopolitics: Foreign Secretary's Mansion House speech at the Lord Mayor's 2022 Easter Banquet', 27 April 2022.

41 See for example Nick Childs, 'UK Littoral Response Group: the shape of things to come?', IISS Military Balance Blog, 25 June 2021.

42 A rare exception was the *Financial Times* article 'The four routes to easing Northern Ireland's political impasse' by Jude Webber, 31 October 2022.

43 Statement by James Cleverly, 'British Indian Ocean Territory/Chagos Archipelago', 3 November 2022.

44 Tom Hazeldine has written about how Correlli Barnett entertained such a position in the 2000s. For a discussion of Barnett's legacy, see 'Pride and Fall', *NLR-Sidecar*, 30 September 2022.

45 Politicians from both leading parties (Iain Duncan Smith and Tom Tugendhat in the case of the Conservatives, and Lisa Nandy a Labour example) have occasionally dabbled in hawkish anti-China rhetoric, but it has never approached the levels seen in the US. An anti-China position has not yet become even a minority political platform within the elite.

2. Someone Else's Empire

1 One of the MI6 officers, identified as SiS 4 in the Iraq Inquiry, spoke of the danger of intelligence analysis becoming 'a pencil we were sharpening for HMG use', and later (in evidence session two) of WMD 'being asked to carry more weight at the bar of history, and all this stuff, than it possibly could be expected to bear'.

2 Patrick Porter, *Blunder: Britain's War in Iraq,* Oxford University Press, 2018.

3 Ben Barry, *Blood, Metal and Dust: How Victory Turned into Defeat in Afghanistan and Iraq,* Osprey Publishing, 2020.

4 Available at: gov.uk/government/publications/operation-telic-lessons-compendium.

5 Simon Akam, *The Changing of the Guard: The British Army since 9/11*, Scribe, 2021.

6 In figures given in the 2022 edition of the Stockholm International Peace Research Institute Fact Sheet, UK military spending was the third highest in the world: only the US and China maintained higher military spending, with India and Russia occupying the fourth and fifth positions.

7 This incident is discussed in Chapter 3 of Leigh Neville's *Special Forces in the War on Terror*, Bloomsbury Publishing, 2015.

8 Brown University, Costs of War, 'Human Costs of post-9/11 wars: direct war deaths in major war zones, Afghanistan and Pakistan, October–August 2021.

9 Mike Martin, *An Intimate War: An Oral History of the Helmand Conflict*, Oxford University Press, 2014.

10 *Defence in a Competitive Age*, Ministry of Defence, March 2021.

11 Robert McNamara conceived of the agreement to sell Britain F-111 aircraft as helping 'to lock the British into a meaningful role East of Suez.' See 'Telegram from President Johnson to Prime Minister Wilson', *Foreign Relations of the United States*, 1964–1968, Vol. XII, Western Europe. McNamara and Dean Rusk also claimed that the US could not be 'the gendarmes of the universe', at least not without some European logistical assistance.

12 '236. Memorandum of Conversation', Washington, 7 December 1964 in *Foreign Relations of the United States*, 1964–1968, Vol. XII, Western Europe. Denis Healey also said that British military operations outside of Europe carried the risk of looking like 'the dying legacy of an imperial power' and that 'when the UK had intervened in other parts of the world it had simply looked colonial'.

3. The British Defence Intellectual

1 See Michael Codner 'High Noon for British Grand Strategy', *War Without Consequences: Iraq's Insurgency and the Spectre of Strategic Defeat*, RUSI, 2008, p. 129. Jonathan Eyal, 'Europe and the United States: An End to Illusions' in *RUSI Whitehall Papers*, Vol. 59, May 2003. Michael Clarke, 'Blair was "optimistic not criminal"', RUSI Blog, 29 January 2010.

2 *Accidental Heroes: Britain, France and the Libya Operation*, RUSI, September 2011.

3 Former War Studies faculty member James Acton, for example, has made several notable contributions, not least among them *Abolishing Nuclear Weapons*, September 2008.

4 *Global Britain in a Competitive Age: The Integrated Review of Security, Defence, Development and Foreign Policy*, Cabinet Office, March 2021.

5 John Bew, *Citizen Clem*, Hachette, 2016.

6 Lawrence Freedman, *Command: The Politics of Military Operations from Korea to Ukraine*, Allen Lane, 2022.

7 In *The Art of Creating Strategy*, Chapter 17, Oxford University Press, 2017.

8 'Chicago Speech: Some Suggestions', published by the Iraq Inquiry.

9 'A reversal in Iraq will not protect us from terrorists', *Financial Times*, 2 August 2005.

10 John Keegan, *The Mask of Command: A Study of Generalship*, Pimlico, 2004.

11 Lawrence Freedman, *Strategy: A History*, Oxford University Press, 2013, p. 244.

4. The Anglo-Settler Societies and World History

1 Richard Kerbaj, *The Secret History of the Five Eyes: The Untold Story of the Shadowy International Spy Network, through Its Targets, Traitors and Spies*, John Blake, 2022.

2 James Belich, *Replenishing the Earth: The Settler Revolution and the Rise of the Anglo-World*, Oxford University Press, 2009.

3 Clinton Fernandes, *Sub-Imperial Power: Australia in the International Arena*, Melbourne University Press, 2022.

4 Bryan Clark, 'The Emerging Era in Undersea Warfare', *Center for Strategic and Budgetary Assessments*, 22 January 2015.

5 '"We can get this done quickly": Australia set to build its own missiles', *Sydney Morning Herald*, 14 October 2022.

6 A position led by the Foreign Minister Nanaia Mahuta.

7 A talk at Policy Exchange in June 2018.

5. Green Bamboo, Red Snow

1 See 'Military and Security Developments Involving the People's Republic of China 2020', Annual Report to Congress, 2020.

2 The Conservative government's 'Strategic Defence and Security Review' of October 2010, for example. Britain was to 'play a strong role in the Nuclear Non-Proliferation Treaty Review Conference, and press for continued progress on multilateral disarmament.'

3 'United Kingdom Nuclear Weapons, 2021', in *Bulletin of the Atomic Scientists*, Vol. 77, 2021.

4 For a full discussion see 'The cost of the UK's strategic nuclear deterrent', House of Commons Library, 25 May 2022, by Claire Mills and Esme Kirk-Wade.

5 'Lakenheath Air Base Added to Nuclear Weapons Storage Site Upgrades', *Federation of Atomic Scientists*, 11 April 2022.

6 Christine Chinkin and Louise Amritsu, 'Legality Under International Law of the United Kingdom's Nuclear Policy as Set Out in the 2021 Integrated Review', LSE, 28 April 2021.

7 At a speech at RUSI on 20 May 2011.

8 In his speech of 16 June 1962, at the University of Michigan, Ann Arbor.

9 Lorna Arnold's *Britain and the H-Bomb*, published by the Ministry of Defence in 2001, contains an invaluable account of the British nuclear programme.

10 Hansard, Vol. 669, Thursday 13 December 1962.

11 See George Warner, 'The United States and the Western Alliance, 1958–63' in *International Affairs*, Vol. 71, No. 4, October 1995, pp. 801–818.

12 See *The British Nuclear Experience: The Roles of Beliefs, Culture and Identity*, Oxford University Press, 2014, Chapter 10, by John Baylis and Kristan Stoddart.

13 Thomas Schelling, *The Strategy of Conflict*, Harvard University Press, 1960.

14 'Theresa May's first job: decide on UK's nuclear response', Richard Norton-Taylor, *Guardian*, 12 July 2016.

15 'United Kingdom Nuclear Weapons, 2021'.

16 In 1981, in 'The Spread of Nuclear Weapons: More May Be Better', Kenneth Walz argued this eventuality would have its benefits.

17 See '406. Memorandum of Conversation, Nassau, December 20, 1962', in *Foreign Relations of the United States 1961–1963*, Vol. XIII, Western Europe and Canada.

18 In December 2014, the Old War Office building was put up for sale and converted into a hotel and restaurants.

19 'BAE Systems and Rolls-Royce win £2bn UK nuclear deterrent contracts', *Financial Times*, 9 May 2022.

6. The Economic Weapon

1 Matthew Klein and Michael Pettis, *Trade Wars Are Class Wars: How Rising Inequality Distorts the Global Economy and Threatens International Peace*, Yale University Press, 2020.

2 'The US is using sanctions more than ever. But do they work?', *Washington Post*, 24 October 2021.

3 'Pompeo calls it "just nuts" to allow Iran to trade in arms as UN rejects embargo extension', *Washington Post*, 14 August 2020.

4 Richard Nephew, *The Art of Sanctions: A View from the Field*, Columbia University Press, 2017.

5 See 'European Union sanctions', eeas.europa.eu/eeas/european-union-sanctions_en.

6 The standard history of Section 311 is Juan Zarate's *Treasury's War: The Unleashing of a New Era of Financial Warfare*, Public Affairs, 2013.

7 Nicholas Mulder, *The Economic Weapon: The Rise of Sanctions as a Tool of Modern War*, Yale University Press, 2022.

8 Robert Pape, 'Why Economic Sanctions Do Not Work', in *International Security*, Vol. 22, No. 2, 1997, pp. 90–136.

9 Tom Ruys and Cedric Ryngaert, 'Secondary Sanctions: A Weapon out of

Control?' in *British Yearbook of International Law*, September 2020.

10 Jiang Shigong, trans by David Ownby, 'Meng Wanzhou Surely Won't be the Last: The Hidden Logic of the American 'Hand-Over'', *Asia Pacific Journal*, Vol. 19, 1 December 2021. Originally published in the *Beijing Cultural Review* in August of 2019 under the title 'The Long Arm of Empire's Justice: The Legal Underpinnings of US Economic Hegemony'.

11 'Remarks by President Biden on Russia's Unprovoked and Unjustified Attack on Ukraine', White House, 24 February 2022.

12 'Economic Sanctions as Collective Punishment: The Case of Venezuela', Mark Weisbrot and Jeffrey Sachs, Centre for Economic Policy Research, April 2019.

13 Sam Heller, 'Syrians Are Going Hungry. Will the West Act?', World Food Programme, 7 June 2021.

14 'The Treasury 2021 Sanctions Review', October 2021.

7. Keys to the World

1 See Arthur J. Marder, *The Anatomy of British Sea Power: A History of British Naval Policy in the Pre-dreadnought Era, 1880–1905*, Knopf, 1940.

2 David Bosco, *The Poseidon Project: The Struggle to Govern the World's Oceans*, Oxford University Press, 2022.

3 'Radio Address Announcing an Unlimited National Emergency', 27 May 1941.

4 From 39 ships in 1649 to 80 in 1651, see Paul Kennedy, *The Rise and Fall of British Naval Mastery*, Scribner 1976, p. 46.

5 See Lance Davis and Stanley Engelman, *Naval Blockades in Peace and War: An Economic History Since 1750*, Cambridge University Press, 2006, p. 28.

6 'Memorandum from the Executive Secretary of the Department of State (Eliot) to the President's Assistant for National Security Affairs (Kissinger)', Washington, 12 March 1970.

7 Paul Kennedy, *Victory at Sea: Naval Power and the Transformation of the Global Order in World War II*, Yale University Press, 2022.

8 The Essex-class carriers launched in 1944 were: USS *Hancock* (CV-19), USS *Ticonderoga* (CV-14), USS *Randolph* (CV-15), USS *Bennington* (CV-20), USS *Shangri-La* (CV-38), USS *Bon Homme Richard* (CV-31), USS *Antietam* (CV-36), USS *Lake Champlain* (CV-39), and USS *Boxer* (CV-21).

9 'Advantage at Sea: Prevailing with Integrated All-Domain Naval Power', December 2020.

10 'Military and Security Developments Involving the People's Republic of China: A Report to Congress', November 2021.

11 'US says most of China's claims in South China Sea are unlawful', NBC News, 14 July 2020.

8. The Proxy Doctrine

1 Donald Trump to Republican Donors, 17 January 2020.

2 See David A. Deptula, *Effects-Based Operations: Change in the Nature of Warfare*, Aerospace Education Foundation, 2001.

3 Joseph Votel and Eero Kevorkian, 'The By-With-Through Operational Approach', *Joint Forces Quarterly* 89, 2nd Quarter, 2018.

4 Speech on the 'Integrated Operating Concept' at Policy Exchange, September 2020.

5 See *The Three Wars of Lt. Gen. George E. Stratemeyer: His Korean War Diary*, d. William T. Y'Blood (ed.), Air Force History and Museums Program, 1999.

6 Stephen Endicott and Edward Hagerman, *The United States and Biological Warfare: Secrets from the Early Cold War and Korea*, Indiana University Press, 1998.

7 Eli Berman and David Lake, *Proxy Wars: Suppressing Violence through Local Agents*, Cornell University Press, 2019.

8 Tyrone Groh, *Proxy War: The Least Bad Option*, Stanford University Press, 2019.

9 Niccolò Machiavelli, *The Prince*, Chapter 12, Penguin, 1999.

10 Andreas Krieg and Jean-Marc Rickli, *Surrogate Warfare: The Transformation of War in the 21st Century*, Georgetown University Press, 2019.

11 'International Strategy for Cyberspace: Prosperity, Security, and Openness in a Networked World', White House, May 2011.

9. On Thermonuclear War

1 The classic text is Samuel Glasstone and Philip J. Dolan, *The Effects of Nuclear Weapons*, 1957.

2 Fred Kaplan, *The Wizards of Armageddon*, Stanford University Press, 1991.

3 Bernard Brodie, *The Absolute Weapon: Atomic Power and World Order*, Harcourt, 1946.

4 A thermonuclear device, RDS-6, was detonated earlier, in August 1953, but it never achieved megaton yields and was not the basis for a deployable weapon.

5 Fred Kaplan, *The Wizards of Armageddon*, Stanford University Press, 1991.

6 Kaufman made contributions to debates over nuclear strategy. His 1954 study

'The Requirements of Deterrence' was influential, as was a subsequent review ('The Crisis in Military Affairs') of Henry Kissinger's derivative work.

7 See Robert Osgood, *Limited War: The Challenge to American Strategy*

8 See *Challenges in US National Security Policy*, 2014, Chapter 10.

9 Herman Kahn, *On Thermonuclear War*, Princeton University Press, 1960.

10 Daniel Elsberg, *The Doomsday Machine: Confessions of a Nuclear War Planner*, Bloomsbury, 2017.

11 Fred Kaplan, *The Bomb: Presidents, Generals, and the Secret History of Nuclear War*, Simon and Schuster, 2020.

12 See 'Report on the Nuclear Employment Strategy of the United States, 2020'. (Also known as the Section 491 report).

13 See James Baker's account in *The Politics of Diplomacy: Revolution, War, and Peace, 1989–1992*, G.P. Putnam's Sons, 1995.

14 At his first address to the UN General Assembly in September 2017.

15 Daniel Elsberg, *The Doomsday Machine: Confessions of a Nuclear War Planner*, Bloomsbury, 2017.

16 Robert Jervis, *The Meaning of the Nuclear Revolution: Statecraft and the Prospect of Armageddon*, Cornell University Press, 1989.

17 Keir Lieber and Daryl Press, *The Myth of the Nuclear Revolution: Power Politics in the Atomic Age*, Cornell University Press, 2020.

18 Edward Luttwak, 'An Emerging Postnuclear Era?', *Washington Quarterly*, 1988.

19 See, for example, Alan Robock, Owen B. Toon et al., 'How an India-Pakistan nuclear war could start – and have global consequences' in *Bulletin of the Atomic Scientists*, Vol. 75, No. 6, 2019, pp. 273–279.

20 'Global Trends 2040: A More Contested World', March 2021.

10. Astrostrategy

1 'Report of the Commission to Assess United States National Security Space Management and Organization', 11 January 2001.

2 'Top enlisted leader Towberman officially joins the US Space Force', by Sandra Erwin, *Space News*, 2 April 2020.

3 Thompson spoke to David Deptula at the Mitchell Institute for Aerospace Studies on 12 May 2020.

4 Hyten was making this point as early as 2000, in for example 'A Sea of Peace or a Theater of War: Dealing with the Inevitable Conflict in Space', *Air and Space Power Journal*.

5 See 'The Malign Influence of the People's Republic of China in International

Affairs', *Journal of Indo-Pacific Affairs*, General Kenneth S. Wilsbach, Commander of the Pacific Air Forces, Summer 2021.

6 'The Congress: Lyndon at the Launching Pad', *Time*, 17 February 1958.

7 Congressional Record: Proceedings and Debates of the Congress, p. 411, US Government Printing Office, 1958.

8 'National Security Strategy of the United States of America', December 2017.

9 'Space Capstone Publication, Spacepower (SCP)', Headquarters United States Space Force, June 2020.

10 'Qian Xuesen, Father of China's Space Program, Dies at 98', *New York Times*, 3 November 2009.

11 Quoted in Namrata Goswami and Peter Garretson, *Scramble for the Skies: The Great Power Competition to Control the Resources of Outer Space*, Lexington Books, 2020.

12 The total mass of the asteroid belt is estimated to be 2.39×10^{21} kilograms (see E. V. Pitjeva and N. P. Pitjev, 'Masses of the Main Asteroid Belt and the Kuiper Belt from the Motions of Planets and Spacecraft'). The mass of the earth is $5.972 \times 1{\wedge}^{24}$ kilograms. A more precise estimate would thus put the total mass of the asteroid belt at roughly 0.04 per cent of the mass of the earth.

13 Everett Dolman, *Astropolitik: Classical Geopolitics in the Space Age*, Routledge, 2001.

14 James Oberg, 'Toward a Theory of Space Power: Defining Principles for US Space Policy', lecture, Army and Navy Club, Washington DC, 20 May 2003. John Klein, 'Corbett in Orbit: A Maritime Model for Strategic Space Theory' in *Naval War College Review*, Vol. 57, No. 1, Winter 2004, pp. 59–74.

15 James Klein, *Space Warfare: Strategy, Principles and Policy*, Routledge, 2006, p. 95.

16 Bleddyn Bowen, *War in Space*, Edinburgh University Press, 2020.

17 Daniel Deudney, *Dark Skies: Space Expansionism, Planetary Geopolitics, and the Ends of Humanity*, Oxford University Press, 2020.

18 Carl Sagan and Steven Ostro, 'Dangers of Asteroid Deflection', *Nature*, Vol. 368, 7 April 1994.

11. What Are We There For?

1 'Draft Memorandum to President Truman', *Foreign Relations of the United States: Diplomatic Papers*, 1945, The Near East and Africa, Vol. VIII.

2 Winston Churchill, *The World Crisis, 1911–1918*, Charles Scribner and Sons, Vol. 1, 1938.

3 'The Assistant Secretary of State (Berle) to Brigadier General Boykin C.

Wright', *Foreign Relations of the United States: Diplomatic Papers*, 1943, The Near East and Africa, Vol IV.

4 Interview on C-SPAN, 4 September 1986.

5 'A New Grand Strategy', Benjamin Schwarz and Christopher Layne, *Atlantic*, January 2002.

6 David Wearing, *AngloArabia: Why Gulf Wealth Matters to Britain*, Polity, 2018.

7 Stewart to secretary of defence, 21 March 1969, National Archives, FCO 8/975.

8 David Spiro, *The Hidden Hand of American Hegemony*, Cornell University Press, 1999.

9 Some high-income countries have had important successes increasing the share of power production from renewables. But even those few have achieved little industrial replacement of hydrocarbons in production processes. Norway produces 99 per cent of its domestic electricity from hydro- and wind power; its economy is substantially based on the sale of oil and gas.

10 *Global Trends: Paradox of Progress*, January 2017.

12. The Benefits of Lawlessness

1 In 1999, six nurses, five Bulgarian and one Palestinian, were sentenced to death in Libya. They were eventually released as part of a deal brokered by European Union.

2 Event at the Carnegie Endowment for International Piece, Washington D.C., 25 January 2017.

13. In Egypt's Prisons

1 'Alleged leak points to military interference in Abu Zaabal police trial', *Mada Masr*, 28 December 2014.

2 Alaa Abd el-Fattah, *You Have Not Been Defeated: Selected Works 2011–2021*, Seven Stories Press, 2022.

3 Asef Bayat, *Revolution without Revolutionaries: Making Sense of the Arab Spring*, Stanford University Press, 2017.

14. Successors on the Earth

1 Hugh Roberts, 'The Hijackers', *London Review of Books* Vol. 37, No. 14, 16 July 2015.

16. Kinetic Strikes

1 Maj. Zachary Morris, 'US Drones: Smaller, Less Capable Drones for the Near Future', *Military Review*, May–June 2018.

Postscript

1 One instructive case was supplied by Michael Mandelbaum, who argued for many years that the United States could not be characterised as an empire. In 2022, Mandelbaum claimed that 'the United States became an imperial power' and then a 'hyperpower' (in *The Four Ages of American Foreign Policy: Weak Power, Great Power, Superpower, Hyperpower*, Oxford University Press, 2022) but this status terminated in 2015, because of the rise of China, the expansion of NATO towards Russia, and the Iraq war. For further examples see David Klion, 'The American Empire Is the Sick Man of the 21st Century', *Foreign Policy*, 2 April 2019; or 'The Downside of Imperial Collapse', Robert Kaplan, *Foreign Affairs*, 4 October 2022.

2 *Spacepower: A Doctrine for the Space Forces*, 2020.

3 Carol Bertaut, Bastian von Beschwitz and Stephanie Curcuru, 'FEDS Notes: The International Role of the US Dollar', 6 October 2021.

4 'Germany bans Iranian airline from its airspace after US pressure', Reuters, 21 January 2019.

5 'International Criminal Court officials sanctioned by US', BBC, 2 September 2020.

6 'Japan to divert LNG to Europe amid Russia-Ukraine tension', Reuters, 10 February 2022.

7 The basic outline of an American-dominated world was first sketched by Franklin Roosevelt's staff: Sumner Welles, Cordell Hull, Adolf Berle and others.

8 This policy influenced the deployment of tens of thousands of American troops to China in 1946, the invasion and carpet bombing of Korea, the catastrophic wars in Indochina, and the assisted overthrow of Suharto in Indonesia, leading to genocidal massacres. In Africa, the usual method was proxy warfare, with instigated invasions of Congo, Angola, and Ethiopia by local auxiliaries.

9 See Richard Rhodes's account of Curtis LeMay's agitation for a preemptive nuclear strike against the Soviet Union in 'The General and World War III', *New Yorker*, 11 June 1995.

10 The Sunak government made a point of pride out of being the first Western power to supply a very small number of main battle tanks to Ukraine, before

the US and Germany agreed a more substantial deal for M-1 Abrams and Leopard tanks.

11 The primary sites being the Council on Foreign Relations, the Kennedy School at Harvard, the Woodrow Wilson Center at Princeton, the Nitze School at Johns Hopkins, the Naval War College, Georgetown University, and the Brookings and Carnegie Foundations. There are, it must be said, also unmistakable signs of degradation. Richard Haass has now been head of the CFR for nearly twenty years, a period that few would argue has added to that institution's reputation.

12 At the MIT Center for International Studies, Robert Art brought a sharper focus to military force as the central component of American power, with dominance over Middle Eastern hydrocarbons.

13 G. John Ikenberry, *Liberal Leviathan: The Origins, Crisis, and Transformation of the American World Order*, Princeton University Press, 2012.

14 Barry Posen, *Restraint: A New Foundation for US Grand Strategy*, Cornell University Press, 2014.

15 Stephen Brooks and William Wohlforth, *World Out of Balance: International Relations and the Challenge of American Primacy*, Princeton University Press, 2008.

16 Some of the growth in interest in declinist theories of American power was a hysterical reaction to Trump's election, but it was also useful in other ways. In the *Financial Times*, Janan Ganesh later provided a forthright description of how useful the illusion of a 'withdrawing' United States had been as propaganda. 'I think there is something to be said for talking up the risk of a withdrawn US,' Ganesh wrote. 'That fear is driving up the military ambitions of Europe. It is ending the "neutrality" of some democracies. And framing isolation as a Trumpist thing in particular rallies the global left behind a cause – defence spending – that it might otherwise oppose. Keep the trope going, then. Just don't believe it.' See 'A Republican-led US would not shrink from the world', *Financial Times*, 7 February 2023.

17 When the election results came through, the *Frankfurter Allgemeine Zeitung* carried the news under the headline 'Demonstrativ Staatsmännisch', reflecting a belief that a Biden victory represents a return to dignity and rectitude. In the *Washington Post*, Josh Rogin wrote that Biden held the promise of salvation from the Trump days: 'a return to a bipartisan, internationalist foreign policy that moderate Republicans and Democrats have long championed'. For the *New York Times*, the moment would be accompanied by 'sighs of relief overseas'.

18 'Biden victory is a mixed blessing for Britain', *The Times*, 5 November 2020.

19 Speech to the Union League of Philadelphia, accompanied by a pledge to reverse minor limitations on military spending imposed under Obama.

20 See, for example, 'Is the US Withdrawal from Afghanistan the End of the American Empire?', Jon Lee Anderson, *New Yorker*, 1 September 2021.

21 For an influential instance, see Elbridge Colby, *The Strategy of Denial: American Defense in an Age of Great Power Conflict*, Yale University Press, 2021.

22 'US freezes Afghan central bank's assets of $9.5bn', Al Jazeera, 18 August 2021.

23 Ivan Krastev, with characteristic restraint, declared in the *New York Times*, 27 February 2022, the end of the '30-year peace' and that 'we are all living in Vladimir Putin's world now'.

24 The *Financial Times*, on 10 March 2022, called this 'the biggest arms push since the Cold War'.

25 'Joint Statement on the US-Ukraine Strategic Partnership', White House, 1 September 2021. And its fulfilment in the 'US-Ukraine Charter on Strategic Partnership', 10 November 2021.

26 Lloyd Austin said explicitly that the goal was 'to see Russia weakened'. For a longer discussion see 'America and Its Allies Want to Bleed Russia. They Really Shouldn't', *New York Times* 11 May 2022.

27 'National Security Strategy', White House, October 2022.

28 The US embargo on the transfer of semiconductor technology to China has been widely reported as part of an 'economic war'. Eric Levitz argued, in 'Biden's New Cold War Against China Could Backfire', *New York Magazine*, 14 November 2022, that the policy amounted to a commitment to thwart China's development.

29 And have since been advocated by the much admired Canadian politician Chrystia Freeland.

30 At George Washington University in October 2015, Biden said: 'I actually like Dick Cheney . . . I get on with him. I think he's a decent man.'

31 'China will "eat our lunch," Biden warns after clashing with Xi on most fronts', Reuters, 11 February 2021.

32 For an egregious example of the desperate efforts to find multipolar powers, see Ivan Krastev's 'Middle Powers are reshaping geopolitics', *Financial Times*, 18 November 2022, in which the examples include Kazakhstan and Saudi Arabia: states penetrated at all levels by Russian and US intelligence agencies respectively.

33 From Sun Zhe, 'Four major effects of the Russia-Ukraine conflict on the global landscape', *Ai Sixiang* [Chinese], April 2022.

34 The Ukraine war has certainly brought with it some small signs of neutrality in the international system, but by any measure they remain embryonic.

Index